KT-369-731

JANNER'S
COMPLETE SPEECHMAKER

including compendium of
draft speeches and retellable tales

GREVILLE JANNER

JANNER'S COMPLETE SPEECHMAKER

*including compendium of
draft speeches and retellable tales*

Cartoons by Calman and Tobi

BUSINESS BOOKS
London Melbourne Sydney Auckland Johannesburg

Business Books Ltd
An imprint of the Hutchinson Publishing Group
17–21 Conway Street, London W1P 5HL

Hutchinson Group (Australia) Pty Ltd
30–32 Cremorne Street, Richmond South, Victoria 3121
PO Box 151, Broadway, New South Wales 2007

Hutchinson Group (NZ) Ltd
32–34 View Road, PO Box 40–086, Glenfield, Auckland 10

Hutchinson Group (SA) (Pty) Ltd
PO Box 337, Bergvlei 2012, South Africa

First published 1968 under the title *The Businessman's
Guide to Speech-making and to the Laws and
Conduct of Meetings*
First published under present title 1981
Reprinted 1982

© GREVILLE JANNER 1981

Set in Times

Printed in Great Britain by The Anchor Press Ltd
and bound by Wm Brendon & Son Ltd
both of Tiptree, Essex

British Library Cataloguing in Publication Data
Janner, Greville
  Janner's complete speechmaker.
  I. Title
  808.5'1   PN4121

ISBN 0 09 142980 3

Cartoons in Books One and Two by Calman
Cartoons in Book Three by Tobi

For
MY FATHER
with admiration
and affection

OTHER BOOKS BY GREVILLE JANNER, QC, MP
(EWAN MITCHELL) INCLUDE:

Janner's Practical Guide to the Employment Act, 1980
Janner's Compendium of Employment Law
Janner's Employment Forms
Janner's Product Liability
Janner's Handbook of Draft Letters of Employment Law for Employers and
    Personnel Managers
The Employer's Guide to the Law on Health, Safety and Welfare at Work
The Director's and Company Secretary's Handbook of Draft Legal Letters
The Businessman's Guide to Letter-writing and to the Law on Letters

*   *   *

Details of Greville Janner's public courses and in-company training
programmes are available from Mr Paul Secher, LLB, JS Associates, 230
Grand Buildings, Trafalgar Square, London WC2. Telephone: 01-839 6985.
    The following audio cassettes by Greville Janner are available from Water-
low Publishing, Waterlow (London) Ltd, Holywell House, Worship Street,
London EC2:

The Health and Safety at Work Act, 1974
The Buyer, the Seller and the Law
Product Liability
The Arts of Public Speaking and Chairmanship
Safety Representatives and Committees
The Employment Act, 1980 – in its practical context
The Executive and Manager – how to survive within the current laws
The Arts of Letter Writing

Video cassettes by Greville Janner in the series 'Managers in Law' are
available from CST Ltd, Bushey Studios, Melbourne Road, Bushey, Herts:

Coping with the Employment Act, 1980
Handling Redundancies and Dismissals
Accidents at Work

Contents

Book Two   DRAFT SPEECHES

Part 6   MODEL SPEECHES FOR VARYING OCCASIONS

Part 7 CLASSIC SPEECHES

Book Three   COMPENDIUM OF RETELLABLE TALES

x *Contents*

Introduction

In business or in social life, competent speech-making brings success. But disaster on your feet will land you on your back. This book is designed to provide the maximum of practical help with the minimum of misery. It is based on a vast and varied experience of hugely varied audiences in many parts of the world.

The book divides conveniently into three sections. The first describes the basic arts of speech-making – construction and delivery, audiences and occasions, technical aids . . . the complete range of basic knowledge and guidance – the essential equipment of the speechmaker.

Whether you are addressing a meeting of staff or of shareholders . . . a family gathering or a political rally . . . making a presentation or presenting a guest speaker or prizes at a school . . . the techniques are the same, but their application is vital. Book One deals with them all.

You may have to chair a meeting, as major as a mass gathering or as minor as a company committee? Here in Book One are the rules on good chairmanship, explained with the minimum of fuss and jargon and the maximum of practicality.

Book Two contains models – a selection of draft speeches for varying occasions. Some revive great moments from the works of mighty orators. Others are modern guides. Use both as guides or precedents. They should help you to make the best of your opportunities to shine – and minimise your prospect of collapse.

Finally, in Book Three, I offer a compendium of my own favourite retellable tales. Listening to literally thousands of speeches, too many of them excruciatingly boring, I have carefully accumulated an array of gems – stories, jokes and epigrams which shine with wit or with vivid language; which captivated audiences; and above all, which made me laugh or rejoice. Select and adapt with care those that suit your mood and style, and with a modicum of that good fortune which every speaker always needs but which is granted only on unpredictable and joyful occasions, they should provide you with a treasurehouse of spice for the seasoning of *your* speeches.

I have many to thank. First: Business Books. My long and best selling *Businessman's Guide to Speech-making and to the Laws and Conduct of Meetings* now retreats into cold storage – along with my

Ewan Mitchell pen name. My thanks to Mrs Pat Garner and to my son, Daniel Janner, for their help in the preparation of this book and to my wife for her encouragement, help and guidance – as well as to those countless others whose speeches provided us with examples – good and bad, worthy and laughable, splendid or sad – from which I have culled both advice and retellable tales.

If you enjoy this book and find it useful, then you might like to hear the principles illustrated in my three speech-making tapes, published by Waterlows Ltd.

May 1981   GREVILLE JANNER

Book One

YOUR GUIDE TO SPEECH-MAKING

Part 1

The speech – its structure and contents

Introduction: thinking on your feet

The art of good public speaking is to be able to think on your feet. Whether you are debating or orating, you are not engaged in an exercise in reading, elocution or recitation. You are trying to put across ideas or thoughts to an audience, in your own words. And if your speech has been written for you, there is even more reason to attempt to make it appear your own.

There are many reasons for avoiding too careful preparation of the precise wording of a speech. Interruption (intentional or otherwise) can so easily throw you off your stride. Your ability to draw from your surroundings . . . to refer to speeches that have gone before or speakers that are to come after . . . these are inevitably affected. The speech loses spontaneity – and hence much of its charm and effect.

Here, then, are the techniques of thinking whilst speaking – an art which every public speaker must acquire, if he seeks success.

1 The skeleton of a speech

The human spirit can live, flourish and be much admired even when the human body is frail, ugly or misshapen. There are some brilliant minds which can capture and hold an audience with a rambling, poorly formed oration. Meaning and sincerity shine through and all is forgiven. But to the businessman who wishes to make a speech in a businesslike way . . . to the average speaker who wishes to put on an above-average performance . . . to the poor timorous orator, forced into public speech-making . . . the structure of the speech is of supreme importance. Create the skeleton, clothe it with sensible thought and all that remains is to put it across. But without a healthy skeleton, the entire speech collapses. So here are the rules on forming a well built talk.

*   *   *

Any speech may conveniently be divided into three parts – the opening, the body and the closing. Let us take them in turn.

The first and last sentences of a speech are crucial. The importance of a clear, resounding and striking first sentence and a well rounded peroration cannot be over-emphasised. You must catch the interest of your audience from the start and send them away satisfied at the end. So, when building your skeleton, spend time on the 'topping and tailing' process. Many speakers actually write out their opening and closing sentences, even if the rest is left entirely in skeleton form.

Assume, now, that you have established a relationship with your audience. You have led in with your thanks for the invitation to speak . . . your topical references . . . your personal remarks, introductory witticisms and greetings to old friends. Now comes the substance of the speech – any speech. It must flow.

Like a first-class book or chapter or article, most fine speeches start their substance with a general introductory paragraph which sums up what is to come, catches the attention of the audience and indicates the run of the speaker's thought. Each idea should then be taken in sequence, and should lead on logically to the next. Just as each bone of the human body is attached to its fellow, so the ideas in a speech should be jointed. The flow of ideas needs rhythm. Disjointed ideas

. . . dislocated thoughts . . . fractured theories . . . these are the hall-mark of a poor speech.

So jot down the points you wish to make. Then set them out in logical order, so that one flows from the next. Connect them up, if you like, with a general theme. Start with that theme – and then elaborate, point by point.

Suppose, for instance, that you are explaining the virtues of a new product to your own sales staff. You begin in the usual way by asking for silence, smiling, looking round your audience and saying: 'Ladies and Gentlemen, sales staff of the X Company . . . it is a pleasure to see you here today, in spite of our reluctance to deprive the company's customers of your services. . .'. Refer to Mr Y and Mr Z by name, congratulating them on their successes. Put your audience at ease. Tell them a joke, if you like. And then launch into your theme.

'I have called you together today to introduce our new product.' (There it is, in a sentence). 'Our research department has produced it. It will now be up to you to sell it. If you understand and exploit its full potentialities, you will not only benefit the company but you should also add considerably to your own earnings. I only hope that the Chancellor of the Exchequer will not consider this in any way unpatriotic in the light of the country's present financial situation. For surely there was never a time when a substantial volume of home sales was more essential to help us build the productive capacity we need to produce our goods sufficiently cheaply to capture the vast export markets which we all desire.' (So you have offered your audience a real incentive to listen . . . have introduced a touch of humour . . . have whetted your listeners' appetites for what is to come.)

Now for the speech proper. First, you name and describe the product in broad terms. Next, preferably with the assistance of diagrams or slides, you describe the product in detail. Then you take its selling features, one by one. 'The following features are entirely new. . .'. Spell them out and explain them. 'But the following features are retained – they were too valuable to be lost. . .'. (Once again, the logical sequence is maintained.)

'So there, Ladies and Gentlemen, we have our new product – and you are the first to know about it. You will be supplied with full sales literature within the next week. It will be available for your customers by the first of next month. The rest is up to you. I wish you the very best of good fortune.' A good, sound ending to a well constructed speech.

Precisely the same rules of construction can be applied to any other sort of discourse. Whether you are pronouncing a funeral oration over a deceased colleague or congratulating an employee on completing 25 years' service . . . whether you are making an after-dinner speech or haranguing your workers at the factory gates . . . whatever the circumstances, wherever the speech is made, if its skeleton is sound and solid, then even if the body is not as strong as it might be, there's an excellent chance that the audience will not notice. But ignore the skeleton and the odds are that the speech will prove a rambling disaster.

2 The end of a speech

There is nothing that so becomes a good speech as a fine ending. And nothing can be more ruinous than a weak termination trailing off into silence. Just as much care needs to be given to the tail of a talk as to the top.

Consider some common flops:

Mr Brown rushes his last few sentences, gathers his notes and slides almost surreptitiously back into his seat.

Mr Black ends his talk in what appears to be the middle of a sentence or the centre of an anti-climax.

Mr Grey, who had been allotted thirty minutes to speak, ran out of material after twenty but was determined 'not to let the audience down', and said: 'In conclusion', 'finally', 'before I conclude', 'lastly', and 'to end up with', at least twice each – each time rekindling hope in the minds of his audience that he really meant it.

Mr Green thought that he was narrating a serial story and left his audience in suspense by overrunning his time, panicking and then forgetting to propose the resolution which was the sole object of his speech.

Mr Blue realises that he is not going to conclude his prepared talk if he keeps going at the same speed. So he runs out of script and breath at the same moment, leaving his audience miles behind.

Mr Dark forgets that a peroration should be brief – and drags it out interminably, embellishing thoughts which were in the body of the speech, introducing new ideas in the guise of a summary of what he had said and is not only woolly minded but shows it.

What, then, makes a really good ending or peroration? It should round off the speech and, in most cases, include the following:

1 A summary, in a sentence or two, of the main purport of the speech.
2 Any proposal or resolution arising out of the body of the speech, and
3 A call for support or warm words of thanks, as the case may be.

Some say that if you were to attach the peroration to the opening, they should between them contain the core of the entire speech. The opening says what is coming; the closing says what has gone and what is to come.

Here are some examples of good closing gambits:

'So this project does have great possibilities for our company. But to achieve success, it is essential that we at once take the steps I have suggested. I therefore ask you all not merely to support the resolution which stands in my name but to help put it into useful and urgent effect.'

'And so, Mr Chairman, my argument is closed. I have tried to suggest the appropriate action which this company could now take. I believe that if the resolution which stands in my name is passed and put into urgent effect, it will transform the company's finances. I trust that no one will vote against it without the most careful thought. I submit, Mr Chairman, that it presents the best possible way out of our current difficulties.'

'And so this company stands in grave peril. To my mind, the way out is clear. The action I recommend could transform the situation. I am pleased to have had the opportunity to put forward the resolution which stands in my name and I am grateful to all of you for having listened so attentively to my arguments. I trust that they will not be lightly rejected.'

'There is, then, no need for despair. The future presents great opportunities. But we must not only resolve to carry out the procedure proposed in my resolution but also ensure that the action which must follow will have the urgent and active support of us all. I therefore move that. . .'.

'So those are the possibilities open to us. And only one of them really carries any hope of real success. It is the duty of this Board to protect and advance the interests of our shareholders. That duty can only be performed if steps are taken in accordance with the resolution which stands in my name. I urge, with all the earnestness I can command, that it be accepted – fully, wholeheartedly and without amendment.'

*　　*　　*

There are many roads to Rome and countless ways to construct the end of the same speech. There is no need for the old clichés: 'My time is running short. . .', 'I see that my time is nearly up and I must close . . .'. Still worse: 'I see that you are beginning to get restless. . .', 'I have no wish to bore you any further. . .'. Make your summary and your appeal – for support, for money, for understanding.

Try not to mix your metaphors. 'We have so many irons in the fire that some of them are bound to come home to roost . . .' brings laughter. But by all means adapt a well known metaphor to your own use. 'This company is the finest in the chicken business . . . and our shareholders will continue to see the profits come home to roost. . .'. Or 'Thanks to the happy relations between management and labour in this business, our many irons are kept white hot in the fire. . .'. The new twist on the old words brings life to many a dead topic.

*　　*　　*

Other recommended endings:

'And so, Mr Chairman, I would like to end as I began – with my warm thanks for your kind hospitality.'

'Ladies and Gentlemen, it has been a delight to be with you. I hope that my words will have been of some help in promoting the cause for which you work and in which I – like you – believe so firmly. I wish you, Mr Chairman, your honorary officers, executives, members and workers, every possible success in your great venture.'

'And so our Conference is over. It has been a tremendous experience to meet you all. I trust that we shall see each other on many more such happy and useful occasions. Meanwhile, I know that I am expressing the warm feelings of all of us when I wish you God-speed on your journeys home, every success in all your ventures, and a speedy return to our midst.'

'I know that the views I have put forward are unusual and, in some quarters, unpopular. But I know, too, that you would not have wished me to do otherwise than to speak my mind. That I have done, most earnestly. I do hope that the suggestions I have made will be adopted, or at least adapted. But whatever decision you take, I would like you to know how much I have appreciated the kind attention which you have given to me – and how much I have the future of this organisation at heart.'

*   *   *

Some people end by saying: 'Thank you' or 'Good night'. But a climax is better. A last, powerful phrase, left hovering in the air – and beckoning on the applause. Then do not rush back to your seat, flop quickly down into your chair, whip out your cigarette-case and light up. Like any good trouper, wait for the applause. If it comes, smile or bow slightly in acknowledgement. If it does not, then look your audience straight in the eye. Pause. And then sit down. The end of your speech should make quite as solid an impact as its start.

3   *Notes*

Some speeches are so important that they have to be read. Every word counts and the occasion is so fraught with peril that you cannot risk setting a foot wrong. But read speeches tend to be a bore. Even Parliament, some of whose debates are an agony to endure, forbids the reading of speeches. The Mother of Parliaments has to suffer enough without allowing its members to exchange debates for a series of written essays, probably the product of the minds of others. Remove the element of the impromptu and the likelihood of the speech proving interesting is minimal. As the audience knows this truth, instead of looking forward to hearing the speaker it prepares for slumber and boredom. As soon as the speaker starts reading from a script, his audience begins to curl up – mentally if not physically.

But to the average, non-professional speaker, the difficulty of constructing a speech as he goes along is almost insurmountable. Even for the expert, preparation is a necessity – and the more complex the speech, the more essential it is to be reminded of its main points, so that none is left out. The compromise, then? Notes. The skeleton of the speech (see Chapter 1) committed to paper, leaving the speaker to clothe it with words, embellish it with new ideas and thoughts, and enliven it with wit as he goes along.

What, then, should good notes contain? The first sentence plus the last sentence plus the skeleton. The flow of ideas. The thread of the speech. Brief phrases to indicate the contents of even lengthy paragraphs. And notes to remind you of themes. Pegs on which to hang your thoughts.

What you need are brief headings for the eye, to direct the flow of speech but not to interrupt it. Except where you must indulge in quotations, the shorter and clearer the note, the better. By all means divide up the note itself by using block capitals for the main headings and a small type of script for subsidiary items. Underline in red, blue, green. Set the notes themselves into columns and lay them out so as to catch your eye, just as you seek to lay out your speech to catch the minds and imaginations of your listeners.

Notes are best made on cards, preferably not larger than normal postcard size. Each theme, each paragraph, each range of ideas can then be put on to a separate card. Use one side only. When the ground on a card has been covered, you turn it over. If you have a desk, table or stand to operate from, well and good. But if not – as when you are speaking from the floor, at a meeting – then you are not burdened by clumsy sheets, paper that tends to slip through your fingers, scraps of notes which you lose at the crucial moment, so sending yourself into that very fluster which the notes were intended to avoid. You simply return each card to the bottom of the pack as soon as you are through with it. Just in case you drop your notes, number each card clearly, at the top, right-hand corner.

Another advantage of the card system is that if you run out of time, the chances are that you can simply skip two or three of the less essential cards – or at least summarise them in sentences and turn them over at speed. They provide your guide without restricting you to an itinerary. They leave you room for manoeuvre, and the ability to think on your feet.

4 Brevity is the soul of success

Mr Mort Mendels, long-time Secretary of the World Bank and sufferer from the speeches of others, boasted a cartoon on his office wall. It showed a man being carried out of the Senate on a stretcher. *'Talked to death'* was the caption. The corpse might just as easily have been emerging from any one of hundreds of meetings anywhere in Britain.

The man who stands in front of the mirror admiring himself for long periods, is rightly regarded as a freak. But at least he disturbs no one else. The man who so rejoices in the sound of his own words that he imposes them at great length upon his fellows should be relegated to the same privacy.

Have you ever heard an audience complain that the speaker did not go on long enough? On the contrary, far more listeners complain at the sluggishness of their watch hands. And on the rare occasions when they do want more from the speaker – well, he can always be invited again.

'If you cannot strike oil within 15 minutes, stop boring', the oil man is alleged to have told his apprentices. He could have been talking to a course on public speaking.

Incidentally, the importance of this chapter should not be judged by its brevity.

5 Wit and humour

Every comedian works extremely hard for his living. If he is renowned for his wit, then he may be able to make his audience laugh (if they are in the right mood) where no laughter is really deserved. Part of the art of any speaker is to let his hearers know what is coming . . . to lead them up to the climax . . . to prepare them to react as he intends. The well known wit has his groundwork laid ready for him. He no sooner comes to the stage or the platform or up to the microphone, shakes his head or performs some other famous gesture – and the audience begins to giggle. Whether his first sentence refers to 'The Diddy people', his mother-in-law, or simply includes some renowned catch-phrase – the audience is off.

But speak to even the most famous men of comedy and you will soon discover how carefully their impromptu laughs are prepared . . . how fickle and unpredictable an audience – any audience – can be . . . how even the best-made stories can fall apart at the seams. You will then realise, if you do not already know it, that of all the skills of the public speaker, putting across humour is one of the most difficult of all. For the most experienced of humorists, the path is tough. How much more difficult must it be for the beginner?

On the other hand, the humourless speaker is a menace. There are few occasions when a word of wit is not appreciated, and the longer the speech, the more vital the touch of humour. The more sombre the subject, the more appropriate the tactful, tasteful touch of light relief will be. Humour, then, is a weapon that every speaker should have readily available. Here are some suggestions on how best to put it across.

*   *   *

The humour must be tailored to the audience and to the occasion. This applies most obviously to the *risqué*, the rude or the plain vulgar. There is never any excuse whatsoever for the use of the obscene. But the element of dirt can sometimes add spice to the meal. When?

Obviously, the stag dinner is the place for the dirty story. Conversely, those who introduce the *risqué* tale into solemn or sombre occasions are inviting contempt. In between come all the rest. You must judge each occasion as best you can. If in doubt – keep it clean.

Similar considerations apply to the dialect story. There is still a place for the saga of the Scotsman, the Irishman and the Jew. But to copy someone else's accent is generally an error. The only speakers who can do it without undue risk are those who belong to the group satirised. Scotsmen, Jews, Irishmen, Negroes – they all delight in stories about themselves, but usually only when told by themselves. If you enjoy the friendship of Jewish people, for instance, you will soon find that they poke merciless fun at their own foibles. Part of their armour, acquired through centuries of persecution, is the ability to make laughter shine through the tears. No one, in fact, can tell an anti-Semitic story with half the relish of the Jew. But then, masochism is reasonable. *Volenti non fit injuria* – the volunteer cannot complain of injuries brought about of his own free will. We cause no injury to ourselves when we makes jokes at our own expense.

Sadism, on the other hand, is always unpleasant, and even a hint may be harmful. Minorities may consider themselves the subject for good humour. But the laughter is often thin when the shafts come from tongues other than their own.

So there are two sides to the coin. First, be tremendously careful not to obtain cheap laughs at the expense of others. Second, many of the best jokes – and those most appreciated – are those about oneself.

'We Welsh. . .', says the speaker with a smile, 'have, through our very name, given birth to an important word in the English language . . .'.

'As you all know', says the speaker in broad Scots, 'I yield to none of my compatriots in the meanness of my approach. . .'.

'We foreigners find it very difficult to understand you English. I know that m-i-s-l-e-d spells misled. But when I pronounced t-i-t-l-e-d the same way, everyone laughed at me.'

None of this is great humour. All of it has been heard before. But then, as one famous comic put it: 'There are basically only two jokes – the mother-in-law and the banana skin'. What matters is to make the joke fit the occasion and the audience, and to put it over effectively.

The best way to suit the occasion is to extract the humour from the surroundings and from the people present (for examples, see Book 3). But how do you put it across? Here are some hints, culled from some well known, humorous speakers:

First, you must give every impression of confidence. It is a mistake to say: 'I was going to tell you the story about. . . .' and then to tell it, half apologetically. However thin the tale, it requires firmness in the telling. You must believe in the comedy or you will never get your audience to do so.

The confidence must be retained, even in the face of defeat. If a joke falls flat, never mind. Pretend it was not intended as a joke at all – and carry straight on. Alternatively, face up to the situation and say: 'Sorry . . . it wasn't a very good one, was it? Never mind – how about the tale of. . . ?' Or: 'Sorry about that – I'll do better next time. But you must admit that after a meal such as we've just had, it is really the height of sadism to expect anyone to attempt to entertain you!'

Timing is all-important. This means that the joke or witticism or humorous thrust must be well placed in relation to the speech, the content of the talk or lecture, the mood of the audience. But it especially means that the joke must be told at the right pace . . . with the correct emphasis . . . with the appropriate pauses. Listen to any first-class comedian at work. Half his effect is achieved by timing. He knows when to wait and when to rush forward. So listen to the experts – and copy them.

Some speakers keep a book of stories, notes of humorous tales which have gone down well and which they would like not to forget. Certainly the jotting down of the punch line on the back of a menu card or in the front of your diary can provide useful ammunition. It may also have the opposite effect – it may help to save you from the gross error of telling an audience the same story that it heard the last time it met. To avoid this fate, you can take some regular attender into your confidence. 'I'm thinking of telling the story of. . .', you say to the chairman. 'Do you know it?' If he says no, then the chances are that you will be safe. If he has heard it, then find out whether it was told at the same gathering. And avoid it, anyway, if you can.

Jokes are for others to laugh at. If you giggle at your own stories the chances are that you will detract from their effect on your audience.

The best stories have a sting in their tail. The laughter should build up. The audience should expect the laughs. But if the first climax brings laughter and turns out to be a false one, giving rise to an unexpected twist, then the story has been a success.

The formal tale also has its place. But the bright phrase, the witty aside, the colourful remark – these are more important. If you cannot think of a suitable, funny story for the occasion, never mind. The odds are that some humorous thought will come to you as you speak. If it does not, at least make sure that your speech is shorter than if you had been able to lighten its darkness with a few shafts of light-hearted laughter.

6 *Quotations*

Your audience have come to hear you. But that is no reason why you should not pepper your speech with apt quotations from the thoughts of others. Quoting, however, is an art of its own. Here are some suggestions on how best to perfect it.

*   *   *

Keep quotations short. To quote at length from memory is a form of 'showing off' which is seldom appreciated. You are not engaged in a stage soliloquy. To read someone else's words at length is seldom an alternative to putting thoughts and ideas into your own words. The reading of speeches – or even lengthy parts of them – is usually an error. And the error is compounded when you are not even reading that which purports to amount to your own original thought.

Quotations are only worth using if they are thoroughly apt. If your audience is flagging, it is sometimes helpful to 'drag in a joke by its ears'. This is a legitimate gambit to reduce strain, but if the joke were apposite, it would be a good deal better. To thrust an inappropriate quotation into your speech merely because you have a fond feeling for it is a great mistake.

By all means attribute the quotation to its true author, if you can. If in doubt, you could try: 'Was it George Bernard Shaw who said. . .?' or 'I think it was Oscar Wilde who once remarked that. . . .' or if the attribution is to someone in your lifetime, you can seldom go wrong with: 'I once heard Winston Churchill remark that. . . .'. Or 'Did you read the saying, attributed to Mr Kruschev, that. . . .'. Who is to prove you wrong?

Make sure that your speech really is strengthened by putting the statement concerned in quotation marks – and as coming from the particular author. When trying to convince a British audience to adopt an American practice, it is sometimes better to adopt the transatlantic arguments, without stating their origin. Conversely, for any foreigner to express a preference for a candidate in an American election is to impose the kiss of death upon him. By all means use the foreigner's arguments, but if you must put them into quotation marks, try: 'One great American was said to have remarked. . .'. Do not quote Satan to condemn sin.

The best quotations of all, of course, are those from the mouths of your opponents. 'Today, Mr Jones condemns amalgamation. But who was it who said, just two years ago – and I quote "Our future depends upon achieving amalgamation. We cannot survive as a small, independent unit"? None other than my friend, Mr Jones!'

Quotations from yourself should be avoided. 'Did I not say, six months ago, that. . .?' Or 'May I repeat what I said at our trade conference last month?' Unless a speaker has previously been accused of inconsistency and must quote from himself to show that he has not changed his mind, this sort of self-quotation is generally regarded as pompous and egotistical. If you have something to say today, say it. Let someone else point out that you are marvellously consistent . . . wise before the event . . . a man whose advice should be taken. The

best you can do is to make that insinuation. Quotations are too direct
a method by far.

7   *Files and ideas*

First-class journalists (especially freelances with no access to
newspaper files) keep careful files of clippings, cuttings, photographs
and ideas which they can later incorporate into articles, features, or
books. Speakers should take a leaf out of their file.

Take jokes, for instance (see Chapter 5). There are books of
allegedly humorous tales for every occasion, but one sometimes
wonders how anyone ever laughed at the bulk of them. But then each
of us has his own style . . . his own sense of humour . . . his own
preference. Do not be afraid to steal the tales of others. They will be
flattered (see Chapter 6). Jot them down and file them. You never
know when they may come in handy.

Then there is specialist material, which can be used time and time
again. Most popular speakers are invited to talk on their particular
specialities. The first time, research must be done . . . facts prepared
. . . statistics unearthed . . . notes prepared. But if those notes are
carefully filed, next time will be a walk-over, though naturally they
would have to be adapted for different audiences (see Part 3). But the
basic groundwork need not be repeated.

Some speakers favour a filing-cabinet, others one of those new-
fangled metal boxes with files inside. Still more make do with loose-
leaf notebooks for stories and quotations, ideas and suggestions.

The object of it all is to reduce your homework to the minimum.
You have no time to repeat any drudgery. So, however boring the
keeping of files or notebooks may be, it is well worth some effort in
the present if it cuts down work in the future.

8 Overstatements

Hyperbole – that is, exaggeration for effect – has its place, and is often used by humorists. There is nothing funny about a thin man – but a matchstick man, a creation of skin and bone, a fat head on a puny frame – that's different. About the only time that deliberate exaggeration helps the presentation of a serious case is when that case is thin. 'If something is too silly to say, you can always sing it,' says the operatic librettist. 'If logic and argument are surplus,' says the skilled speaker, 'then it is just possible that if you shout loud enough, exaggerate sufficiently, thump with sufficient force, you may numb the minds of your audience.' This sort of behaviour is the last resort of the advocate and should only be used when *in extremis*.

Otherwise, your exaggerations are likely to boomerang . . . to cause laughter . . . to ruin such a case as you have. Some horrible examples:

Reference to a speech immediately preceding: 'That magnificent and moving oration which we have just heard . . . that tugged at our heartstrings and must now open our purses. . . .' The charity goes without money.

'I only saw her passing by, but I shall love her till I die', said Sir Robert Menzies, then Prime Minister of Australia, enthusing at a dinner in honour of the Queen. However well loved the Queen undoubtedly is, Sir Robert's hyperbole brought only ridicule in its wake.

*   *   *

Words, like drugs, may be highly beneficial in the correct quantity and dosage. But over-indulgence may cause death. Moderation pays.

9 Repetition

A former Duke of Wellington is reputed to have said: 'I dreamed that I was speaking in the House of Lords. I woke up and found that I was.' Repetition and long-windedness may not only demoralise your audience but yourself as well.

On the other hand, it does have its place: 'Brutus is an honourable man...'. Shakespeare knew how to build a speech upon the repetition of a theme, without ever approaching boredom.

Some of my personal dislikes:

The man who starts his speech by saying: 'Mr Jones has made all the points which I wished to put forward'. A better approach would have been: 'Mr Jones has put forward his case with immense skill, and I commend it to the meeting. However, there are several aspects of his remarks which, I think, require further emphasis.'

'I will not bore you by reploughing the furrows so thoroughly covered by Mr Jones.' Watch out. Boredom is on its way. That sort of introduction, combining mixed metaphor with cliché, is a sure sign of impending audience distress. Leave the meeting if you can.

Then there's the man who repeats his points in the same words. Most well constructed speeches should begin with a summary of what's coming: a full-blooded exposition of those points in the body of the speech and another brief summary at the end. 'To summarise, then; if we are to achieve success, we must take the following steps. First . . . second . . . third . . . and, above all. . .'. But English is a rich language. If you cannot think of similies, consult the invaluable *Roget's Thesaurus* – which should be on the desk or at least in the library of every speaker. And if you must repeat yourself, at least try not to do so in the current and boring clichés, which are merely a sign of speeches made without thought, and so reveal the thoughtlessness of the speaker.

10   The cliché

One way to while away the speeches of others is to compile a list of clichés. Some examples, culled from a recent company meeting:

'In this day and age. . . .'
'Each and every one of us. . . .'
'We are escalating towards disaster. . . .'
'We must give of our best. . . .'
'No politicians are to be trusted. . . .'
'We must stem the tide of ill-will. . . .'
'The ship of State is heading for the rocks. . . .'
'Blood, toil, sweat and tears – that is the only recipe. . . .'
'The present system of taxation is destroying us. . . .'
'Our expansion plans are going full steam ahead. . . .'

There is really no limit to them, is there? And each one is common, hackneyed, trite and commonplace (see *Roget's Thesaurus*, paragraph 496). Even though the sentiments expressed may be wise, sage, true, received, admitted, recognised (same paragraph), that flexibility of the language which can cloak even the most uninspiring and unoriginal thought with at least the appearance of charm or originality has not been brought into play.

After a particularly monotonous cliché-ridden speech, made by a dull guest in the Cambridge Union, Mr Percy Cradock brought the house down with the following: 'I know that we have all greeted each sentence expressed by Mr — with something of the wretched anticipation felt when one notes the approach of an old but extremely seedy acquaintance.'

Contrast the effect made on the dowdy woman by a new hairstyle, a chic outfit and modern accessories and the moral needs no emphasis. No longer is she seedy. Her familiarity has a new and interesting flavour. She is now worthy of our attention. She is ready for the wooing. And it is no hyperbole to say that the oldest thought in the newest dress can have a rare and surprising appeal. 'There's nothing new to say about this subject' is a cliché. 'Consider the problem from this new angle', is a worthy start – and if the angle is sufficiently acute, its familiarity may well be forgotten. You may not regard yourself as a bore. What matters is that your listeners should share your view.

And a good start to this hopeful process is to learn to recognise clichés in the speeches of others and ruthlessly eliminate them from your own.

11   *The great I am*

Every speaker should treat the sound of his own voice as a drug to be taken in moderation. The restrained use of the first person singular is worth some careful thought.

There are two possible reasons why you have been asked to speak. Either your audience wanted to hear you or they thought that they ought to. These categories subdivide.

If you have been invited to speak in the hope that you will have something interesting to tell, then you are lucky. But do not push your luck too far by retelling what you are, rather than what you know. Leave it to your introducer to sing your praises. To do so for yourself is to court ridicule. 'Start loving yourself', Oscar Wilde once remarked, 'and you are in for a lifetime of romance'. Fine. But do not do your courting in public.

If you are asked to give advice, you can usually manage it without ever mentioning yourself directly. If you are requested to tell tales of the trade, you must, of course, draw on your own experience and, indeed, a joke told against yourself can be immensely successful. But you do not need to tell your listeners how good you are. Do so and they will not believe you. Fail to do so and they may think up the idea for themselves.

Naturally, if you have been the rounds of similar businesses, factories, offices or workshops to your own, at home or abroad, and are asked to give your impressions . . . if you wish to express views and to make it clear that they are yours and not those of your organisation or, perhaps, of your board or partners . . . if you wish to lighten the darkness of some drab subject with a personal anecdote – then do so. 'I once met . . . in Birmingham,'; 'I was told the tale of. . .'; 'these are my views, I repeat, and if they turn out to be wrong, you will know where to place the responsibility. . .'. All fair game.

But 'when I last saw the Prime Minister. . .'; or 'now, I don't like to drop names, but when I was spending a weekend recently with Lord and Lady Blank in their country estate. . .'. Both are unforgiveable.

Remember the story of the famous general whose first-person anecdotage was accepted because of his undoubted greatness? He was telling an audience about his battle tactics. 'I could not decide what to do next,' he said. 'I thought to myself: "My God what is to be done now?" "General," came the answer, "You decide. I have every confidence in you." So I did.'

Of course, people like to be given the inside information (for traps, see Chapter 13 on how to handle the Press). It is all a question of sensibly putting on a cloak of apparent modesty.

All this becomes even more important when you are the Guest of Honour – which is not necessarily the same as the honoured guest. Maybe your hosts want your money . . . your support . . . your services . . . your backing. Maybe they are simply hoping to lubricate you sufficiently to obtain some useful information which, in a less cordial or obligated moment, you might never give. Whatever the reason, you are on show. So play up to it. Be grateful that – whatever the reason – you are to be honoured and not reviled. Help to keep it that way by making your speech extremely modest. Or try the favourite of Lord Janner: 'After all those kind words, Mr Chairman, I can hardly wait to hear myself speak!'

'It is extremely good of you to honour me in this way,' you might continue. 'I fully appreciate that your intention is, through me, to honour my company . . . my organisation . . . my entire Board. . .' (or as the case may be). 'We are all deeply grateful to you.'

In the body of the speech, tell them about the work your organisation is doing. Give them as much inside information as you decently can. If you are being honoured for long service, then reminisce – and mention as many individuals amongst your audience as you can. 'Now Bill Black over there . . . he'll rememeber when we were both involved in an embarrassing disaster in 1967 . . . Sir Michael Brown – whom we are all very pleased to see amongst us – shared many an exploit . . . Richard Jones, whose sobriety is a proud tribute to the breathalyser. . .' and so on.

Everyone mentioned is flattered – assuming that he receives an honourable mention. You have achieved the all-important, informal touch. Your audience are your friends. The ice is completely shattered, and you are shown to be a man of the people and not the complete egoist everyone had thought you to be. And if they are after something which you are not prepared to give, try this line: 'You are indeed lucky to have in your active ranks tonight and always, Reginald Property . . . Mr James Industry . . . and that lady, famous for her good deeds, Mrs Jewel.' The guest who gives honour will receive it.

'I now must close. . .' (one hopes because of the time of the clock and not the time you have taken in your speech) – 'but, before doing so, I would like to thank you once again, most sincerely, for the great kindness and generosity you have shown to me. I have thoroughly enjoyed being with you. I hope that we shall meet again many times, always on happy occasions. And may this organisation/company/ institute (etc.) flourish for many years to come under your leadership, Mr Chairman.'

A resounding ending to a good speech. Your hearers will tell you so – and mean it.

12 The spoken word

The old, pedantic rules for writing have largely been discarded in favour of freedom of expression. Freedom of speech has followed in its wake. Sentences without verbs . . . split infinitives . . . they offend the ears of some but are generally forgiven. Still, here are some general rules which may prove helpful.

*   *   *

The most common grammatical error of all arises in the use of the first person. 'Between you and I' is wrong. So is 'Dr Brown and me were most impressed with our welcome' and 'You and me must give some careful thought to this problem.' If this sort of problem worries you, discuss it with a friend whose grammar is impeccable.

Swear words and obscenities are best excluded, even from the stag-dinner oration. There will always be those who are offended. But slang and modern idiom are to be expected. If in doubt, you can always put them 'in quotes', so to speak.

If in doubt about the precise meaning of a word, either avoid it or look it up beforehand in a dictionary. If given the choice between two words, one long and one short, choose the shorter. Good old Anglo-Saxon monosyllables are usually the most effective.

Sentences, too, should be kept short. Quite apart from your audience losing the thread, you may do so. 'Now, where was I?' is a dreadful admission of a speaker's failure.

Avoid precise statistics if you can. Apart from the possibility of being found out, the effect of an understandable approximation is much greater than the spelling out of some lengthy figures. Clichés should be 'conspicuous by their absence'. You should 'leave no avenue explored' in your attempt to avoid phrases of this sort (see Chapter 10).

There are occasions upon which it is necessary to use material which is full of sound and fury but signifies nothing. The higher you get in the government of a country or of an organisation, the more frequent those occasions become. But in general, direct speech is better than indirect, the active voice better than the passive, the striaghtforward greatly to be preferred to the insinuation.

13   Dealing with the Press*

Publicity is the life-blood of any trade. 'I don't care what they say about me', said one famous magnate, 'just so long as they say something'. 'There's no such thing as bad publicity', said another. Exaggerations, both. Still, if things go well with you, your greatest difficulty may be to get the Press to come at all. Once there, you must know how to deal with them.

The Press may come in many guises. They may be both wanted and invited. Alternatively, they may be unwanted – and represented by your own members or colleagues with a taste for the pen or for the payment that the Press offers for appropriate tit-bits. The chances of an important and interesting meeting really being private are fairly remote. Someone is likely to 'leak'. So choose your words accordingly.

Unfortunately, there are few speeches which read as well as they sound (or *vice versa*). The witty jest which provokes friendly laughter may read like a jibe. The sincere appeal may sound good but look limp in print. The flamboyant utterance which rouses or enthuses the

*See also Chapter 43.

audience may land you in deep waters when it appears in the local paper.

'I didn't say that', exclaims the scandalised speaker. The reporter refers to his notebook. 'Sorry', he says. 'I have it all down'. 'You took it out of context.' (Always the next ploy.) 'The context is your entire speech. Anyway, the sub-editor did a job on it. It's what you said, isn't it?' You are powerless. Condemned out of your own mouth.

Of course, if there is some gross mis-statement or unfair representation of your words, you could report the paper to the Press Council. If your complaint is considered to be well founded, the newspaper will be honour-bound to publish the finding in its own columns. And no doubt you will get an appropriate apology. But far more often, it is the speaker who is in the wrong. Reporters are only human. They make mistakes. But it it far rarer for them to get carried away by enthusiasms of the moment than it is for those whom they are paid to report.

That is the important point. Press men earn their living by supplying material for the Press. They follow a code of conduct which helps them to obtain background information, inside stories and retain goodwill. Tell them something 'off the record' and it is highly unlikely that your trust will be betrayed. But do not try to get them to conceal that which the public should know.

'I must now deal with a most serious matter', says the speaker. 'I know that our friends of the Press are present and I must ask them to treat what I am about to say as confidential.' The chances are that they will.

'We have just heard from our chairman. What he said was entirely confidential and must not in any circumstances be reported.'

Why not? What right have you to impose censorship on the Press? If what the chairman said was intended only for private ears, it should have been left for a private occasion.

Conversely, 'What I have just said is of the greatest public interest. I trust that our friends of the Press will give it full publicity.'

They may. It all depends on whether their assessment of the interest of your words matches your own.

The private interview with the Press man needs careful handling, too. Accuracy is essential. Consider some common pitfalls.

'Do you think that this industry is heading for disaster?' you are asked.

You think. 'Well,' you say, hesitatingly, 'I suppose that in one sense you could say that.' Next day's headlines: *James Caxton says: 'Industry heading for disaster.'*

Or: 'Would you say that the industry is heading for disaster?'

'Oh sure,' you answer, your voice thick with sarcasm. 'With exports such as we have recently achieved, I would say disaster is just around the corner, wouldn't you?' And you both have a good laugh about it.

'Disaster just around the corner', says William Hicks.

Extreme examples, of course, but none the less a warning to choose your words with care. After they have appeared in the Press, it helps little to write saying you have been misquoted . . . that you meant something else . . . that the report was inaccurate. . . . Some people may believe you, of course.

How about those items, then, that the Press get hold of but you would prefer to have kept out? At worst, the wife of a senior executive has been caught shop-lifting . . . the company secretary is in matrimonial distress . . . the senior partner was drunk and disorderly. Whether you like it or not (and you do not) the Press will be there at the trial. What to do?

Send along a Queen's Counsel to defend the accused on the minor, magistrates' court charge and you are bound to alert the watch-dogs. Put in a plea of mitigation, say how vital it is for the accused to have his car because he is such an important company official, and you are begging to be reported. But just keep as mum as possible and allow the proceedings to slide through along with the rest of the queue and with a little bit of luck, no one may think the matter worth reporting. But the man who tries to bribe or to threaten a reporter into silence is almost certain to be fully reported. Cajolery and an appeal to the better feelings of the Press man might succeed – but if the story is a really good one, the odds are heavily against you. Silence is undoubtedly your best hope, in most cases.

Of course, the Press may be put on its honour if entrusted with your private secrets, as we have seen. But if the secrets really are not yours . . . if they have come into the public eye . . . if they are not, in fact, secret – then it is luck rather than good judgment which will keep them off the front page. The laws of defamation are unlikely to do so – as we shall now see.

14 Defamation – the laws of libel and slander

It is defamatory to publish anything about another person which would tend to 'lower him in the eyes of right-thinking people'. You must not bring others into 'hatred, ridicule or contempt'. To defame someone in writing or some other permanent form (including, incidentally, a statement made on television) is a libel. To speak ill of another is slander. The public speaker – even when he thinks that he is talking in semi-private, as in a meeting of his Board or any other committee – must beware of both.

The fact that a statement is true does not prevent it from being defamatory. But no one is entitled to a good name which he has not earned. So, if sued for a defamatory statement which you can prove to be true, you may plead 'justification'. But the effect of a plea of justification is to repeat again – and even more loudly and publicly – the very same defamatory statement that you made before. Hence if a plea of justification fails, your offence has been severely aggravated. The damages awarded against you will be greatly increased.

A much more helpful defence for most businessmen on many occasions is that of 'qualified privilege'. The law recognises that certain statements must be made, for the public good. People must be entitled to speak their minds. Hence 'privilege'.

No action in defamation will lie in respect of any statement made in a court of law by anyone, whether it be judge, juryman, witness, or counsel. Absolute privilege also attaches to all statements made in Parliament. Our legislators must be able to speak without fear of legal reprisal. However malicious, untrue or unjustified a statement in court or Parliament may be, it can never give rise to a defamation action.

Similar privilege attaches to occasions upon which the law recognises that the maker of the statement has a public or private duty to make it and the hearer a direct interest in receiving it. For instance, references are necessary if the wheels of business are to be kept turning. So the giver of a reference is protected. He is under a moral duty to speak his mind to the inquirer (although, note, he is under no legal duty whatsoever to supply the reference). The recipient of the reference obviously has an interest in knowing its contents. The occasion is 'privileged'.

Or suppose that you have to discuss at a board meeting the possible sacking of a member of staff. It is alleged that he was dishonest . . . slovenly . . . disobedient . . . stupid . . . in a word, unfit to be in your company. Every time anyone speaks ill of him, he is defamed. But clearly, this sort of discussion must be allowed to take place. It is no mere idle gossip. It is essential company business. The occasion is 'privileged'.

But whilst the privilege of courts and Parliament is 'absolute', that of the businessman speaking to his colleagues or supplying a reference is 'qualified'. The qualification? That if it turns out that the statement was made out of 'malice', the privilege evaporates. 'Malice' simple means some wrongful motive. If it can be shown that the object of making the statement was to harm the person defamed rather than to assist the Board in coming to a sensible conclusion, or the prospective employer to decide whether or not to employ the man, the privilege goes. The law is not designed as a shield to guard the spiteful.

Normally, however, you can speak your mind without too much worry, provided you do so at a private gathering of people with similar business interests. The larger the gathering and the less obvious the community of interest, the more risky the defamatory statement becomes. If in doubt, consult your solicitor. Or bring him to the meeting and let him make the statement for you, if he sees fit. He will be acting as your agent, but the chances of any defamation action being brought against him are remote in the extreme.

So what other defences remain to the speaker of evil words? 'Fair comment on a matter of public interest.' In a country where free speech is treasured, people must be allowed to comment on matters of general concern.

Note, first, that what you say must be a statement of opinion and not of alleged fact. If the words complained of were partly opinion and partly fact, then in so far as they consisted of fact, they must be substantially correct. Comment to your heart's content, but do not mis-state facts.

The comment must be 'fair'. But this does not mean that your audience or the person named must consider it reasonable. In practice, this word provides little restraint upon your comment. Provided you are not simply using the occasion to forward a private grudge rather than to comment on a matter of public interest, you have nothing to worry about. But I repeat: The Englishman's right to comment must not be confused with his continued liability in damages if he confuses fact with fiction and, under the guise of comment, propagates false statements about his enemies. The speaker, then, should watch his words, whenever he is speaking evil. Remember the three little monkeys? The one with his hands clapped firmly over his mouth is the most intelligent of all. Speak no evil and you need fear no action in slander. All this works, as usual with the law, also in reverse. If you are at the receiving end of unkind words, apply these principles and you will know whether, in theory at least, you might have a good action in defamation against the speaker. But do not be surprised if you are advised by your lawyer not to sue, even though an action may lie. Defamation proceedings tend to be perilous in the extreme. Even if you win, you are in for a good deal of worry, aggravation and probably expense into the bargain. While orders for costs are customarily made in favour of the winners, these rarely cover all the costs incurred. There is usually a balance over which has to be paid by the winning litigant to his own lawyers, in any event. So litigation is a luxury. Nor can defamation proceedings ever be brought with the help of Legal Aid. Together with actions for breach of promise, they lie at the suit of the litigant at his own potential risk and expense.

Then, of course, your action may go wrong. The lesson of Oscar Wilde should be read by all potential plaintiffs in defamation actions.

Then there was the recent case of the leading plastic surgeon who was defamed in print by an erstwhile colleague. He sued. Now, juries have almost entirely disappeared from the civil courts, but they still remain in defamation proceedings. In the plastic surgeon's case, the first jury failed to agree. The case had to be retried. The second jury failed to agree. Once again, the worry, nervous strain and expense recommenced. Only on the third round did the plaintiff win. It was a handsome victory but the cost in frayed nerves and sleepless nights was extreme and the financial risk quite staggering.

So look well before you leap into proceedings arising out of the evil words of some other speaker. And hope that when you are guilty of defamation, the person referred to will, like yourself, have taken this chapter to heart.

Still, those who speak in public cannot be too careful about their words. As we shall now see.

15 Personal attacks*

The word 'gentleman' has been defined as meaning 'one who is never unintentionally discourteous'. But just as the mature speaker never unintentionally loses his temper, so he does his utmost to cause offence only by design.

Outside the realm of politics, most wounds are both regrettable and regretted. 'The moving finger writes; and, having writ, moves on: Nor all thy piety nor wit shall lure it back to cancel half a line, nor all thy tears wash out a word of it.' With one, off-guard moment, you may acquire an unnecessary enemy for life. Regret it as much as you wish. The uttered word cannot be erased. So be careful.

Humour and wit are vital to the speaker (see Chapter 5). But many a jest, however kindly meant, has been taken amiss. There is all the difference in the world between pulling someone's leg in private and tweaking his sensitive tail in public. The same joke which went down splendidly at the dinner table may be a disaster when told from the platform.

No section of the public is more concerned with its own dignity than the men of commerce. Lawyers are reputed to be pompous. But they recognise as part of their trade the bitter court battle – which has no reference to their personal friendship outside the court. Barristers from the same chambers fight as bitterly as need be for their clients. The personal jest is seldom resented.

But the businessman whom you attack in public is unlikely to wish to speak to you in private.

The seasoned politician revels in the 'cut and thrust' of debate. In most cases, he is able to dissociate the nature of an opponent from his public words.

But there is no such code in the world of business.

It follows that (quite apart from the laws of defamation – see Chapter 14) it is as well to keep the discussion at the level of ideas, rather than personalities. If you do attack your opponent, be sure of your ground. Make certain that his discomfiture is intended – and that it has a reasonable chance of leading to the results you seek. The thoughtless, careless, unprepared and vicious outburst in public can

*See also Chapter 29 on Rudeness.

wreck a friendship, a partnership, a board, a project. Whether you are speaking at a comparatively small meeting or a mighty gathering, be careful. You are not alone. But if your attack is ill-chosen, you soon may be.

On the other hand, if you must attack a personality, then prepare your case with special regard to documentation. Letters, quotations, firm facts – these are what should accompany your theme. The more bitter your resentment, the quieter and more apparently reasonable your tone should appear. If you lose control of yourself, you will probably lose control of both the situation and the organisation, in due course.

It is also a good idea to find out in advance whether your words are likely to be well received. There is no worse time to be shouted down than during a personal attack.

The chances are that if you must tell a man what you think of him, it is better to do so – and not to tell others.

If you are satisfied that rudeness is in season, then make full use of the power of ridicule. Shortly after the last Great War, there were bitter arguments as to whether the Fascist movement should be banned – 'after all, have we not just finished a war against it? They would not give us our freedom, if they had their way – so why should we give them theirs?' But the 'leave them alone and let us hope they die of attrition' group won the day. they poured scorn, ridicule as well as contempt upon Hitler's British imitators. And so far at least, the recipe has worked.

But if the time does come for a personal vendetta, then the time and place must be most assiduously selected. By launching an attack, you invite a counter-attack. By mentioning the name of your opponent, you give him not only the publicity that he probably seeks but – in the eyes of those who believe in fair play – a moral right to reply. Instead of being in sole occupation of the platform, you may have to surrender it to an opponent who would be better off to lurk unseen.

16   Negligence – and those who speak without due care

To drive without due care is an offence dealt with by a magistrates' court. If someone else suffers damage as a result of a careless statement, it may lead to trouble all round. That was one effect of a recent, important decision of the House of Lords, sitting in its judicial capacity.

The story? A well known merchant bank was asked for a reference. The inquirers wished to know whether a certain company was worthy of credit. The bank supplied the information; and when this turned out to be quite incorrect the inquirers lost their money. They sued the bank, claiming that although they (the inquirers) were not customers and the information was supplied gratuitously, the bank still 'owed them a duty of care' – that is, was under a duty to them to exercise such care as was reasonable in all the circumstances to ensure that the information given was correct.

'Nonsense', retorted the bank. 'We supplied the service at no charge and you cannot expect us to have the same liability to you as we would have had, if you were a customer or we had charged you. And anyway,' they added, 'there was a disclaimer on the reference saying that is was given "without responsibility" on the part of the bank or its officers'. And they denied negligence.

The trial judge held that they had been negligent but that the effect of the disclaimer was to let them off the hook. They were under a duty of care, even though the service was given gratuitously. This decision was eventually upheld by the House of Lords.

The basic principle was established long ago. We each owe a duty of care to our 'neighbour', and a 'neighbour', in this sense, is any person whom we ought reasonably to anticipate would be likely to be affected by our negligent act. If, then, you are a manufacturer, you have a liability in contract to the people who buy your goods. If the goods are faulty, then you are in breach of contract. If you are negligent and they suffer injury, loss or damage, then you may be held liable.

But your responsibility does not end there. It extends to 'the ultimate consumer'. Suppose that you manufacture drink. It must be obvious to you that the person who is likely to drink it is not the wholesaler or retailer to whom you actually sell the stuff. The man behind the bar may drink some of his brew, but if he drinks it all there will be no profits. The 'ultimate consumer' – the customer of the retailer or caterer – is the man who will be poisoned if the drink is defective. He is the 'neighbour' of the manufacturer.

So there is a liability in the law of negligence not only to those whom you know but even to complete strangers.

'And the bank', said the House of Lords, in effect, 'must be taken to have realised that the reference was asked for with a purpose in mind. The intention was that the reference be acted upon. So the bank ought to have realised that if the reference was incorrect, the result might well be that the recipient would suffer damage. So the bank "owed a duty of care" to that recipient, even though the service was given gratuitously.' The milk of human kindness may prove a very costly commodity.

So negligence had been found against the bank and a duty of care was owed. The damage was also proved. That left the disclaimer. The bank had given the reference upon the explicit and clear under-standing that it was not to be held responsible for the accuracy of the document. The recipient could not go behind that disclaimer which was fully effective to protect the bank. As a result, the House of Lords did not have to consider the question of whether the defendants had been guilty of negligence. The bank escaped because of its disclaimer.

Ever since that case, all sorts of people have shivered slightly in their shoes – and rushed off to insurance brokers to get cover. The giver of every sort of reference must take care not only to avoid defamation in circumstances in which malice may be imputed to them (see Chapter 14) but must be careful to see that, if asked for a reference for one Peter Smith, he does not provide it in respect of another. He owes a 'duty of care' to the recipient.

Now suppose that you are making a speech. You are supplying information or advice. You owe a duty to your audience to be accurate. You are not guaranteeing complete accuracy in every word. The law only requires of you that you take such care as is reasonable in all the circumstances to ensure that what you say is correct. You will be expected to be as careful and accurate as an average, reasonably skilful speaker, dealing with your area of country. But you do owe a duty of care to your audience. You could, of course, start your speech by saying: 'Everything that I say to you is without responsibility on my part'. The audience will then be in the same position as the man who accepts a lift in a car with a sign up inside: 'Passengers carried entirely at their own risk'. But normally, you must exercise care because if you do not and as a result damage is suffered, you may be held liable in law. If you are obliging your audience by speaking . . . doing an unpaid kindness . . . doling out free information out of the goodness of your heart . . . the result may strike you as distinctly unfair.

Of course, it is not enough to prove that you were negligent in giving the advice or information concerned. To obtain damages against you, your hearers would have to prove two other matters. First, they must show that the statement concerned was acted upon. Second, they must prove that they suffered damage foreseeably arising from the negligence.

Infallibility being a divine attribute, everyone makes mistakes. But happily, most of them lead nowhere. We ourselves may even benefit from them – one wit observed that the great advantage of making a mistake is that next time you may recognise it. If others do the recognising, then that is unfortunate. But it is only if they do not realise that you have been in error and actually take action as a result of your mistake that they will be able to claim a legal remedy.

Suppose, for instance, that you make a misleading statement in a speech to a trade gathering. As a result, one of your hearers consults his Board, his solicitor, his accountant, his management consultant and then – bolstered by the expert approval – takes action along the lines you have suggested. The chances are that he could not blame you. There were too many intervening people, facts and ideas.

Alternatively, suppose you make some provocative statement. It may never enter your head that anyone would be stupid enough to act upon it without further research or inquiry. But then maybe you were being obtuse. The question is: Would the 'reasonable man' have expected you to have foreseen that your hearer would act upon your words? Should you reasonably have prophesied, had you applied your mind to the situation, that your words would give rise to someone else's actions? If not, then your mistake will lead nowhere – at least so far as you are concerned.

Assume, now, that your hearer can overcome both these hurdles. He has still not reached the end of the trail. He must show that the damage was not too remote. Take an example from an ordinary road traffic accident. Your employee caused it through his careless driving. If the man was driving in the course of his employment, you are as responsible as if you had yourself been at the wheel. Therefore you would have to compensate anyone who suffered injury, loss or damage as a result – provided that this was foreseeable.

So the cost of repairing the other vehicle . . . or reimbursing the injured man for his lost wages . . . paying damages in respect of his personal injuries – all these can be laid at your door.

But suppose, on the other hand, that the other driver had missed an important appointment and hence a potentially profitable contract. That will be his misfortune. The damage was 'too remote'.

All this involves some very complicated legal considerations. If by any chance your speech-making leads to the threat of legal prosecution, the sooner you get to your solicitor, the better. Meanwhile, just treat this chapter as a warning – and take care. Even if you are not paid for making your speech, you still owe a duty to your audience. Bore them and they get no recompense – except to take their revenge either by returning the compliment or by not renewing your invitation ever again. But cause them actual loss or damage as a foreseeable result of some careless mis-statement and the sound of your own voice may be a very expensive product indeed.

17 Blasphemy, sedition, injurious falsehood and other spoken traps

There are various other respects in which the law interferes with freedom of speech. They are all comparatively uncommon in practice, but still require a weather eye from the speaker. So here is a miscellany of civil and criminal consequences which can arise out of use of the wrong word.

*   *   *

It is a serious offence 'to speak or otherwise to publish any matter blaspheming God'. You must not 'deny His existence or providence or contumeliously reproach Jesus Christ, or vilify or bring into disbelief or contempt or ridicule Christianity in general or any doctrine of the Christian religion, or the Bible, or the Book of Common Prayer'. But it is no longer a crime merely to 'propagate doctrines hostile to the Christian faith'. The question is – how do you do so? You must not 'exasperate the feelings of others' through any element of 'ridicule, irreverence or vilification'. You must not cause a breach of the peace.

Note that you may reproach Buddha, Mohammed, Abraham, Isaac or Jacob . . . Moses, Vishnu, the Gods of the Medes or the Persians . . . and the law will (unless you are provoking a breach of the peace or anything contrary to *The Race Relations Act, 1978*) do nothing. But then it does nothing, in practice, about blasphemy either. *The Blasphemy Act, 1697*, is still technically on the Statute Book . . . 'if any person or persons having an education in or at any time having made profession of the Christian religion within this realm shall by writing printing teaching or advised speaking . . . maintain or assert there are more Gods than one or shall deny the Christian religion to be true or the Holy Scriptures of the Old and New Testament to be of divine authority . . . and shall be convicted thereof, he shall be stripped of his public offices and if convicted again, he shall cease to be entitled to be guardian of a child, executor or administrator of any person, holder of any office, civil or military or beneficently ecclesiastical for ever within this realm. . . .' He may also be imprisoned for up to three years. This curiosity of the law was unearthed, of course, in the recent *Gay News* case.

The offence of sedition embraces 'all those practices, whether by word, writing or deed, which fall short of high treason but directly tend to have for that object to excite dissatisfaction or discontent . . . to create public disturbance, or to lead to civil war . . . to bring into hatred or contempt the sovereign or the government, the constitution or the laws of the realm . . . to excite ill-will between different classes of the sovereign's subjects . . . to incite people forcibly to obstruct the execution of the law. . . .' and so on, and so on.

In theory, this offence may put a heavy rein on free, political discussion. But in practice, it, too, is almost as dead as the proverbial dodo.

Not so perjury. If any person who is 'lawfully sworn as a witness or as an interpreter in a judicial proceeding wilfully makes a statement material in that proceeding, which he knows to be false or does not believe to be true. . .' he is a perjurer and may be imprisoned for up to seven years or fined an unlimited amount – or both. So when appearing before any 'tribunal, court or person having by law power to hear, examine and receive evidence on oath', mind how you speak (and see also Chapter 45 on witness-boxing).

Although there are prosecutions for perjury, bearing in mind the number of perjurers, it is obvious that the fear of committing this offence has about as little effect on the dishonest witness as any terror of purgatory, caused by flouting the witnesses' oath.

Now for some civil results of uncivil words.

As we have seen in Chapter 14, defamation may lead to trouble.

But has it occurred to you that to speak ill of a person's goods may be defamatory of his person? Suppose, for instance, that you say: 'Jones is turning out really shoddy stuff these days and selling it at a very high price'. You are hardly heaping compliments on Jones's goods. You are saying, in effect: 'That man Jones is a rogue – he is selling low-quality goods at a high price'.

But quite apart from libel and slander, words may themselves give 'a cause of action' if they cause damage to a person 'in the conduct of his affairs' or are calculated to cause him pecuniary loss.

Suppose, first, that any sort of property is up for sale. A man 'without lawful motive' untruly alleges that the property is charged or that there are liabilities upon it or that the vendor is not in a position to sell. This is 'slander of title'.

Again, to say of someone that he is selling goods in infringement of copyright or patent, you may be alleging 'slander of title'. But nowadays, there are various statutory remedies available to those accused of this sort of behaviour (as by Section 65 of *The Patents Act, 1949* – which says that a person who is threatened with proceedings for infringement of the patent may bring an action for declaration that the threats are unjustifiable, and may also claim an injunction and – if he has suffered any – damages as well).

Again, falsely and maliciously to disparage the quality of a man's goods may give rise to a cause of action – if the disparagement prevents their sale. By all means indulge in 'mere trade puffery', but 'knocking' may lead to trouble.

So where a false statement is made maliciously (out of a desire to injure and without lawful authority) and produces as its direct result 'damage capable of legal estimation', an action may lie for slander of title, or of goods 'or other malicious falsehood'.

Finally, just a note on 'malice'. 'Maliciously' has been defined as meaning 'without just cause or excuse'. Unlawfully and intentionally to do 'without just excuse or occasion' an action which causes damage may lead to trouble. But it is certainly malicious to act out of some improper or dishonest motive or with the intention of causing injury. Where there is 'a distinct intention to injure the plaintiff apart from honest defence of the defendant's own property', an action may lie, without there being any defamation as such. (For 'malice' as affecting the defence of 'qualified privilege' see Chapter 14.)

What it really comes to is that if you improperly or dishonestly attack the title or property or products of your competitors, they may have a good claim against you. The law approves of competition but frowns upon the more unpleasant forms of 'knocking' of the goods and property of others.

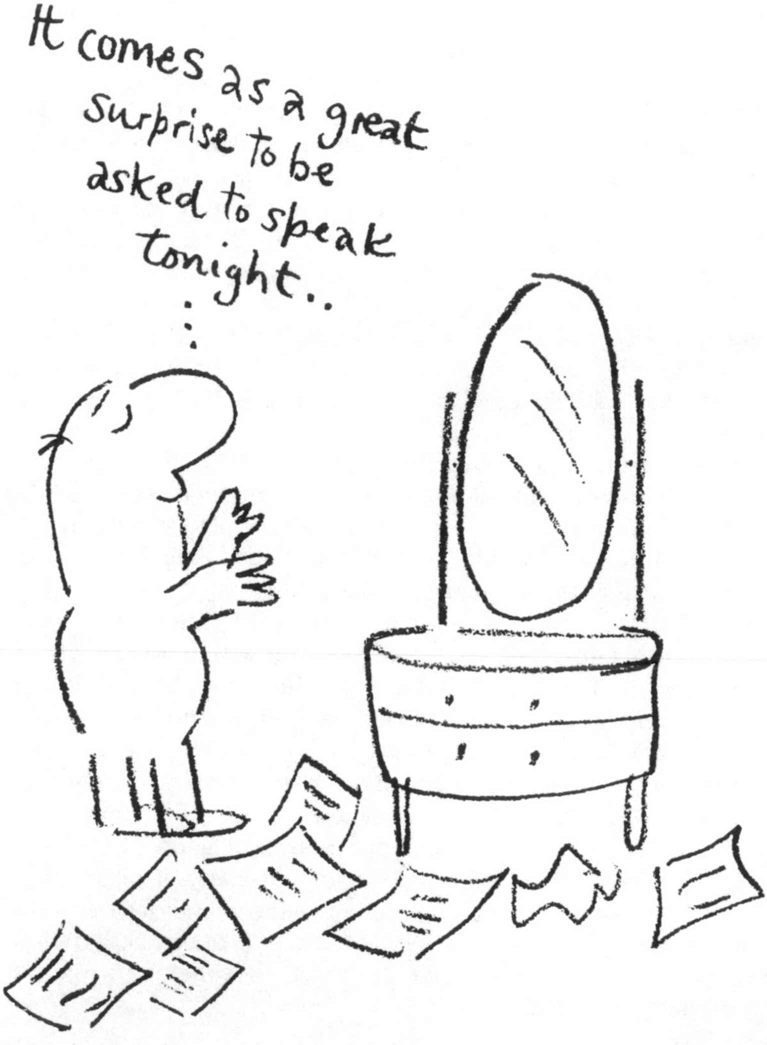
It comes as a great surprise to be asked to speak tonight..

Part 2

The arts of delivery

18 Advance organisation

In Italy, opera singers employ a claque. They have to. They pay the organisers who then ensure that the star receives the appropriate (or even inappropriate) applause, at the right time. If any star sees fit not to pay up, then (as one of them recently remarked), 'they are quite capable of whistling instead'.

Those who speak in public may also have a claque – paid or unpaid. And if the opportunity arises, no harm is done by ensuring that you get off to a good start or that your words appear to be treated with such delight that (with luck) your opponents may not like to speak out. People are like the proverbial sheep, particularly in public. They like to be on the winning side. Few have the courage to speak their minds openly in the face of a vociferous majority. 'What's the good of it?' they say – not realising that if they only spoke out, they might well win the day. And they might discover that the noise-makers were in fact nothing more than a loud-mouthed minority.

The most inoffensive type of claque work is easily organised. 'For heaven's sake show me some support', you say to your friends. 'If you do not give me some loud "Hear Hears", I shall stop trying. I refuse to be shot at on my own.'

Alternatively: 'This is going to be a very difficult audience to warm up. If you would be kind enough to start the clapping when I am called upon to speak, I shall remember you in my will!' (Have you ever noticed that it only takes one or two people to clap the speaker and the rest join in – but if no one starts, he goes on 'cold'?).

Again: 'I am going to tell them the story about the. . . . For heaven's sake laugh!'

Of course, you may carry your claque along with you because they are under some obligation. Maybe you employ them . . . are the kind benefactor on whom they rely . . . have patronage in your gift. In that case, no preparation should be needed. Wise barristers soon learn to laugh at the judge's jokes – and whenever possible to produce any of their own ideas in the guise of words of wisdom dropped by Their Lordships.

But if you are on strange ground or amongst an unfamiliar audience, do not be afraid to ask your friends to give you the appropriate leg-up. One day you may be able to return the compliment.

Of course, advance 'softening up' of an audience may often go far deeper than this. If you have a case to put forward, you should do your best to sound out your audience in advance. If you have a resolution to propose, make sure that someone will be prepared to second it. The proposer without support is a miserable fellow and, in most cases, would have been better off to keep silent. A good speaker not only prepares his case, but also his audience.

Of course, none of this preparation should show. One reason why inexperienced speakers often take too little care in the preparation of their material is that they have seen how apparently easy the experienced speaker makes it all seem. Be not deceived. In general, the higher the polish, the greater the elbow grease . . . the more relaxed and effortless the style, the more careful has been the preparation.

Of course, there are natural speakers who need to take less care than the rest. But follow one of them round. Note how his performance varies. The odds are that when he stumbles, repeats himself, goes on for too long, breaks the basic rules of good speaking and starts to bore his audience – then he has not prepared his speech.

The better the preparation of the material and of its reception, the less it will show. The more it shows, the less its effect. In fact, if audience preparation shows at all, the insincerity of the claque may rub off on your speech. And that could be a disaster.

So choose your supporters with as much care as your words. But do not be too proud to prepare both with equal attention.

*   *   *

Incidentally, if you are the chairman, do make your preparations with special care. If there is to be a question time, prime someone to break the ice and to ask the first question – otherwise the silence may be unreal and embarrassing and ruin the evening. If you have to appear neutral but would like to espouse a particular viewpoint, make sure you get the best proponent possible to be ready with his speech at an early stage – and someone else available to do a later mopping-up operation. If preparing a team, the basis used by most athletes for relays could be helpful. The anchor man – your best – goes last. The next best goes first. The third does the third leg. And the worst goes second. You may want to put your anchor man first, of course – particularly if he has a right of reply (see Chapter 24).

If you are not the chairman, but are particularly interested in a particular topic or anxious to speak on it (or if you have to leave early or arrive late) do get the arrangements set up in advance. Most chairmen will oblige. They will probably be glad to have advance

notice of your intentions, so that they can plan operations accordingly.
  There is nothing like a pre-arranged plan to produce a happy result – provided the pre-arrangement is done with care and common sense.

19   Practice – and nerves

The more practice you get in public speaking, the better. But you will never chase away the butterflies for ever. 'Nerves' are part of the equipment of every public speaker.
  The finest athletes are liable to feel decrepit and wobbly before their big event. But the moment that they line up at the start, or are in position for the game to begin, their nerves fall away. Nature has done its job. Adrenalin has been pumped through the body. The athlete is keyed up and ready to give of his very best.
  The same process precedes the making of an important speech. Its importance may have nothing to do with the size of the audience (see, for example, Chapter 43 on Interviews). It may assume special gravity because it concerns your reputation or your future – or because you are dealing with a new and unfamiliar audience. There are very few of us who escape that nasty feeling in the pit of the stomach before some big speech.
  So the beginner can comfort himself with the thought that even those who appear to have the most confidence and experience may well be feeling much like himself. Of course, they will not show it. The skilled man will not twist his hat, chew his finger-nails or tear up bits of paper. Part of his art is to dissemble his feelings. To some extent, the public speaker is an actor – but one who must normally write his own scripts.
  Far from worrying about your 'nerves', you should be grateful for them. They are causing the adrenalin to build up and to prepare you for your ordeal. If you have no nerves . . . no feeling of apprehension . . . no pre-speech worries – then the odds are that you will not give of your best.
  So banish those terrifying fears that your throat will dry up, your voice crack, your mind go blank. Provided you have prepared your

speech . . . that you have your notes handy (see Chapter 3) . . . that you know what you are to be talking about – all should be well. Under no circumstances must you panic, or all will be lost.

The more practice you get, the more your basic confidence will grow. If you are at a meeting, steel yourself. Ask questions of the speaker. If you are offered the chance of proposing the vote of thanks, accept. If a small group wishes you to address it, agree to do so. If you have been dealing with some new and interesting project . . . if you have gone on a lengthy and unusual journey . . . if you have something out of the ordinary to say – then let this be known. The chances are that your club, friendly society, pet charity, political group, trade organisation or other body which you have previously merely belonged to, will be only too delighted to invite you to speak to its members or some section of them.

Or maybe you have a social function of your own: a dinner party, a cocktail party, or a company lunch. This time, stand up and say those few words of welcome, of thanks, of genuine greeting. If the speech is to be of any length, then (whatever the social occasion) the rules in Chapter 33 (on After-Dinner Speaking) will provide you with some useful guides. Remember: the higher you rise (or would wish to rise) in any field, the more vital it is that you should be able to express yourself on your feet. The only way to gain experience is to get up on those feet and, as the Americans put it, to 'sound off'. You will then cease to be afraid of becoming the centre of public attention; you will get used to the sound of your own voice, raised in public. You will stop worrying about 'making a fool of yourself'. And you will eventually learn how you can even cash in on your own mistakes.

So speak. The odds are that, however much you were previously kicking yourself for having agreed to do so, your nervousness will fall away when your words come through, loud and clear, and you see that your audience is listening to them. To borrow the words of President Roosevelt, you have nothing to fear but fear itself.

20 Handling an audience

Many an outstanding speaker does not talk to his audience at all. He looks around for some friendly face, and even amongst the most hostile gathering, there is usually someone from whom he can extract a friendly or tolerant smile. He then talks to that person. The speaker who looks over the top of his audience, out into space, seems to be indulging in soliloquy. But even he is better than the man who keeps his head lowered and mumbles into his notes.

Audiences are people. They want to be entertained. In most cases, they have come to the gathering, whatever it may be, because they are interested – if not in what you are going to say, then in what the meeting is to undertake. You keep their interest by talking to them – and not over their heads, literally or metaphorically. Look at them. Speak to them.

If asked to address a particular gathering, try to find out the sort of people to whom you will be talking. By all means inquire what the size of the audience is expected to be. Your preparation may differ considerably according to the number of your listeners. But even more important, try to find out whether they are skilled or unskilled, simple or learned, well versed in your topic or new to it, likely to be friendly or hostile.

After all, if you are attempting to put through a business deal, in private, you would not give the same 'spiel' to everyone. You would try to tailor your talk to the nature, personality, interests and sensitivity of your hearer. 'That's only common sense', you say. Well, if more public speakers would apply that same sense to their audiences, the market for public speaking would not be spoiled as it is. People would turn up to meetings, instead of preferring their television sets. And speakers would be a great deal more successful than they are.

Whatever and whomever your audience may be, you must watch them while you speak. You can easily see whether they are concentrating or shifting around in their seats. If you have held them still for some time, then stop. Pause. Take a sip from your glass of water. Fiddle through your notes. Give your audience the chance to shift about and then to resettle. No one can concentrate for any lengthy period of time without a break.

If, on the other hand, your audience is restless when you do not intend it to be so, you must restore your hold upon it. If you have been pretty serious, then throw in a joke, a story, an anecdote. If you have been speaking at high volume, then switch to a confidential tone. If nothing works, then wind up – either permanently or for an extended question time. There is no more important rule for the public speaker than to keep a hawk-like watch on his listeners. It is different, of course, if you are talking to yourself – and if you ignore this rule, you soon will be.

Postscript – *looking them in the eye*

As we have already seen, one of the speaker's problems is where to look. Facing your audience and looking them in the eye is a problem. But why should it be? Know the reason and the problem becomes easier to beat. Consider, then, one paragraph in that most revealing of books, *The Naked Ape* by Dr Desmond Morris:

> 'A professional lecturer takes some time to train himself to look directly at the members of his audience, instead of over their heads, down at his rostrum, or out towards the side or back of the hall. Even though he is in such a dominant position, there are so many of them, all staring (from the safety of their seats), that he experiences a basic and initially uncontrollable fear of them. Only after a great deal of practice can he overcome this. The simple, aggressive, physical act of being stared at by a large group of people is also the cause of the fluttering "butterflies" in the actor's stomach before he makes his entrance on to the stage. He has all his intellectual worries about the qualities of his performance and its reception, of course, but the massed threat-stare is an additional and more fundamental hazard for him.'

There it is. We fear those who stare at us. But if you want to lift your head above the crowd, you must expect people to stare at it. Learn to stare right back.

21   Your friend, the microphone?*

In the old days, you had to speak to be heard. (For details, see Chapter 22 on Voice Production.) Nowadays, a whisper will do. The microphone has definitely arrived. What matters is to know how to use it. Well employed, it is a trusty ally. Over-employed or misused and it will blast away your audiences for ever.

A voice was a pre-requisite for a singer. No more. With the aid of the 'mike', the men of alleged music can make their fortunes without, in many cases, enough power in their lungs to fill a telephone box. Alternatively, they may belt out the tune – but the nuances and expressions which the opera singer spends years learning to create are absent. The effects which brighten so many otherwise even more miserable music moments are created by the microphone – through the tricks of the trade.

Now, not every businessman required to speak in public is blessed with the voice of a Churchill. Some of us have voices which refuse to be produced. Never mind. We can learn a good deal from the pop singers.

First, make sure that your mike is switched on. Tap it with an inquiring finger. The sound of the tap should reverberate. And you should hear it. Nothing is more embarrassing than to talk into a microphone which is dead when you think it is alive but your audience knows that it is not.

Next, adjust the microphone to your height. Whether it is a standing or a table model, the chances are that there is a turning ring near the centre which – with a bit of luck and some reasonable wrist power – should enable you to fix the microphone at just below the level of your mouth. The top of the speaking part of the instrument, then, should be almost level with your lips. You may, of course, be lucky and be given one of those marvellous, modern gadgets you simply hang around your neck. Then you have no worries at all – assuming that it works. But otherwise, adjust for level.

In the artillery, there's a routine. You line up your gun as follows: roughly for elevation; roughly for line; cross-level; accurately for line;

*See also Chapter 38 on Microphone in the Open Air and Chapter 45 on Radio and TV techniques.

47

accurately for elevation. Hours of incredibly boring drill drum this routine into the mind – so that even years later, the odds are that the order is approximately accurate. There should be a similar routine for the mike-user. Roughly for height; roughly for position; volume; accurately for position; trial words.

So position the microphone in front of you, even if this means keeping people waiting while you adjust the cord or, if at a table, whilst it gets lifted over the wine and whisky. With the position and the level right and the mike switched on, you now check for volume.

You should be able to stand (or, in some cases, to sit) comfortably and perhaps six inches away from the microphone and still have your voice come through loud, clear and undistorted. If there is a scream, a whistle or a shriek, then it is on too loud. If there is a whisper, it is on too soft. If your voice sounds as if it were coming from outer space, with a Martian echo or an eerie ululation, then something needs adjusting.

This, of course, is not an engineer's summary. It is simply the result of years of acquaintanceship with microphones. So get hold of the mike, position it, and speak out. If the sound is wrong, then stop and have it adjusted before you launch into your speech.

'Fellow directors. . . .' Silence. Lift up your voice: 'Will someone kindly switch on this mechanical marvel?' Laughter. With a bit of luck, the engineer scurries around and flips the appropriate switch. 'Thank you.' Screams and whistles from the machine. More laughter. 'There's no need to overdo it.' The engineer tries again. 'Fellow directors. . . .' Silence. 'Are you receiving me?' you say, smilingly tapping the dreaded instrument. 'Do you hear me at the back?' Loud cries of 'No, no' and more laughter. But note: They are laughing with and not at you. You have command of the situation. You are waiting until the conditions are as you wish them to be before you start speaking.

With luck and perseverance, the microphone will be put into proper order. If it is not – or if reception is intermittent or unpleasant – then you must make up your mind as to whether or not your voice will carry. Is it better to risk being unheard than to submit your audience to squeals and screeches from the machine? Will you succeed in interesting your audience, when the microphone is playing up? Have you, perhaps, a genius in the place who can adjust the amplifier, the loudspeaker, or some other unmentionable or unpronounceable part of this gadget? Think on your feet – fast.

'I shall do without the microphone', you belt out. 'And I hope that you will all hear me.' Applause.

Alternatively: 'I apologise for the inefficiency of this modern marvel. I think I had better submit you to the occasional grunt and growl, so that at least I may have the pleasure of letting you hear what I have prepared to say!' Hear, hear!

One way or another, you are off – even if it is to a late and unhappy start. But your audience have seen that you have complete confidence. More good speeches are ruined because the speaker is not prepared to take his time and make his preparations with the microphone than for almost any other reason.

Once you are speaking into the mike, remember that (usually) you are limited in your movement (see also Chapter 21). When you shift away from the mouthpiece, the volume falls. Turn your head either way and your words may be addressed to the entire hall but heard only by those at your feet. Find your distance from the machine and stay there. Within limits, you can relax. But move outside those limits and a lot is lost. Hence, of course, the special virtue of the hanging mike. Use one of them and (assuming, as before, that it is properly adjusted) you can move wherever the cord will allow.

For this reason, the hanging mike is infinitely to be preferred to the standing variety, whenever there is to be a lecture or other long speech which may require the speaker to move to blackboards . . . to wield a pointer at slides or diagrams . . . to alter his position. The man who speaks into a standing microphone, then rushes across the stage to point silently to some screen and then back to the microphone once more, is asking for trouble. He is also, of course, breaking his thread of speech and the audience's thread of thought. The good speech has continuity. The attention of the audience remains with the words spoken or, at the least, with the speaker's thoughts and not with his movements.

Experience will show each speaker how best he may make use of the microphone. But most of the above rules apply to us all. Make the mike your ally. Never panic when it goes wrong. Be prepared to fall back on your own voice power, if you have to – so that you are really not afraid of the microphone not working. Take your time when you start. Make friends with the engineer so that he is particularly careful to have the gadget fixed to your convenience, your height, your voice. And you have a trusty friend that King Henry V, Elizabeth I, Mark Anthony and Julius Caesar would have welcomed. Come to think of it, how did any of those great speeches ever get heard by more than a fraction of the alleged multitudes ready to receive them?

22 Voice production

We may not all be opera singers, but we must make the best of such voice as we have. With luck, this happens naturally. Even the maximum of training, coaching or attention would prove useless without a basic flair for speech. But the unheard word would be better to remain unheard.

Basically, we are told, the chest is a sound-box. The voice should reverberate and carry, in the same way as a stringed instrument acquires its volume through the resonance of its sound chamber. The human voice, then, is an instrument and may be used properly or otherwise.

Try saying the word 'war'. First, talk through your nose. A puny sound. Then, speak the word from the front of your mouth. That's a little better. Now take a deep breath and expound the word until you can feel the vibration in your chest.

'If war comes again', says the speaker, 'then it must mean disaster for us all'. 'War' is a word which receives no special attention and produces little drama.

'Disaster . . . faces us all . . .' says the orator. 'We are standing . . . perilously close . . . to the menacing brink . . . of . . . WAR!' Now, this may produce a 'ham' effect, but if the well produced, deep and resonant sound is used from time to time to vary the more general conversational tone of the speech, it can be immensely effective.

The opposite also applies. To get and to hold the attention of an audience it is not necessary always to shout at them. The dramatic effect of a whisper can be intense. 'What greater menace is there than . . . the industrial spy?' Proclaim the last three words and they have an untrue ring. But whisper them and you can give them a snake-like quality.

But above all, however much you change the volume and tone of your speech, you must be heard. Speak to the rather deaf-looking lady in the back row. If she can hear you, you need not worry about the gentleman in the front. Be particularly careful not to drop your voice at the ends of sentences. The final few words should generally be spoken even more loudly and clearly than the rest – it is the inexperienced speaker who drops his last few words into his beard.

Assuming that you can be heard, what really matters is to avoid monotony. Vary your tone . . . the speed at which you speak . . . the volume of your words. Your job is to keep the attention of your audience. While to do so you must produce your voice with reasonable skill, the odds are that the less you actually think about voice production while on your feet, the better. Concentrate instead upon what you are saying . . . upon letting your audience hear it . . . and upon keeping their attention focused always upon you.

23 Persuading – the art of advocacy

Barristers, said Dean Swift, are men 'bred up in the art of proving that white is black and black is white, according as they are paid'. He left out of account, of course, the ethics of the Bar, which often requires its members to keep faith with the court by acting (and speaking) against the interests of their clients. Advocacy is one thing, deception another. Still, the Swift aphorism is too good to forget. And even the businessman may often be forced to propound or to defend in public, policies or decisions which, in private, he abhors.

It is not only the Cabinet that must stand by its majority decisions. The same normally applies to the Board of a company, the partners of a firm or the committee of an organisation. Either you accept democracy – allow your views to be overruled when the majority of your colleagues are against them – or you resign. If you remain in office, then you must stand by your colleagues. And this may mean engaging in their public defence.

So the advocate may not only have to propound views which are unpopular with his audience, but even those which find little favour with himself. Businessmen customarily attack lawyers and politicians as sophists and word twisters. But just listen to that executive, trying to make the creditors' meeting 'see sense' . . . the chairman attempting to extract himself (and possibly the company secretary) from trouble . . . the sales director, drilling his sales force about an unpopular (and perhaps not very satisfactory) product. There is really no end to the categories of persuasion in which the modern businessman has to indulge.

There is little art in persuading the convinced, preaching to the converted or keeping your team behind you when they all agree with your views or policies. To enthuse is, of course, important. But to argue a difficult case – or even one that seems on the face of it to be impossible – is a very much greater task. And here the businessman may take many a leaf from the brief of the skilful barrister.

Start with the quiet, sincere but firm approach. Call it 'the soft sell' if you like, but the studied lack of histrionics lies at the root of the modern persuader's art. Gone are the days of the ranter, the arm waver, the loud shouter (see Chapter 27). The theatrical tugger at the strings of the heart may still have his place in the revivalist meeting or the Welsh chapel, but he is a stranger to the court of law – and should be equally so to the company or organisational meeting.

The more your audience starts against you, the greater the importance of moderation – especially in your opening. Here are some well tried gambits for the man in a minority:

'I fully appreciate the difficulty of my task in convincing you that. . . . But I hope and believe that if you will be good enough to give my case a fair and full hearing, you will be as convinced as I am that. . . .'

'Mr Black, who has just addressed you, is a skilled and experienced advocate and has presented the case against with skill and eloquence. But there is another side to the picture and, before coming to a decision, I am certain that you would wish that both sides of the story be fully ventilated. . . .'

'I am sure that many of us were extremely sorry to hear the vehemence and, in some cases, even the venom – with which the case for – has been put before this meeting. Whilst many of the points made have at least apparent validity, when you go a little beneath the surface, all is not quite as some of my friends have suggested. There are some very important points to be made to the contrary and I am sure that this committee/organisation/meeting would not wish to take any decision on such a very important matter without having had both points of view put before it. I shall do so, as briefly as possible: but I would be grateful for your indulgence, Mr Chairman, if I take a little longer than usual because one really does have to go into the case against – in some depth in order to establish its essential correctness. . . .'

'This is a small committee of busy people and I really do think that we should expend no more time and energy in surplus pursuit of Mr X. He has made serious mistakes and is in the process of paying for them. Let us look to the future. And would it not be helpful to start with some of the achievements of Mr X. In many ways – some would say in most ways – he let us down badly. But he has laid certain foundations for our future success. First . . . Second . . . Third . . . Fourth . . . Fifth . . . Sixth. . . .' By the time you are finished, Mr X appears to be quite a splendid character, does he not? But if you had started with his virtues, you would have lost all hope of winning your case.

*   *   *

Here, now, are some notorious traps to be avoided:

'Does anyone really think Mr Y has cheated the company?' Cries of 'Certainly. . .'.

'Could it conceivably be in the long-term interest of this organisation to follow the line proposed by Mr Black?' Shouts of: 'Of course'.

'Does anyone really think that I do not know my job after all these years?' Loud cries of 'Yes' – and laughter.

Avoid the rhetorical question.

'I am . . . a man. . . .' pause: shouts of 'No, no,' . . .

The pause is a useful weapon – but watch where you place it (see Chapter 25).

'You may think that the statements you have just heard from Mr Z are about as untrue, misleading, ill-conceived and plain stupid as one could ever envisage.' This sort of attack – especially by someone in a minority – can only lead to vituperation, venom and defeat. Softly, softly, catchee monkee . . . as the Chinese are reputed to put it.

'I am furious. . . .' Then do not show it.

'I could weep when I hear such extravagant attacks.' They all know that tears are not in your line – so away with the crocodiles.

*   *   *

Another move which is nearly always an error is to walk out of a meeting in high dudgeon. There are occasions when there is no decent alternative left to you. If decisions are taken which you regard as illegal, dishonest or so contrary to the welfare of the body concerned that you disassociate yourself publicly from them, then you may have no alternative. But otherwise, stay put and fight. Your chances of winning from without are far less than of working your colleagues or audience around to your way of thinking, from within. If you leave, remember that it is highly unlikely that you will be invited back. The dramatic exit is necessary for the diplomat whose country is publicly attacked in his presence. But it is seldom the answer for the orator spurned.

The threat of resignation is, of course, a powerful and a valid weapon. But it must not be misused or over-employed. Before it is used at all, you must consider whether it has any persuasive power. If your colleagues or the meeting would be happy to see you go, then you should rarely offer to provide satisfaction.

'If this decision is to be made, then I hope that it will not be taken amiss if I say that I shall have no alternative other than to reconsider my membership.' Fairly put. 'I have worked for this organisation for many years and am anxious to continue to do so in the future. I would not wish to sever my ties nor to be forced into such a position that I would have no alternative other than to do so. I do beg you to reconsider. Or at least, please do give me a fair hearing for the other point of view. I would put it like this. . . .' The chances of your not getting a fair hearing are remote.

On the other hand, avoid: 'If you do not change your minds, then I shall resign'. You are inviting the retort: 'Go right ahead'.

24   *The reply*

The debater who contents himself with making his own speech, without reference to those which have gone before, does not know his job. And many discussions – in public and private meetings of companies and organisations of all sorts – are really debates. The skilled speaker must study the art of making a reply.

The proposer of a motion or resolution is normally accorded the 'right of reply'. He opens the debate or discussion, and before the vote is taken, he has the privilege of closing it. His speech should not be a mere repetition of his original effort. He should deal – courteously, clearly and firmly – with the speeches which have intervened.

First, he should thank those who have spoken in favour of the resolution. Directly or by implication he should congratulate them on their perspicacity. 'I was not surprised to have the warm support of that experienced businessman, Mr Brown – but I was grateful for it none the less . . . Mr Green is highly experienced in the trade and I do hope that everyone here will give his words due weight . . . Mr White comes to us from an entirely different side of the trade. It is therefore all the more significant that he approves of this resolution. . . .' 'Mr Green is, as you will all know, an extremely skilled and public-spirited lawyer. We must all be grateful to him for the careful analysis he gave to our problems – and for the legal light which he cast upon the dangers of the course of action espoused by those who oppose this resolution . . .'

Then demolish your enemies. 'I am sorry that Mr Diamond has not appreciated the warnings given by Mr Black. . . .' 'If Mr Stone had really considered the argument that . . . I feel sure he would have come to a different conclusion. . . .' 'Mr Ruby is, I fear, just plain wrong. The facts are not as he has suggested. The true position is. . . .'

Then sum up your arguments once again, in a few sentences (see Chapter 2 on Perorations). Commend your resolution to the meeting. Then hope for the best.

Do not be afraid to use notes when replying. No one will expect you to remember all that has been said without keeping jottings. Once again, the card system may be very helpful (see Chapter 3). You can, if you like, deal with the questioners or opponents in turn. But you would probably be better off to rearrange the comments and criticisms to suit your argument. Remember that a reply is a speech like any other. It needs a good opening; a sound body; and a proper end.

Some suggested openings:

'Thank you, Mr Chairman, for permitting me to reply to some of the points raised. . . .'

'Mr Chairman, I suggest that nothing that has been said against the resolution has in any way destroyed its essential validity. . . .'

'We must all be grateful to those who have taken part in this debate. Even those who oppose the resolution do so with the interests of the company at heart. But as, I think, we have seen from the speeches of Mr Brown, Mr White and Mr Black, its opponents have not really grasped the importance of the course of action suggested – and the risks of following any alternative. . . .'

'The differences between us, Mr Chairman, have been fully aired. Every possible alternative has been thrashed over. But, at the end of the day, are we not still left with only one real possibility? The resolution must be passed.'

*   *   *

The making and answering of toasts is the subject of Chapter 34, but some of the above rules also apply to many responses to toasts. Do not ignore the speeches that have gone before. Do deal with any points of criticism or suggestion raised by previous speakers. Do not fear to use notes to remind you of the words of others. And do make certain that your speech is properly constructed. You have one great advantage over the man replying to a debate. His speech must not only appear extempore but must actually be so. Yours may be carefully prepared.

25　The pause

Churchill used the pause more than any other great orator. It is this interval between words, phrases or sentences that keeps the audience expectantly waiting for the next thought. Whilst the 'er' is normally the sign of a bad and aggravating speaker, and should be avoided like the plague – if you are a good enough orator, you can even use that irritating habit to good effect. 'We . . . er . . . have no intention of allowing that . . . er . . . maniac to control our lives.' Each pause and each 'er' merely whetted the audience's appetite for Churchill's next slashing attack on the Nazis.

But for those of us who are not Churchills the pause without the 'er' is to be recommended. If you cannot think what to say, never mind – say nothing. So long as the audience thinks you are searching for the *mot juste*, even though you know you have a blank mind, all is well. 'Er' not. Stand firm. Look fierce. Look around. And when you are ready with your next pearl, drop it.

At the start of a speech, talk or intervention, you must be silent until you have the attention of your audience. If you are interrupted – whether by a drop of a window, the shrill of a jet passing overhead or the intervention of a colleague or interrupter – wait for silence before you proceed. To pause is not the sign of indecision or weakness. It is the speaker's greatest potential weapon – and the one that most speakers use far too little.

The pause before an important word is a superb trick, provided that it is not used too often. 'Ladies and Gentlemen, if we do not now take the steps I have suggested, I foresee only one result.' Pause. Look round. Wait. 'Absolute disaster for the company.'

'We all remember the terrible days of . . .' pause. You are only using an extension of the suspense motivation, employed at the end of each properly constructed instalment of a radio play . . . the end of the chapter of a tightly written crime story . . . you are keeping your audience on its toes.

'After hearing all the views of this committee, I have come to my decision. I think that we have no alternative other than . . . to . . .' Wait for it . . . keep them waiting . . .

Of course, the pause must not be too long. Just as brevity of a wait may show lack of confidence and cause the pause to lose half its effect, so too great a length may be regarded by the audience as 'pure ham'. To over-dramatise is as bad as to under-play. Only experience can teach the speaker how long to pause. Only practice can show the maximum period for the best effect, But if in doubt, pause longer. Under stress, time tends to pass slowly. Prepare an important speech and rehearse it more or less word for word and time yourself on a stop-watch. Then make the same speech on the important occasion and get someone to time you. Ten to one you get through it quicker under stress. (Only when you must expect and deal with interruptions . . . including, one hopes, applause . . . will the converse apply, of course.)

While gaining that experience, then, consider the most common occasions for pauses.

1 *The opening* Make sure that your audience have settled down and are ready to hear you – whether you are making a major oration at a rally or a minor intervention at a Board meeting.
2 *In mid-sentence* To emphasise a really important point.
3 *After an interruption of any sort* Once again, your audience must be settled in to hear what you have to say.
4 *Before your last few words* 'And now, Ladies and Gentlemen, I beg you once more to support your Board . . .' pause 'so as to ensure . . .' pause '. . . that this great organisation . . .' pause '. . . will continue to flourish.' Pause. Look around at those from whom you expect applause. And then sit down.

Which brings us to the final hint. Applause is a very helpful (not to say invigorating) leg-up for any speaker. If you did not want it, you would not speak. We all like to be liked. We all wish our words to be accepted. The 'hear hear' or clapping is as gratifying to the speaker as the groan is a misery. It is essential to anticipate and to deal with the cheers – and to fish for and to pause after them.

It is rare that a pause should be used against the groaner. By all means look round and glare at the man who has the temerity to jeer at you. But then leap back at him with both feet. 'People who have the interests of the company at heart and want to see this venture succeed will not assist by that sort of behaviour. . . .' Or: 'I do not think that you, sir, are assisting your cause by behaving in that manner'. Or, if kindness seems to be the best way to deal with the situation: 'I am sorry that you should see fit to jeer, sir. If you would be good enough to wait a little, you will hear the reasons for my last remarks. And you will see that they are correct.' Then pause. Allow the effect of the jeer to die away. But do not pause so long that the interrupter is encouraged to have another go. The borderline between the effective and the defective pause is a narrow one. Each case must be judged on its own facts. But far more people rush forward in haste than regret the (apparently) confident wait for silence, attention . . . effect.

The pause is even more vital – and less of a risk – when fishing for cheers. If you are nervous, follow the sound theatrical first-night tradition of organising your own claque. Tell them that when you refer to Mr Jones and his great service to the company, they must immediately clap. 'Be a good chap and cheer loudly when I finish the sentence about. . . .' It only takes one or two people to get the applause moving. 'When old Smith gets up to speak, for heaven's sake help me to give him a good reception. . . .' A fair gambit. So is: 'We must give the impression of vast enthusiasm for the new project. So when I say how confident I am that it will be a success . . .' pause '. . . clap!' (The pause gambit is even useful in ordinary speech.)

An audience generally likes to know when applause is expected. 'We are all pleased to welcome our guest of honour from abroad, Monsieur Jaune.' Pause and you will get a clap. Rush on and you will not.

'Here, Ladies and Gentlemen, is the first sample of our new product. I present it to you . . .' pause '. . . with pride . . .' pause '. . . I trust that you will sell it, to your profit and that of the company . . .' pause. Look round. Someone will probably say 'hear hear . . .' if only to please you.

One possible approach if no one applauds is to attack them for their silence. 'Gentlemen, the success of each of you, as well as that of the company, depends upon the way you push this product. So I trust that your silence is no indication of any lack of enthusiasm. I invite you . . .' pause '. . . to greet with pleasure this new success from our research department.'

If that does not do the trick . . . if you cannot drag up the applause you want, then never mind. Move on. Change your tack. Alter your approach. Try again. But do not rush. Wait. Control your audience. Do not be afraid of the pause. The old saying, 'silence is golden', has no more vital and accurate application than in the world of the spoken word. Silence is sometimes a weapon as valuable as speech itself.

26 *Interruptions*

Sometimes speakers welcome interruptions – in the right places. Apart from giving the speaker the chance to show his mettle, the heckler can rouse the audience and put them on the speaker's side ... the unexpected break can bring variety to a dull occasion and spark off an easy flood of laughter ... and sometimes, the interruption can make a point better than the speaker could do on his own. But you have to be alert to reap the benefit. If you are tied to a script, written or memorised, you may be thrown off your balance. If you cannot think on your feet, you are better off sitting down.

First, take the heckler. The shareholder comes to a company meeting to criticise. He shouts interruptions at you. How do you deal with him?

You must maintain your dignity. Quiet but firm appeals for a fair hearing usually bring applause. 'I appreciate that the gentleman has a point of view to express and he will be given every opportunity to do so. Meanwhile, I would ask him to have the courtesy to listen.' Alternatively: 'If, sir, you would be good enough to listen to what the Board has achieved in the present difficult circumstances, you might learn something to your benefit'.

If the moment has come to be rude, try: 'If you would listen to me, sir, instead of to yourself, you may be doing yourself a favour, as well as the rest of us'. Or: 'For heaven's sake have the courtesy to be quiet'.

Naturally, if the meeting gets too rowdy and you cannot control it – or, to be more precise, the chairman cannot deal with the interrupters, in the atmosphere which you created or in which you are speaking – then the chairman may have to call on the stewards to evict the interrupters. He is not bound to let your meeting be wrecked (see Chapter 59).

Still, it is rare that a wide-awake speaker cannot keep his audience in reasonably good humour – or at least obtain a hearing, literally as well as metaphorically, without the use of force.

Some interruptions are healthy and helpful – whether or not they were intended to be so. The humorist's outcries can often be turned against himself – assuming that the man on the platform is alert. The scream of a jet engine overhead may drown you for the moment, but give you the opportunity to draw some moral about the point you are making. Even a friendly remark addressed to a member of your audience arriving late may save you both from embarrassment, as well as giving you the opportunity you may in any event need to sort yourself out . . . to vary the pace of your talk . . . to give your audience the chance to relax for a moment, to shift about in their seats and to prepare for the rest of your speech.

What is required, of course, is self-confidence from the speaker. He must pretend to be in complete command of the situation – and will probably discover that in fact he is. The more you feel like panicking . . . the more likely you are to lose control . . . the more you must smile, pause and give the appearance of absolute 'unflappability'. The rowdier the meeting . . . the more disconcerting the interruption . . . the more aggravating the break in your train of thought – the more important it is for you to demonstrate to your audience that you are not to be thrown off your guard. When they see that you are determined to remain in control, the chances are that they will help you to do so.

Go to any first-class political meeting – if you can find one these days – and watch the skilled politician at work. Listen to how he prompts his audience to get cross with hecklers . . . to tell them to 'Shut up' . . . to demand from others in the audience that they give the speaker a fair hearing. Half the good political speaker's work is done for him when he has a few inefficient hecklers in his audience. They rouse supporters, bring the uncommitted to the speaker's side and enliven what might otherwise be a dreary occasion.

The more spontaneous the reply, the wittier the retort, the speedier the counter-attack, the more effective the speaker and his speech. A weak riposte now is better than that brilliant barb which you afterwards wish you had thought of at the time.

So do not be put off your stroke by the interruption. Make use of it.

27 Passion

There are certain matters about which we all feel particularly strongly. It may be something affecting one's personal integrity . . . one's family . . . the entire basis of one's work. It may be a personality . . . an idea . . . a scheme. If our passions are shared by others – all others – then they will have no real place in a public speech. But if we have to fight for our ideas and ideals, they are likely to be the subject of motions and emotions, resolutions (in both senses of that word), speeches and harangues. So in case you have to introduce passion into your public words, here are a few suggestions.

*   *   *

Passions must be controlled. The speaker who loses control over himself will fail to handle his audience. Unless your mind is clear, you cannot put on your best performance. Passion clouds the mind.

Studied calm is a powerful weapon. Your audience will be well aware from your demeanour that you feel deeply. But if you make it clear that your mind is guiding your heart, you are far more likely to influence the ideas, votes or pocket-books of your listeners in the direction you require.

You may wish your audience to feel sorrow with you, but you do not want them to feel pity for you. Just as you may seek to have them laugh with you, if they laugh at you all may be lost. So direct your words at your theme – but not at your own feelings. Finish off, if you like, with a thundering peroration – or an icy blast – indicating your own views and calling for support. But do not let your feelings prevent you from making a good, well-constructed, carefully thought out and well presented speech. Crying does not pay. Passionate eloquence may have its place in the pulpit but it seldom produces results at a company meeting, organisational gathering or public conference.

If you must let off steam, do it at home.

28   Stance and gesture

Most speakers hope to put across ideas. Even if engaged in pure entertainment, you still require the attention of your audience. And it is the words that should be having their effect. So nearly all physical movement is a distraction, to be avoided where possible.

We all know the man who strides up and down while talking, like the American lawyer in the television court-room scenes. In England, lawyers stand still. Their speeches are the better for it.

Comedians doing a tumbling act must gyrate and mime. Not so the man who relies upon the words. Consider the mastery of such as Bob Hope, who stands still and pours wit into the ears of his audience.

The more motionless you stand, then, the greater the chance of your speech reaching the minds of your audience.

But what to do with your hands? The more inexperienced the speaker, the more difficult he finds it to dispose of his hands.

It you have a rostrum or music stand before you, then grip the edge. If you are standing by a table, then you can keep your hands down in front of you. If you stand on your own, then you could do much worse than to put your hands behind your back, *à la* Duke of Edinburgh. What matters is that you should be erect and still.

What of gestures?

These should be sparing. The rarer and the more restrained the movement, the greater its effect. The days of the ranting, tub-thumping, rabble-rousing arm waver are gone. The businessman who 'hams' is regarded (not always rightly) as an insincere show-off. A contemptuous shrug . . . an occasional, accusing finger . . . a reference to the heavens and a hand pointing to the sky . . . these all have their place in the skilled speaker's repertoire. Those who use spectacles may find them quite useful weapons. To emphasise a point, remove them gently from your nose. Hold them still in your hand. Bend forward and glare at your audience. Make your point and then replace your glasses and return to your theme. Even the occasional jab with the closed spectacles can be dramatic and useful. Speakers with spectacles need not be shy. Many excellent speakers who could do without their glasses, even for seeing their notes, deliberately wear them. So do not be afraid of your poor eyesight. Like many other defects, it can be turned to good account.

But generally, the speaker should use his tongue, his face and his mind – not his feet or his fingers. Otherwise his audience may take to their heels.

29   Rudeness – and water off a duck's back*

To turn the other cheek is often a desperately difficult proposition. There are those who recommend it as being good for the soul. But for the businessman who speaks in public, to demonstrate the self-control that this sort of reaction to rudeness inevitably demands is almost always also a good gambit. To lower yourself to your opponent's level rarely achieves the desired results.

Your object, after all, is to win your case – to convince your audience of your rectitude . . . of the usefulness of your activities . . . of the excellence of the way in which you are running the business – or, conversely, of the errors of your opponents. The sharp intellect is a far better weapon than the rough tongue. When the theme is laced with incivility, the audience is likely to suspect a lack of factual backing or to deplore a lack of self-control – or both.

If ever you have a half-hour to spare and are in the vicinity of a court of law, watch how lawyer advocates do their job. They must 'handle the judge'. As one distinguished practitioner put it: 'What matters at the Bar is not whether you know your law but whether you understand your judges'. So spare a moment to watch the professionals – good, bad and indifferent – earning their living through advocacy.

Try, in particular, to find a judge or a magistrate who is known to be 'difficult'. Happily, the vast majority of men and women on the Bench, at all levels, are courteous and, in general, kindly. But there are exceptions – most of them well known to the profession. And even the best of men may be suffering from ulcer, backache or matrimonial troubles. So see how lawyers politely but firmly stand up to the rigours of the unfriendly judge. Quietly, firmly and respectfully – and sometimes with considerable courage – they refuse either to be brow-

*See also Chapter 15 on Personal Attacks.

beaten into premature silence or provoked into unseemly loss of temper. They well know that their client's chance of winning his case is rarely helped if they lose their self-control – or even appear to do so.

There are, of course, famous exceptions. Legal memoirs and reminiscences are full of tales of the brilliant barristerial repartee . . . of Sir Patrick Hastings putting the judge in his place . . . of F. E. Smith carrying his client to victory on the shoulders of a deadly rebuke directed at a disagreeable judge. Like good wines, these tales tend to mellow and improve with age.

But for the average public speaker – whether he be the company director, trying to talk sense into the heads of his Board in revolt . . . the salaried director or company secretary, dealing with the irascible chairman or managing director who is seeing fit to dress him down at a Board meeting . . . or an angry shareholder, making loud-mouthed, unwarranted and personal attacks against the company at its Annual General Meeting – the 'other cheek' policy is seldom out of place.

'I am extremely sorry that Mr Jones has seen fit to deal with this serious matter in such a vituperative fashion. . . .'

'If Mr Jones would be good enough to listen to what the Board has achieved, I think he will regret the manner in which he has seen fit to refer to it. . . .'

'We are all here for a common purpose – to advance the welfare of the business. The sort of remarks which have just been made are likely to send it into retreat. They can only give comfort to our competitors. . . .'

'We will answer each criticism, in turn. We will ignore the personal and regrettably offensive manner in which some of these attacks have been made. If Mr Black really is, as he says, concerned for the welfare of this organisation, I trust that when he has heard the case for the steps which he has so bitterly criticised, he will not only have the good grace to withdraw those criticisms, but also to apologise to those whom he has inevitably hurt by his unkind remarks. I hope that such was not his intention. He is, as we all know, a kindly man, and we all appreciate what he has done for the company. We know how deeply involved he is, emotionally and otherwise, in its success . . . and no one will bear him the least ill-will because he has spoken his mind. . . . But. . . .'

'We all appreciate, I know, the customary frankness with which Mr White has dealt with this resolution. We do not appreciate, however, the personal insinuations he has made – which can only detract from the genuineness of his case and the real concern with which he and those who support him – and, indeed, many of us on your board – view the circumstances he discussed. . . .'

* * *

There is a basic psychological truth that hostility breeds hostility, and an aggressive approach nearly always invites a like response. The converse often applies. Surprise your critics with your moderation, understanding, sensitivity and those views may mellow. It is, in any event, an approach far more likely to succeed than the frontal attack.

What is more, once you have let rip with your hostility, not only has the reasonable possibility of future friendly relations been gravely affected, but you have even discounted the off-chance that the critic was really on your side all the time. Any experienced politician will tell you that some apparently hostile questions are asked at meetings so as to obtain an answer for the benefit of those whom the questioner wishes to convince, and not for the questioner's benefit at all. 'All right, don't listen to me. . . . We'll ask old White. . . . He'll tell you a thing or two. . . .' Blast the questioner for being an idiot and you have obliterated a friend and confirmed a foe in his enmity.

If you must lose your temper, then at least do so with deliberation. Choose your moment and your words with equal care. Absorb the chapter on defamation (Chapter 14). Consider the rules on disorders (Chapter 60). And then – if you must tear into your opponent – do it properly.

A judge once said to F. E. Smith: 'What you are saying to me is going in one ear and out the other'. To which F. E. Smith replied: 'That, my Lord, does not cause me any surprise, having regard to that which lies in between'.

But most of us think of the best repartee when the occasion is past. While swift retorts often produce acclaim far beyond their merit, the rude, unkind, offensive or angry outburst . . . the facetious, sarcastic, ironic or spiteful suggestion – these breed contempt, derision, stony silence – and defeat. And not for the individual towards whom the words are directed.

30   *In a tight corner*

Metaphorically speaking, we tend to draw our allusions, in time of trouble, from the worlds of fencing or boxing. A cutting remark . . . a debating thrust . . . out for the count . . . to hit below the belt . . . in a tight corner . . . and so on. . . .

Well, if you are in difficulties, you must choose your words with especial care. To emerge unscathed, you have three alternatives. You can throw in the sponge . . . trade blow for blow . . . or duck smartly under your opponent's fist, and make nimbly away.

You are proposing a toast to the bride and groom? The bride's father is dead? The groom's parents are divorced? What do you do? You can surrender by making no mention of the parents. This is abject cowardice, and generally regarded as such. You may neatly duck the situation by a few, carefully chosen sentences: 'The bride's father . . . we wish he were not here only in spirit . . . but he would have been proud and happy today . . . How pleased we are that our groom's parents are both so well and handsome – and here together for the celebration . . .'

Finally, you can take the bull by the horns (to take an analogy from a sport of another kind). You can start with the sort of comment given above – and then extend it into the appropriate elegy. 'Let us face it, Ladies and Gentlemen – no occasion is completely perfect, no life without its problems. How sad we are that the bride's father is not here . . . but we admire her mother doubly for the fortitude with which she bore her loss and especially for the courageous and splendid way in which she brought up the bride . . . the extent of her triumph is revealed by the radiance of our bride today. . . . We know, too, that our groom's parents, alas, have not been without their differences. But today, as always, they put the happiness of their son above all else – and they sit together with him, united in their joy at his happiness and good fortune. . . .'

There are plenty of equivalent situations in business. The surrender is achieved by an apology. The counter-attack is explained in Chapter 29 (Rudeness). And the form of ducking away from trouble, to be adopted in any particular circumstances, will depend upon those circumstances themselves. Here are some useful, opening gambits:

We fully appreciate the circumstances which have led to your anger and disappointment. But there is another side to the story and we do hope that you will give it your earnest consideration. . . .

You are quite right, on the face of it – but. . . .

I do see your point of view – but am sure that you will give consideration to mine. . . .

Yes, we made a mistake – but in all good faith. The situation nevertheless remains that. . . .

We see your viewpoint. Now please do consider ours. . . .

You have set out your case quite admirably. It is only courteous, then, for me to set out as fully as possible the situation as we see it. . . .

We genuinely feel that your complaint is based on a misunderstanding. We do see that . . . but would urge you to consider. . . .

Yes, you are right. But. . . .

No, we do not agree with you. But nevertheless. . . .

* * *

Have you noticed that the man who uses words as weapons employs very similar tactics to those of the fencer or boxer? You give way a little, so as to attack a lot. You retreat gently, so as to counterattack with firmness. You at least pretend to see the other man's viewpoint, so that he will be prepared to consider yours. Alternatively, you politely disagree – and then show your magnanimity and/or good sense or good will by offering a compromise or giving in on some point, however small.

The French put it well: 'Il faut reculer pour mieux sauter' – You must withdraw, the better to leap forward. As with weapons of war, so with words of forensic skill, written or spoken. You step back so as to throw your opponent off balance (boxing again).

There are occasions, of course, when you have your back to the wall . . . there is no room for retreat . . . all escape routes are cut off . . . Then remember the advice given to policemen, in similar but physical circumstances. 'Tuck yourself neatly into the corner and use your fists, your knees, your truncheon. . . . At least if you are in that corner, they will not be able to get a knife in your back. . . .' Unless, of course, they knock you unconscious and drag you out. . . .

Try these gambits, when absolutely desperate:

If you see fit to make these allegations to third parties, we shall have no hesitation in putting the matter in the hands of our solicitors. . . .

Your threats are as empty as the premise upon which your allegations are based is groundless. Nevertheless, if you wish to take the matter further, we must refer you to our solicitors. . . .

We regard your allegations as both impertinent and groundless. If they are repeated, we shall take such steps as we are advised by our lawyers, to protect both our position and our good name. . . .

If you are so ill-advised as to carry out your threats, then kindly direct all future correspondence to our solicitors. . . .

In one, last, desperate attempt to remedy a situation which (we repeat) is not of our making, our Mr Jones will contact you and try to arrange some convenient time to visit your office. . . .

Our chairman will be in touch with yours. . . .

31   The venue

Very often, the speaker has no say as to where his speech must be made. The company meeting, organisational gathering or dinner-party is to be held in a place chosen by others. But even there, the experienced speaker may be able to make the best of his surroundings, if he knows what to look for. In many other cases, the speaker can influence (if not choose) the venue for his talk.

The first essential is to try and match the size of the room to the number of the audience. If the room is packed, the chances are that an atmosphere will be easy to create and the speaker's task made vastly simpler. If the room is half empty, his difficulties are enhanced. Take fifty people and squeeze them into a drawing-room and you are likely to have a lively, happy meeting. Lose those same fifty in a hall and the evening is a failure before it has even begun. So underestimate your audience. If a few get left outside, never mind. Next time they will come earlier. If some have to stand, or perch, on radiators, that cannot be helped. You must avoid at all costs the echoing emptiness of a half-filled hall.

If you do find yourself with a sparse audience, do not panic. Suggest to the organisers that they ask all those present to come right up to the front. People hate being at the front, preferring to tuck themselves away in a nook near the door, the better to make their exit if they get too bored. And it is not only speakers who are sometimes shy. But a capable chairman can wheedle most people into 'helping our distinguished speaker'. If your chairman is inexperienced, then (having obtained his permission) you ask your audience to 'gather round'.

Many times, it is better to abandon the platform, draw the curtains and come down to your audience. If the formal gathering has failed to draw in the crowds, then at least ensure that you have an informal chat, so that your audience go home satisfied with their evening. It is most unlikely that they would be if they were to be regaled from above with an oration more suitable to a packed and cheering hall than to an almost empty room. Someone overestimated the audience in the first place and created your unfortunate situation. It is now up to you to make the best of it.

Other suggestions? If the room is too hot, stop and ask for a window or a door to be opened. Your audience will bless you. If it is too cold, speak to the organisers and see whether they can do anything about it. The chances are that they cannot. But at least your audience will know that you are thinking of their comfort. If there are aeroplane noises overhead, stop until they pass. To speak on regardless is a sure sign of inexperience. If a carpenter is banging next door, then ask the chairman to use his influence to obtain silence for you. Then wait whilst the results of his efforts appear.

Of course, it is far preferable to have these distractions dealt with in advance. If you can get to a meeting sufficiently early, you can sometimes induce the organisers to rearrange the seating so as to suit your theme or your plans. You may want to avoid the use of a platform or to have the chairs arranged informally in a horseshoe, or conversely, to speak to your audience from a higher level. It helps everyone to have things arranged beforehand.

Again, it may pay dividends to have the sound equipment tested before the audience arrives or the lighting adjusted to suit your requirements (see Chapter 21). No theatre audience expects to have these changes arranged in their presence. No audience for a speech or lecture, a discussion or debate, likes to to see them done after their arrival. Punctuality pays. If you wish to make a triumphal entry at a later stage, you can always disappear from the scene until the appropriate moment. And if your chairman or hosts know their business, they will have organised some small room at the back for

you to use for your coat and hat and for your refreshment.
But so much depends on the occasion. As we shall shortly see.

32   Lessons

The British businessman tends to be an amateur. We have no real equivalent of the Harvard Business School, and the average British speaker has seldom had any formal training. Even the barrister, who makes his living out of advocacy, is entitled to qualify without ever having opened his mouth in public. He learns on the job (or not, as the case may be) – all of which just does not make sense.

We all know that there is, in this country, a certain prejudice against taking lessons in public speaking. A book on the subject is not so bad. (Have *you* put this one into a plain, white cover?) 'But my dear fellow . . . fancy taking lessons in speaking. . . .'

Yet there is no good, logical reason for this curious attitude of mind. Speaking in private may come naturally. Speaking in public does not. It requires experience. And without the appropriate flair, no amount of teaching can produce really outstanding results. But if you find that public speaking is a burden upon you . . . that you need to practice in private, but with an experienced audience . . . then do not despise the lesson. There is no need to advertise to your customers, clients, friends or family that you are indulging in that particular form of masochism. But whether you are simply an inexperienced speaker in need of practice or (and more especially) a sufferer from any form of speech defect or accent impediment, a good teacher is worth his weight in the compliments he will bring upon your head.

How do you find the right man? He may advertise in the local Press. Your local Education Authority or Citizens' Advice Bureau may put him in touch with you. In general, beware of the local school of drama – but an experienced speech therapist may either be your man or know of him. Do not, of course, lay out money for any long series of lessons until you are satisfied that the individual suits your purposes. Try a lesson – and do it on the basis that you will pay a single, once-off fee if you do not decide on a course, but that if you do opt for the longer and more expensive training, then the first lesson will form part of it.

The same principles apply to courses in public speaking which you may want for your staff or executives. Find an expert and call him in. Negotiate a fee and then watch out for results. Given even moderate material, the first-class teacher can be a very great help. The speaker in public may be an amateur, but there is no reason for him to be untrained. If more speakers had more training, listeners would have a much happier time.

33 *Visual aids*

Speech sounds – but the eyes (if you will pardon the Parliamentary pun) have it!

In general, the less the mind and the ear are distracted by movement and gestures, the greater the concentration upon word, wit and wisdom. But vision may produce understanding . . . explain the otherwise inexplicable . . . and even create or maintain interest where the subject (and dare we say it, the speaker?) may not be over-scintillating.

The simplest visual aid, of course, is the blackboard – with chalk and duster. You can also use white plastics 'blackboard', with coloured ink pens. Next comes newsprint – a pad or a flip chart of paper, with crayons or thick fibrepoint pens. For the speech which is also a lecture, discourse or training session, 'newsprint' is normally best.

Still, visual aids are becoming increasingly sophisticated. The training department of every major commercial organisation is equipped with expensive machinery, for the projection of ideas onto screens and into minds. If you have none of your own, you or a colleague can probably borrow all you need. Otherwise, there are plenty of companies only too enthusiastic to hire or to rent.

So consider the major aids available, their use and advantages, their misuse and the merits.

Films

A film may set the scene for your speech – or even emphasise your main theme. But it can hardly be used as a background to your words.

Suppose, for instance, that you are giving a lecture on the perils of smoking. A horror film before or after may convey your message with greater impact than any words of yours. If you are making an appeal for a charity, then a film of its work could be useful. Or if you are presenting the work of an industry or organisation, a company or an authority, then a film could produce wonders better than words.

However, just as the moving finger writes and having writ moves (said Omar Khayyam) so the film may be recalled or halted in mind but scarcely in motion.

Video

While a film is generally projected onto a large screen and a video presentation could be, a television set has more usually a 26-inch maximum impact. But video is becoming an increasingly popular form of industrial and commercial training – though rarely used as a speechmaker's aid.

Less expensive than films, video equipment is now becoming standard. Still: The speech normally comes before or after.

Video cassettes can be stopped and restarted . . . wound back and forward . . . introduced and, if professionally made, endowed with that magical magnetism of 'the box'.

Slides and transparencies

Slides well illustrate lectures – and sometimes speeches. Usually, the lights dim and your audience concentrates on the slides. Modern gadgetry includes the turntable, slipping the slides forward or even backward at the finger's touch.

Transparencies lie on a lit or mirrored surface and are thrown or reflected onto a screen. Far easier to produce, amend and project than slides, they are usually best for the speech or presentation.

Most transparency projectors are fan-cooled – and fans may make a nasty whirr. Not only does this disturb while the projector light is on, but it often continues while the machine is cooling. When the sound ends, so the atmosphere changes. But silent or reflector projectors are now available.

Flexibility

Slides and transparencies and – to a lesser extent – video presenta-tions – all have one vast advantage over films. They can be used to punctuate, illustrate and activate a lecture, talk, speech, presentation or other aural effort to reach the minds of the listener. The eye is harnessed for the foreground or the background, but the mind remains focused on the speaker.

Pointers

The old teacher's wooden pointer is still best for a screen. But telescopic pens, which fit into your pocket, are fine if the room is small. If you are using transparencies, then use an ordinary pencil to emphasise your point and it will be reflected onto the screen along with your words.

*   *   *

Each speaker should develop his own style, approach and methods. Each should use the visual aid as is best suited to his style.

My Lords, ladies & gentlemen—
Pray silence
for ...
HOW TO SPEAK IN 5 EASY

Part 3

Occasions

34 After dinner

A captive audience, well wined and amply dined, should be an orator's joy. But more often than not the speaker is too apprehensive to enjoy his food – and instead makes a meal of his speech. Which is quite unnecessary, if he would only follow a few basic rules. First, wait for silence. When you have it, look around amiably and begin: 'Mr Chairman, Ladies and Gentlemen . . .' or as the case may be. Those few words are useful. You discover that you have not lost your voice after all. And your audience (at that stage at least) is ready to listen – and to be entertained.

However heavy the dinner or the company, however important the occasion or mighty the listeners, no one wants a dry lecture on top of a wet repast. So however important your message, do your audience the courtesy of exerting patience. Start with a joke . . . a witticism . . . a story.

The best jokes are usually impromptu. A friendly jibe at the chairman, the restaurant, the food . . . an oblique reference to the headline in the evening papers (those of the audience who have read it are delighted to be in on the joke). Otherwise, there are many good opening gambits such as:

'A few moments ago, the chairman turned to me and said: "Would you like to speak now – or shall we let them go on enjoying themselves?".'

Not long ago, an after-dinner speaker was greeted by a woman, at the evening's end, who said to him: 'Mr Jones . . . that was a terrible speech!' He composed himself as best he could – and was then greeted by another woman who said: 'I'm awfully sorry about Mrs Brown . . . she has such a long tongue . . . and she's such an idiot – she hasn't got a mind of her own . . . She only repeats what she hears other people saying!'

'I wish you could have seen the chairman, at the nineteenth hole. . . .'

However weak the wit, dry the humour or wet the joke, provided that you put it across with verve, courage or at least a friendly smile, you are on your way to establishing *rapport* with your audience. They will settle back into their chairs, relaxed – and either be receptive to a continuation of merriment or, at worst, they will be the better braced for such message as you care to give.

77

Now you launch into the speech. Brevity should be its keynote. Have you ever heard anyone complain that a post-prandial offering was too short, too condensed? When addressed by the best after-dinner speakers, they may say: 'I could listen to him for ever. . . .' But even if they think that they mean it, practice would prove them wrong.

The lower down you come in the toast list, the greater the premium to be put on brevity. So why is it that many of the most nervous speakers find it necessary to be the most long-winded? Do they think they can make up for their lack of wit, their terror or their dearth of wise words, by length? You may argue your bank manager into submission . . . stifle the opposition of your competitors by talking them into the ground . . . exhibit superb salesmanship by making it clear that you are not going to leave until you get what you want. But all this is in private. Enter into the public arena in general, or the dinner table in particular, and you must be brief.

As for the after-dinner speech itself, it requires the same careful construction as any other. It needs a flow of ideas as well as of words. And the more the words are laced with wit, the more likely that their wisdom will strike home.

So watch your audience. If they drop off to sleep, either tell them a joke or sit down. If they start jiggling the cutlery, wind up your sermon. If you want to be asked again, do not outlive your welcome.

As you approach your end, remember what it is you have been called upon to do. If you are responding to a toast, you should start by thanking the man who made it and complimenting him on his wit and wisdom. And you should finish where you began – by repeating, once again, your delight at having been asked . . . your pleasure at the privilege of responding to the toast . . . and your good wishes to the organisation which has asked you.

More important, if you are making the toast – then do so. Nothing is more discomforting than for the chairman to have to say: 'And now, kindly rise and drink with me . . .'. That is your job. So do it.

The standard formula? 'Ladies and Gentlemen, I invite you to rise and drink with me a toast to the continued success and prosperity of . . . the health and happiness of . . .' or as the case may be. By all means vary it. But by no means forget it.

One toast, incidentally, which should never be varied is that to: 'Her Majesty, the Queen'. If you are privileged to propose the loyal toast, then do so – in those words. No one wants a speech from you, extolling the beauty and majesty of the monarch – still less a defence of hereditary peerages, royal privileges and the like. The same applies to a toast at Jewish dinners: 'Mr Chairman, Ladies and Gentlemen –

the President of the State of Israel'. This is no time for a Zionist out-burst. The presence of an ambassador calls for a toast to the head of his state – but unless a toast to that state is one of the non-formal variety, reserve your eulogy to some proper occasion. Of course: no one should smoke until after the loyal toast and others of the formal, national variety. This explains why some kindly chairmen call on the proposer of these toasts when the waiters are collecting the soup. At least the proposers can thereafter relax and enjoy the rest of their meal, in an aroma of Havana cigar.

35 Feasts and funerals

The businessman may be called on to 'say a few words' on festive and funereal occasions, involving family, friends or colleagues. In general, similar rules apply to those outlined for the after-dinner orator – and elsewhere in the book. But here are some special suggestions for particular occasions.

The funeral

Naturally, no ill must be spoken of the departed. But, as usual, praise should be sincere and, where possible, deserved. Tact is essential. You are really expected to sum up all the pleasant and happy thoughts and memories which your audience would like to recall about the departed . . . to encourage and support those who remain behind, with the knowledge of the affection in which they are held . . . to indicate the immortality of the deceased – through those of his works which will live after him.

The obituary will range in length from a full-blown oration to (more likely) an introduction to a request for the audience to stand in memory of a departed friend. The following might serve as a model:

'Ladies and Gentlemen, Colleagues and Friends. Before we start our meeting, I know that you would want me to express our deep regret at the loss of our well loved fellow director, James Smith. He was a man of enormous enthusiasm, energy and initiative. He was loyal both to his friends and to the company for which he worked so well for so long. The organisation which he created – in particular in our branch factories – will remain as a permanent tribute to his commercial acumen. We – his friends and colleagues – will miss him. So will the company. I ask you all to stand for a moment in memory of . . . James Smith.'

*   *   *

Feasts

Happily, whilst every lifetime contains the seeds of its own sorrow, there are far more gay occasions than sad ones. Births and baptisms, christenings, confirmations and first communions . . . The Brit Milah and the Bar Mitzvah (Jewish ritual circumcisions and confirmation of 13-year-old boys) . . . engagements, weddings (including silver and gold) . . . each is the occasion for a word of congratulation at the start of a meeting or of a speech – or for a celebration at which a speech is required.

Of the full-blown variety, the after-dinner speech may form the model (see Chapter 34). Perhaps the best advice of all is contained in the saying: the secret of talking to the public is the same as that of speaking to your wife – keep your tongue in time with your thoughts; if either gets ahead, you are done for!

36   Overseas speeches – and foreign customers

The isolationist businessman is (or should be) as extinct as the proverbial dodo. If you can export, then you should, says every government the world over. If you must import, then do so – but at the most competitive prices. You must bargain with the foreigner, eat with him, drink with him and even expense-account with him – and, in the ultimate, you may well be thrust into making speeches to or at him.

Naturally, if you are blessed with equal facility in the foreign language as you have in your own, your problems are minimal. Then you only have to follow the rules laid down in the rest of this book and all should be well. Subject, of course, to cutting your forensic cloth to the style of your overseas audience, there is no essential difference between rousing, holding, interesting, convincing – or boring – an audience of Englishmen, Frenchmen, Russians or Greeks.

The proviso is a considerable one. Examples? Melodrama goes over a good deal better in the United States than in Britain. The florid oratory that went out in Britain many years ago still thrives in some parts – and with some audiences – abroad. But not all. And, in general, if you play up to the image expected of you – if you give your audience a touch of urbane wit, rather than roistering slapstick – you are likely to come across best.

In fact, stick to your style when in America and you have every chance of a friendly welcome. I once toured the United States, talking about Britain . . . the Welfare State . . . even what they choose to call 'socialised medicine'. I met a certain surprise that the Englishman was not cold, reserved, humourless, upper crust and frosty. The image of the icy Anglo-Saxon who will only speak when introduced – and, preferably, warmed with alcohol – dies hard. So the friendly, humorous opening acquired an extra significance and importance. Establish *rapport* and you are well away.

Once the overseas audience knows that you really do intend to entertain as well as to instruct – to talk across and not down – they are even more ready than your fellow countrymen to give you a warm hearing. The best tip for heating the atmosphere? To use the language of the country.

English and American is the same? In general, yes. But the idiom differs – and so do the allusions. The American speaker in Britain who takes the trouble to look at his daily newspaper and to joke about the current crime wave, strike outbreak, political disaster or other local misery does well. When you are talking to overseas listeners, return that sort of compliment.

A simple, well tried opening in the USA: 'You will be relieved to know that I am not about to launch into discusson of whether or not that which is good for General Motors is good also for the country as a whole . . . as to the merits or otherwise of the political efforts of the Cabots, the Kennedys or' (*here insert names of local politicians currently in the news*). 'If I am asked whether I support the Yankees, the Dodgers or' (*here insert the name of the local baseball team*), 'I shall refuse firmly to enter into your local politics. We British have enough trouble trying to run our own affairs, without risking another Boston tea-party. No. I shall confine myself, you will be pleased to know, to a discussion of. . . .'

Another invaluable story. 'I have been asked to comment upon your current commercial crisis. I must respectfully decline. You may know the tale of the dying man who was visited by his priest. "My son", said the priest, "do you renounce the Devil, now and for ever more?" "Oh Father", said the dying man, "this is no time to be making enemies – anywhere!" Ladies and gentlemen, as the solitary Englishman in your ranks, I wish to make enemies, nowhere – so I shall tell you about our troubles – rather than venturing to discuss yours.'

Once you have established friendly relations with the overseas buyers, suppliers or fellow traders, if you stick to subjects which interest them, all should be well. They are as anxious to pick up profitable tips from you, as you are from them. Provided that you assume a cloak of modesty, they will wish to hear of your achievements. After all, that is why you have been invited to speak. So do not be shy. Talk freely of your doings – and you never know – the effort may prove more profitable than you had expected.

Now suppose that you are forced to launch into your speech, to people for whom English is not the mother tongue. There are two main possibilities. Either you address them in English and hope that they understand – following the Englishman's ancient theme: 'It's not for me to learn their language – the foreigner should educate himself' – or you may speak in the foreign language. The second possibility is infinitely preferable, provided that you have a command of the tongue concerned.

If you are really talking business – putting across facts, figures, theories or ideas in respect of which words must be given their precise meanings . . . if what you say may create misunderstandings if the words are not used with their correct nuances . . . if shades of meaning matter – then you should stick to English and work through an interpreter, if necessary. It is no tribute to your bravery if you venture into foreign seas without wearing a lifebelt.

On the other hand, it may be that this is the occasion where it would be worthwhile preparing your speech beforehand and having it translated – and then reading it. Make a friendly, impromptu opening (or one which is apparently not read) and the audience will just have to put up with what may not be an oratorical masterpiece but will at least be strictly accurate. That will teach them to invite an overseas expert to speak to them!

In this case, you should do everything possible to mitigate the misery by looking up from your speech as much as you can . . . talking to your audience, whenever you can manage it . . . pausing from time to time, to throw in a joke in English – or an apology for having to read your script . . . and make sure that you do try to put it across in the accent of the native.

We have all heard the Englishman who speaks the foreign tongue as if it were his own. French words read in broad Scots, Yorkshire, Welsh or upper-crust Bath or Tunbridge Wells have a distinctly humorous flavour on the music-hall stage. But to the foreign listeners, it is just plain silly.

There is an exception. If you are going to make your speech in English, then you should always prepare a few words, right at the start, in your host's language – or, if you are the host, then in that of your guests. It matters not how badly you mispronounce the words – that adds to the fun. Nobody cares if you make a hash of the grammar – that will be taken in good part. Even if you manage to make a ghastly boob, which gives words their opposite meaning, all will be well. What matters is that you make the genuine effort to speak to folk in their own tongue. You pay them the compliment of making what is obviously a genuine attempt to be friendly – and in the most genuine possible way.

The best formula? Start with your usual opening, in English. 'Mr Chairman, Ladies and Gentlemen, Fellow Workers in the – industry. . . .' If you then break into the foreign tongue, you will produce just that element of surprise which should give rise to a very friendly reception. 'You did not know that I was learning Greek/Spanish/Hebrew/Chinese . . . did you?' (This, of course, in the language concerned). 'After I'd met Mr . . . in . . . who speaks such marvellous English, I was shamed into trying. I am only sorry that my efforts have been, as you hear, so very unsuccessful. To avoid any future misunderstandings of what I have to say, I hope that you will forgive me if I return – very gratefully – to English!' All that in the foreign language. Memorise it if you can. Otherwise read it. The fact that you will have got the information and the translation from one of the nationals of the country concerned is irrelevant. The compliment you have paid your audience will undoubtedly be appreciated.

There is an alternative. You can launch right into the 'Mr Chairman, Ladies and Gentlemen . . .' in the foreign tongue, following it up with: 'Welcome to Britain – we are very happy to have you and hope that you will have a very good time.' Do that in the foreign language – and then add: 'I know that you will forgive me if I return to English – I have a feeling that the way I pronounce French/Hungarian/Japanese/Italian, you are more likely to understand me in English than in your own tongue.'

If you cannot manage all that in the foreign language, then at least start with: 'Welcome to England' and end with 'Farewell – and come back soon', in the language of your guests. As usual, if you get the start and the finish of your speech 100 per cent right, the rest will fall into shape.

Naturally, if your audience happen to be a mixed bag, then the above rules will have to be modified. I have heard a very successful opening: 'Ladies and Gentlemen, Messieurs et Mesdames, Señores y Señoras, Meine lieben Herren und Damen . . . welcome to you all – and if I have managed to mispronounce even the few words in your language which I have ventured to speak, I know that you will appreciate why I am going to make the rest of my speech in English – I think it will be easier for us all'. Pause whilst the audience nod, smile, and chatter. 'Misunderstandings that are created by speakers – especially by politicians – who stick to their own tongue are only exceeded by those who have the temerity to create vast international misunderstandings by murdering the languages of others – and murder is a crime in every country in the world!'

Finally, an anecdote with a message. There is a famous prison in Massachusetts, USA, called the Norfolk Penal Colony. Although a maximum-security unit, it takes pride in its debating team, which plays no away games but welcomes guests from all over the world, who make speeches in the prison hall before the assembled inmates. Together with another ex-officer of the Cambridge Union, then studying with me at Harvard Law School (and now, incidentally, a distinguished QC), I once debated at Norfolk: 'That this house deplores the advance of the Welfare State'. Our opponents were a forger and a convicted killer. Both were absolutely charming Boston Irish. Their opening gambits were classic and brilliant, tailored for any audience – and especially for the one they had.

'The arguments you have heard from the gentlemen from England', the manslaughter man began, 'are as phony as my partner's cheques!' That brought the house down.

'We live in a welfare state', began the forger. 'Does anyone want to stay?' Roars of 'No, no' were the obvious result.

We did our best. 'My partner is Britain's favourite export . . . Britain asks that you do not send him back. . . .' We lost the debate, but at least we did better than the previous English guests, one of whom had ruined the atmosphere by making the most elementary of mistakes – offending and talking down to his listeners at the same time. 'This is the first occasion that I have spoken to a captive audience', he had begun. His speech collapsed into immediate and well deserved embarrassment.

37 Appeals and fund raising

The art of extracting money from the listener requires careful thought and ready adaptation to the circumstances. The Chancellor of the Exchequer may have political problems, but at least he can enforce his financial requirements. The businessman seeking to raise funds for his trade charity . . . an industrial benevolent fund . . . or even for some less apparently altruistic outlet . . . he must win the cash, pound by pound. How? That depends on the audience and the cause. But here are a few suggestions.

*   *   *

There are those who give out of pure kindness of heart. But guilt and self-interest are usually more powerful motives.

There are those who work very hard for a charity – and others who do not. But the latter may play their part by contributing the money they have earned whilst not striving for the good cause. In their own way, they can do as much for the needy as their more apparently energetic colleagues. Tell them so – by implication.

'There are those of us who are in the happy position of being able to spare time to work for this important charity. There are others who find it impossible to do so. May I make a special appeal to them? Give us the means and we will do the job. It is a job that desperately needs every penny that you can afford to spare – and more. . . .'

What, then, of enlightened self-interest? Maybe it is a question of insurance. The charity deals with the aged, infirm, ill or needy? And you are young, middle-aged or at least fit? That is now. What happens when you get dumped on the scrap heap . . . sacked . . . struck down by (Heaven forbid) some fell disease? You have a pension? Well, maybe the company will not be in a position to pay it . . . it will not suffice for the needs of your widow. So now, when you are in a position to assure your future, do so.

Naturally, this is never said. The approach is more like this: 'I ask you to give as an expression of gratitude for the fact that you do not need to make use of this great trade charity for yourself. I hope that none of us will need at any time to occupy a bed in this convalescent home . . . to receive a payment from this fund . . . to rely upon the benevolence of others in the industry . . . But who knows?' Pause, significantly. 'And even if, as we all hope, we escape the necessity for help of this sort, we can be very proud indeed that those who do require it can look to us. They have given good service . . . they have earned every penny that comes to them . . . they have been smitten by the ili-fortune that we have managed to avoid . . .' And so on. We all spend money on insurance, do we not? Well, this is a healthy and helpful form of outlet for the same, intelligent response to potential misfortune.

Consider always the best way to confer a bargain. This is generally done with the kind aid of the tax man. If a businessman feels that he can give more by paying less, you are far more likely to get your money . . . to have a bed endowed in the trade home . . . to acquire your 'Smith House' or 'Jones Hall'. So check on the covenant schemes, charitable trusts and the like.

'Think of it, ladies and gentlemen. Any person paying income tax at the current standard rate can confer a benefit on this charity, out of all proportion to the amount which he has to give up from his own spending. Here are some examples . . .' Then say how much a gift of £X per year or £Y per year will mean gross, to the charity. Remember, of course, that when a charity receives covenants, these can provide good security for loans, if it needs the money at once. And it is sometimes possible to get people to give a lump sum right away on the basis that it will be grossed up for tax purposes over the years. But this is a matter for the charity's accountants to work out.

Then, remember that lawful blackmail is the charitable fund raiser's most potent weapon. You phone your supplier. 'Jimmy', you say, 'We've had such a tremendous call on our benevolent fund that we simply have to raise an extra £50,000. Can I count on you for a thousand?'

Jimmy groans inwardly. 'Certainly, Bill', he smiles. 'Shall I send an advertisement for the Ball Brochure?'

Use the same tactic in public speech. Look at Jimmy when you ask for funds. He may turn away his gaze, but he may not dare to keep his cheque book closed. After all, when he came to the function or the meeting, he realised that the skinning knives were likely to be out. Or, even better, corner him in advance. Find out how much he is willing to give. Announce it – as a bait for others, or to shame them into raising their donations to an appropriately announceable level. If you have goodwill, then use it for the benefit of the less privileged. No one will ever tell you of the resentment they feel. It's all in a good cause, is it not?

Of course, whether you can use this sort of direct attack or whether you have to be more subtle . . . whether you can announce donations at the meeting or have to let the word go round from mouth to mouth . . . whether you conduct a mock auction at inflated prices, a raffle, a tombola . . . all depends on all factors in the unhappy case. But one rule applies to nearly all: you cannot afford to be bashful, or to worry about rebuffs, if you are looking for money from the pockets of others.

The best time to attack those pockets is when the mind is weak through the stomach being overloaded or the heart touched by your words. If you have people in a happy, receptive and giving mood, then (literally) cash in on the situation. Either ask them for their donation at the time – and pass round the appropriate banker's order or covenant forms – or at least write to them the very next day saying: 'It was very good to see you last night . . . I enclose herewith banker's order . . . I am sure that I can count on your further support. . .'.

Have I strayed from the straight and narrow of the public speech-maker? Not really. The speech can never be regarded as a separate entity, divorced from the project it encompasses. If you want funds, then you may have to appeal for them. But the appeal must be tied in with the campaign before and after. The very nature of the speech will depend upon that of the appeal, its preparation, its follow up, its needs. The production of goods depends upon the market . . . the resources at your disposal . . . the economic situation . . . and all the facts of the case. A speech must be matched to the audience and the circumstances – and no speech more so than that which incorporates an appeal for money.

Postscript

Jews are great givers. Any professional appeals organiser will tell you that if you can interest the Jewish community, you are well away. And whilst Jewish people are willing givers to their own communal and Israeli causes, they take pride in taking part in the appeals of others. Perhaps even more important, they are excellent fund-raisers for charities of all sorts. So I reproduce with gratitude – and with due acknowledgement to the *Jewish Observer and Middle East Review* – an interview in which a successful Jewish appeal-maker gave away some of his secrets:

'I know plenty of people who can make an excellent speech', he said, 'but not an appeal. The technique is quite different. The man who makes a speech can create the right atmosphere for someone to follow on. The appeal-maker must not waste time making speeches. He needs a couple of minutes to say what it is all about. And, of course, an appeal-maker must never be satisfied with his audience. Whatever he says, he must have the people in a frame of mind where they want to give. He should know when to stop.'

An audience, then, should be like a 'juicy orange – you squeeze, but not until the pips fall out. When you stop is a matter of psychology or intuition.'

When you have finished your appeal, can you tell whether the audience is still with you?

'If they applaud you as loudly when you sit down as when you got up, you can be happy with the job done.

'An appeal-maker must never read a speech. What he has to say must be spontaneous. It must come from the heart. He must never embarrass people but make them feel happy about their giving and leave them in a good frame of mind, thanking him for a successful job. People recognise the sincerity of the appeal-maker. An appeal-maker must be somebody who sincerely believes in the cause he puts forward . . .

'Finally, the appeal-maker must set an example in giving.'

Give, and the world gives with you . . . the mean man is not an appealing figure, in any sense of the word.

38   *Out in the open*

The open-air speech is a comparative rarity. But you should be prepared to make one. Maybe it will be at the factory gates, at the dockside, or at some open-air trade show. Perhaps it is only a vote of thanks at your local sports day . . . a talk or a lecture on site . . . or maybe you have to speak at a rally in Hyde Park, Trafalgar Square or at your local war memorial? Whatever the place and whatever the circumstances, there are certain basic rules on open-air oratory which should help you succeed in any such appearance.

*   *   *

Human voices carry poorly in the open air. So the prime essential for the outdoor speaker is to be heard.

If you have a microphone, use it. The same sort of rules apply as set out in Chapter 21. But more so. The chances of outdoor amplifying equipment going wrong are far greater than with their indoor brethren. The variety that hooks on to a motor-car battery is particularly vulnerable. Listen to the men of politics, next election time. Pity their attempts to be heard – especially when a crowd is all around them and the amplifying equipment points only to the front. If you have a microphone, remember its outdoor limitations. For instance, if ever you have to speak in a moving vehicle – perhaps from the front of a car or the back of a truck – talk very slowly and distinctly and get the driver to proceed as slowly as possible. People do like to hear what is being thrown out at them from a moving object. But they get extraordinarily aggravated when it flies by without giving them the chance to pick up the words – however banal or trite those words may be. Usually, there is time for a slogan only. 'Today's the day . . . come to the carnival . . . 12.15 p.m. at the Rectory . . . .' Then you are gone.

Still, most outdoor speaking is stationary. And – mike or no mike – many of the indoor rules go out the window. For instance:

The outdoor speaker can be far freer with movement and gesture.

Old-fashioned oratory – of the rabble-rousing variety – is much more effective and appears far less insincere when out of doors.

Instead of having an audience ready made, you may have to collect it. Whereas indoors there is no point in speaking to yourself, outdoors you may have no alternative – so the louder and more provocatively you rant, the greater your chances of an eventual audience.

But some rules of indoor speaking require special emphasis out of doors. For instance:

Do not be afraid to pause . . . to wait . . . to give every possible indication of complete calm and confidence.

Never panic, no matter what may be thrown at you – even if this is more than mere words. Remember always that the man on the platform has a vast advantage over his hearers. If he is firm and refuses to be ruffled, in the long run he should be bound to win (but see Chapter 26 on 'Interruptions').

Make certain that your voice carries. If you use a battery-operated, hand megaphone, pull the trigger tight. As one famous Harvard professor used to put it: 'Take your voice and throw it against the wall at the back of your audience and make it bounce off'. If you get hoarse as a result, do not worry. You have joined the ranks of the outdoor speakers. You have hit one of the hazards of the trade. Lose your voice and it will come back. But lose your audience and it is gone for ever.

39   Presentations and awards – as giver and receiver

The giver

You may come at presentation or award speeches from two angles – that of the giver and that of the receiver. In either event, 'a few words' will be expected of you. But in either case, the keynote of the speech is sincerity.

Everyone likes to be honoured. The art of the well turned compliment is appreciated more than almost any other. Flattery given freely and wholeheartedly is always welcome – but it must be given in moderation.

'Mr X is the most brilliant businessman, straightforward and sweet-tempered, a paragon of commercial virtue. . . .' Rubbish. No one will believe it – not even Mr X. Compare this: 'On the one hand, Mr Smith has been the head of a large and successful commercial concern. He has had to see that business became and remained thoroughly competitive. His has been the unpleasant duty of striking the hard bargain, ensuring that the business was tough and competitive, enabling the enterprise to survive and flourish in spite of all the economic circumstances, the bitter and fierce rivalries within the trade, the battle for manpower.

'On the other hand, Mr Smith has sought to preserve the good name of the company and its good relations both with its suppliers, customers and competitors and with its own staff.

'That he has succeeded in building up the business without destroying the foundations of goodwill . . . that he has promoted the economic welfare of the business without demoting or undervaluing the honour and integrity or the goodwill of the Board . . . that he has earned such a warm regard not only for the company but for himself – those are the reasons why we are delighted to honour him this evening – and why we are so sad at his impending retirement.'

Or take the manager, foreman or operative, leaving after long service, or receiving an award for distinguished, long-term conduct.

'We were thinking of presenting Mr Jones with a watch. But we do not believe our staff really want to know the time just when it has become least important to them. And so we felt that this electric tea-maker would be more appropriate and much more useful. It comes with the thanks and admiration of the company – and its gratitude. But it is also given with the affection and goodwill of his fellow members of staff. They have contributed towards it and I know they hope, as much as I do, that it will remind him – and his wife and family – of the affection and esteem in which we all hold him, and of our thanks to him for his loyal service. We wish Mr Jones, together with his charming wife, a long and happy retirement, blessed with the very best of health. And we hope that he will visit us whenever he comes this way. He will always have the warmest of welcomes from all of us, his colleagues and friends.'

No flowery insincerities. No 'schmaltz', as the overdone compliment is sometimes called in the United States, but straightforward, sincere and sensible words which are bound to be appreciated by the person concerned.

Sometimes, of course, the presentation of an award is really an excuse to encourage people to come to a dinner or other function, knowing that they would not wish to offend the recipient by being absent. With this sort of award or presentation, it is expected that the toast to the recipient will be coupled with a eulogy of the organisation which he represents – and/or of the virtues represented by the organisation which is conferring the award. This sort of excuse for an oratorical jamboree is becoming increasingly common, and is a not altogether welcome transatlantic importation. The public relations man has created a new vehicle. But if it comes your way, you must be prepared to steer it.

'In the new and expanding sauna bath industry, we are proud of our pioneers. This dinner is in honour of Mr Finn, whom we are all delighted to welcome to England.' Hear, hear!

'Mr Finn has helped to put our industry on to the British map. Close on the heels of the central-heating boom has come the realisation that sauna-bath treatments bring health and true family relaxation. Whilst no public authority should be without one, there is an immense, untapped demand for them in the larger private homes throughout the country.' (The Press start scribbling.) 'What better occasion could there be than this to launch the great new drive for British-built sauna baths – we shall create a home demand so as to build up an economic, export potential. . . .' And so on. 'And we wish to express our admiration and thanks to our honoured guest, Mr Finn, to whom I am delighted to present this gold pin, in the shape of a sauna bath, as a token of our respect and gratitude.' Loud cheers. The audience rises. Flash bulbs pop.

This is only a slight exaggeration of the sort of award occasion which occurs somewhere, every day of the week. If you are the presenter, the more fatuous the occasion . . . the less deserving the recipient . . . the bigger the publicity hoped for – the more your sincerity becomes vital, if the occasion is not to deteriorate into sickening slush.

How, then, do you appear sincere, even when you are not? By playing down. By avoiding exaggeration. By excluding melodrama, theatricals, tears in the eyes or choking in the throat. 'I am so moved that I can scarcely speak. . . .' Then don't. 'Mr Jones is fabulous, fantastic, magnificent. . . .' Superlatives are seldom either sincere or accurate. A few, quiet words of praise are worth paeans of exultation.

The receiver

With a bit of luck, you, too, may be at the receiving end of an honour, an award, a presentation or a toast. Praise may be heaped on your receptive shoulders. How do you cope with it?

'I am very grateful to Mr Smith for his most generous obituary.' (*Adlai Stevenson*)

'There is one difference between a speech of this kind heaping praise on the living, and a funeral oration, extolling the dead. In the former case, but not the latter, there is one listener who is ready to believe in the truth of all that was said.' (*Chaim Weizmann*)

More common: 'I would first like to thank Mr Jones for his very kind references to my wife and myself. We are very grateful – and only wish that half of it were true.' Or: 'I am deeply grateful to you, Mr Chairman, for the very generous way in which you have referred to my organisation and to myself. We shall do our best to live up to your high regard.'

What it comes to is this: just as it is vital for the maker of the speech of praise to be patently sincere, so the recipient must be clothed in decent modesty.* It would be ungracious to say: 'It's all untrue . . . you shouldn't have said those things. . . .' And anyway, no one would regard that sort of attitude as bearing the true mark of sincerity. On the other hand, one can hardly say: 'Every word is an understatement. . . .' You may be immodest about your wife: 'All that has been said about my wife is true. I am very proud of her – she's a gem!' But then you must go on to say: 'I only wish that I could believe the same of the words about myself. Nevertheless, I am most obliged to Mr Smith for having spoken them. Maybe he convinced my wife of their truth, even though he left me in a good deal of doubt.'

The next stage is to return the compliment by speaking well of the individual or organisation that has had the good sense to honour you.

*See also Chapter 11.

'I have been very lucky to have had the opportunity of serving this company over the years. . . . It has been a privilege to work with you all . . . I shall miss you . . . I hope that we shall meet again, very often. . . . . .' Or: 'Whilst this fraternal organisation has been good enough to make an award to me, I should in fact have been making a presentation to the organisation. The honours are flowing in the wrong direction. I shall try to redress the balance a little by saying why it is that I regard the work of this organisation to be of such enormous significance, especially in the present state of the industry. . . .'

Or: 'It was very good of Mr Smith to speak so well of me. As everyone here knows so well, most of the virtues that he was kind enough to attribute to me were in fact his own. This company is very fortunate to be led by a man of his calibre. . . .'

Sincerity and the nicely turned compliment, then, should not be the prerogative of the giver.

Finally, the conclusion. 'And so, Mr Chairman, my speech – like my time with the company – has drawn to its close. Thank you, Mr Smith, once again for your very kind words. Thank you, my colleagues, for your goodness to me, over the years – and for your most generous gift. My wife and I will treasure it always – as we shall the memories of our association with you. Good luck to you all.'

Or: 'And so, in accepting this award, I thank you all for the compliment you have paid to me – and through me to my organisation. My colleagues and I are all happy to have been able to carry out our work – and we undertake to attempt in the future to exceed the achievements in the past which have caused you to honour us in the present. Our gratitude to you all.'

The sentimental anecdotes you have slipped into the body of your speech . . . the reminiscences, memories, tales with a moral – all of which go down so well in this sort of situation . . . these are all rounded off with a final word of thanks. To end, where you began, with your gratitude. It has been a fine occasion – and an excellent speech.

40   Credits

Few men object to being thanked or resent receiving credit, even where it is not strictly due – and in this instance at least, 'Man' (as Churchill once put it) 'embraces Woman'. But most people get upset from time to time if their merit is not recognised or thanks are withheld – especially if credit due to one goes to another. So the good advocate is as liberal with his praise of others as he is parsimonious with his praise of himself (see Chapter 39). The listener who feels that you recognise – and are prepared publicly to laud – his worth is far more likely to be receptive to your arguments.

Here, then, is a good opening attack upon an audience, even if it happens to be friendly towards you:

'First, I would like to express my appreciation to various people here. Were it not for Mr Brown, this gathering would never have been organised at all. Were it not for Mr Black, the company would be in grave difficulty. Were it not for Mr White, the scheme we are about to discuss would never have been born. In paying tribute to them, I express my gratitude to all of you for giving them the support and backing without which they could not have put forward this essentially constructive project.

'Now, let us look at the project.' Your audience is softened up. They are ready to listen to some constructive criticism from you.

Alternatively: 'Under the chairmanship of Mr Green, this project has made great headway. With Mr Brown as treasurer and Mr Blue as honorary secretary, it is hardly surprising that it has gathered momentum. And now it is up to us to help them by applying constructive minds to the scheme they have created. I know they welcome criticism designed to forward their work. We all appreciate that their enthusiasm is only increased by suggestions, coming from people like ourselves who only want the scheme to succeed. They know that there is no element of destructive intent in the views that some of us hold. Mr Chairman, we are with you all the way – and if we take the liberty of suggesting that the way may not be quite as simple as some think, I am sure that you will give careful consideration to our submissions.' Flattery? Certainly – but legitimate. Praise? Yes, indeed, and with every appearance of sincerity. Credit, thanks, tact – and all designed to prepare the ground for your forthcoming attack. It is not only armies that do best when they advance from the side, and there is no shame in a swift strike from the rear.

To see the importance of these rules, all you have to do is to listen to someone who ignores them. Beware the benefactor scorned . . . the doer of good deeds which go unrecognised . . . the creator whose idea, invention or brainchild is fathered on to another.

There exists, of course, the occasional *eminence grise* – the spectral backroom boy who takes as much pride in praise going to others whom he has built up as does the father who basks in the reflected glory of the exploits of his child. But even he appreciates the oblique reference to the power that made the throne secure, the modest mind that 'wishes to remain anonymous but must not go without being thanked . . . Those of us who are fortunate enough to realise just how and by whom the work has been done salute our silent and modest friends – we are indeed grateful to them.'

Just as the editorial mention and the praise of a product which appears in the general pages of a newspaper are the public relations man's delight – and worth a good deal more to him than the advertisement which he has to pay for – so the 'plug' given in the course of a speech and as part of it is often a good deal more valuable to the maker and appreciated by the person referred to than the formal and expected vote of thanks. But even that is a weapon not to be despised in the campaign to get your own way – as we shall now see.

41 Votes of thanks

The formal vote of thanks to the speaker is a mark of courtesy and just as necessary as the word of gratitude to the hostess at the end of the evening. You may not have enjoyed your meal. The company may have been excruciatingly dull. Unlike the fabled hostess who was said to have made her guests feel at home even when she fervently wished that they were, Mrs Black may have caused you to be thoroughly ill at ease. Nevertheless, as you leave you thank her – and no doubt compliment her as warmly as you can on the excellence of her cooking and the pleasure you have had in the company of her other, well chosen guests. Because the compliments are apparently unrehearsed, they may well be believed. Anyway, they must be given.

So it is with the guest speaker. He must be thanked. In America, it is customary to make handsome payment to those who lecture, even to Rotary Clubs, friendly societies or business or charitable organisations. They are given tangible thanks, in financial form. In this country, the speaker is thought to have been the recipient of a compliment. When he says: 'It was very kind of you to invite me to this splendid, peaceful Highland resort', he probably means, 'I wish I could have thought of some way to refuse your invitation to trek up to your God-forsaken development area slum'. So at least bathe him in the warmth of your thanks.

Incidentally, have you remembered to offer to pay the man's expenses? He would probably be too embarrassed to ask for them and he may even refuse your offer. But to beg for and receive the benefit of the time of a busy speaker and then to expect him to pay for his fare or accommodation is a typically British stupidity. All speakers know the wretchedness of being dragged many miles for a few minutes of speech to a minute audience. That is one of the hazards of the trade. But when he does so entirely at his own expense, in money as well as in time, it is hardly surprising if he feels bitter.

What, then, of the vote of thanks itself? How do you best put it across?

Sincerity is the keynote. This rests upon a genuine (if possible) and topical (certainly) assessment of the positive and helpful aspects of the visitor's speech. Refer, perhaps, to the speaker's wit and wisdom, the full and frank way in which he has dealt with the subject, the particular interest which you have had in that portion of his talk which dealt with ... By all means elaborate on a point or two, to show that you have really taken it in – or to indicate that you have been taken in, as the case may be. But do not use the occasion to launch into a tirade of your own. Your job is to thank. Do it.

A vote of thanks is a mini-speech. So the general rules apply, in abbreviated form.

By all means write out your first sentence and the skeleton of the speech (see Chapter 1). But to have the whole speech written in advance is a travesty. 'We have all been extremely impressed with the wise words of Mr Stout', the speaker reads from his typed card. 'He gave us a very clear exposition of the subject. We have much to think about as a result.' Terrible. Obviously written before the speech was heard and not worth the paper it was written on. In fact, of all the speeches which should never be written out, votes of thanks head the list.

'We are very honoured to have had Mr Slim with us this evening. We realise and appreciate how far he has come. We know and understand the effort that it has cost him. And I know that I am expressing the feelings of everyone here when I tell him how deeply grateful we are to him.' At this stage, you must pause for applause. If you rush on, your audience will not know what is expected of them. There will be a few embarrassed hand-claps and the speaker will not be complimented.

'We listened with great interest to Mr Slim's views on . . . Personally, I was especially impressed with the concept of . . . If my own company does not take steps to put this system into effect, it will not be through any lack of enthusiasm on my part, nor any failing on the part of our distinguished speaker. He has paid us the compliment of laying out before us in the clearest terms the essence of the organisational method which he has distilled through years of trial, error and experience. The greatest tribute which can be paid to him will be through our adoption of his ideas.' Every speaker likes to feel that he has sown a good seed on fertile soil. Treat his words as pearls and he will not think of you as the proverbial swine.

'But perhaps our greatest delight, Mr Chairman, has been in the way in which Mr Slim has succeeded in bringing his somewhat recondite subject to life. He has proved that to tell a tale of . . . need not be dull. He has enlivened our evening with wit and humour.

'And so, in thanking Mr Slim for his good words this evening, I can only hope that we shall have an early opportunity of hearing him again. We wish him every success in his ventures – and a speedy return to our midst. Thank you, Mr Slim, very much indeed.'

And thank you for a terse, appropriate, sincere, friendly and well constructed vote of thanks. Just to think that the audience inwardly groaned when you were called upon to speak, worrying in case you were about to make the late hour even later . . . to cause them to lose the last bus or train or the services of their aggravated chauffeurs . . . or, possibly, to embarrass them by saying what they really thought about their guests. So they were pleasantly surprised – and are likely to invite you to perform the same service again. Or maybe they knew all the time that you would perform this underrated chore with aplomb, which is why they asked you to do it. In that case, their trust was not misplaced. Thank you indeed.

42   Brains trusts

Curiously, even very prominent people are prepared to sit on so-called 'brains trusts'. The audience gets at least two views for the price of one evening. The speaker – who might otherwise resent the competition and the feeling that his audience really should be satisfied with an evening of him – accepts, perhaps because he is delighted not to have to prepare any set speech. Each or all of the speakers are often fooled into accepting because they think that the others on the panel have already done so – or they turn up because they have been asked by someone whom they cannot refuse. Whatever the circumstances, most speakers have to perform at brains trusts some time or another. So here are some suggestions.

*   *   *

The organisers ought to provide each speaker with a pencil and pad. But they often fail to do so. You should never turn up at any meeting without pen and paper, but both are absolutely vital for a brains trust.

When a question is asked, jot it down. Alongside it, put any random ideas which leap to mind. If you have none, then indicate to the chairman that one of your colleagues should open the batting. Something will come to your mind whilst the answer is given. If it does not, then do not be afraid to say: 'I agree', or 'I'd rather not comment on this one, thank you'. And there are questions which may provoke all sorts of possible answers, none of which you think it politic to give. Do not be browbeaten into words you may later regret.

Each answer you do give should be a small, neat speech. It should have a beginning, a body and an end. But it must be concise. And precisely because it must be extempore, you may find it considerably more difficult than the ordinary, set effort. There is a definite art to brains trusting.

You may have to cope with interruptions from your colleagues or from the chairman. You must take them in your stride. React to the informality of the occasion. Do not be afraid to break your train of thought – or, if you cannot return to it, say: 'Now, where was I, before Mr Brown's witty intervention?' Someone will remind you.

Conversational informality – that is the key to a successful brains trust performance. You are performing at a dinner party, with an audience to play up to. Make use of your powers of showmanship. React to your audience. By all means fish for applause and laughter. Relax and enjoy yourself – and the odds are that your audience will do the same.

Well chosen brains trust panels include people with different backgrounds, viewpoints and ideas. With any luck, there will be a friendly clash. Speakers can engage in gentlemanly teasing. Jokes against yourself will be appreciated. And smart retorts to points made by other speakers seldom go astray. But the tradition is still that of the dinner party and not of the political tub-thump. Aggressive and unfriendly rejoinders . . . rude or unkind rebuttals . . . personal remarks to or about other speakers, which hurt (whether or not they are calculated to do so) – these are all to be avoided. The object is to demonstrate your brains, not to tear out those of the other panelists.

On the other hand, if things get too dull, some provocative remarks are appreciated. Well prepared brains trusts have some questions provided in writing at the start, so as to get things moving or to fill in dull moments. But if the dread moment arrives when the audience is silent and the questions do not arise, say: 'I wonder whether I could take this opportunity to ask Mr Large something I have wanted to get out of him for some time? I appreciate, Mr Chairman, that he might prefer to answer this question in private. But if you would allow me to put it to him, at least we shall see whether or not he is prepared to allow his views on this subject to appear on the platform.' The chairman will doubtless be delighted. And Mr Large will probably be pleased and flattered to know that his opinions are sought. Speakers, on the whole, are a pretty vain lot, who like expressing their views for all to hear. Those on brains trusts are no exception.

43   Interview techniques – from both sides

The difference between speaking in public and in private depends largely upon the formality of the former, the informality of the latter. Some private occasions are sufficiently formal to require the speaker to give careful thought to his statements. Into this category come most interviews. Some public occasions are so informal that the speaker can conveniently 'chat' to his audience. Here we have some private gatherings, perhaps around the hearth – or, on occasion, when what was expected to be a large public meeting turns into a small gathering. The speaker can save the day by turning to complete informality, asking his audience to sit around him, himself remaining seated – and throwing his notes out the window.

There are nearly as many techniques for interviewing as there are interviewers and situations. The head of an organisation that specialises in supplying sales teams for industry and who spends the bulk of his days interviewing prospective representatives reckons on a five-minute maximum. Take any longer, he claims, and you start overlooking the defects of the interviewee because you find common ground with him. The chief personnel officer of a giant retail organisation reckons on each interview taking at least fifteen minutes and preferably thirty. 'It takes you a quarter of an hour', he says, 'to put the interviewee thoroughly at ease and to be able to start finding out what he is really like'.

Each of us, then, acquires a technique to probe the talents and character of the interviewee. The only vital rule is to allow the other man to do the talking – and to prod him into speech.

What guidance, then, have we for the interviewee?

First, he must be as natural as the situation allows. Ideally, of course, he should have a shrewd idea of what the interviewer wants to find – and then hint as broadly as possible (but with the maximum appearance of subtlety) that he is everything that is required. But one can be a good deal too clever. So relax as much as you can. Be yourself. And if that is not good enough – well, even if the interview had proved more successful perhaps you would not have fitted the assignment anyway. One door closes. Another will doubtless open before long.

Do not prepare a speech in advance – unless, of course, you are being interviewed for a Parliamentary candidature and are expected to deliver a ten-minute set piece. In that case, the ordinary rules of speeches would apply. But in the more common circumstances – where you are facing, perhaps, a Board of interviewers – the interview will take the form of question and answer. The less you are tied to a memorised script, the more natural you are likely to be, and the less inhibited.

The only question you are almost certainly to be asked is why you want (or think that you are suited for) the particular job, scholarship, assignment or position for which you have applied. Be as frank in your answer as you can. If you think it will give you the opportunity to serve, in a way that you have always desired, then say so. If you are at present in a rut and feel that the new situation will provide an exciting outlet for your enthusiasm, then speak up. Tell them. But be careful not to over-play your hand. An interviewee was applying for a senior executive post in a particular European country. 'Why do you want to go to that country?' he was asked. 'Because I have always found it fascinating', came the ready answer. He then discovered that one of his interviewers was an expert on that country's affairs – about which, despite his alleged fascination, the interviewee (as soon became pathetically apparent) knew practically nothing. He had failed at the first hurdle.

How much better he would have done had he answered: 'I have the terrible feeling that I am in a rut. I have always wanted to work abroad and have never had the opportunity. I must admit that I do not know a great deal about conditions and circumstances in the country in question. But I am anxious and willing to find out. I have had to adapt myself to all sorts of work in England, and I am sure I could take to the situation which you have to offer abroad.'

Regard an interview as an examination, and prepare for it. If, to return to the same example, you wish to obtain an appointment abroad, at least take the trouble to read a book or two concerning the country in question, its political, commercial and economic situation and the state of the particular trade or industry with which you are concerned, in that foreign land. Make sure that you are able to discuss the prospects . . . the work . . . the difficulties. By all means play down your knowledge – but put yourself in a position to surprise the interviewing panel with what you do know.

You are selling yourself. So apply the ordinary rules of good salesmanship. In most cases, the 'soft sell' is infinitely preferable to a show of immodesty, pomposity or omniscience. You may be better than your interviewers, but it is tactful not to make this too obvious. Of course, if your interview concerns a product, then the fact that you are dealing with an interviewing panel rather than with one potential customer only means that you must spread your usual wiles more widely.

Before you come up for the interview, sit down and think about its purpose. Be prepared to answer questions clearly and comprehensively. Consider the sort of background information which you would require if you were doing the interviewing. Make sure that you have it available at the front of your mind.

Answer the questions you are asked, in an informal, conversational style. Avoid oratory, rhetoric or platform fineries. By all means show a sense of humour, but do not be 'too clever'. Do not be afraid to show enthusiasm, ideas, imagination. The chances of your failing the interview through over-enthusiasm are as nothing compared to the fair certainty of failure for those who appear indifferent, unenthusiastic, uninspired.

Of course, what you really need at an interview is good luck. But good speech certainly helps.

44   Lectures and visual aids*

A lecture has been defined as 'a discourse before an audience or class upon a given subject, usually for the purpose of instruction' (*The Shorter Oxford English Dictionary*). The lecturer, then, is expected to instruct or, at least, to describe. He is likely to have to speak for at least twenty minutes and possibly up to an hour. He will probably be forgiven if his notes are more extensive and his reading and quotations more lengthy and apparent than would otherwise be expected. But the word 'lecture' is not synonymous with the word 'bore'. All the rules as to preparation, notes, humour, the structure of the speech and the like apply. But the lecturer will normally be expected to be expert in his subject – and to demonstrate his expertise.

If you do have to 'read a paper' and prepare a speech, word by word, you can generally reckon that, at the ordinary rate of delivery, you will need somewhere about 110 words a minute. But by all means check your own delivery time by reading out the first few paragraphs and using a stop-watch. Remember that you will probably speak faster when the time comes. But remember also that a good speaker varies his pace (see Chapter 25) as well as his volume and tone. Like a first-class record player, his output is variable.

One great advantage of the properly briefed lecturer is that he may make use of visual aids and these are well worth preparing, especially as a lecture (unlike most speeches) can often be repeated.

Slides and films are useful. But do make sure that you would have a projector or, if you bring your own, that the appropriate electrical supply, plugs and the like will be available. If you have to 'get set up', then come early.

*See also Chapter 33.

You may also be able to obtain film strips. Or your hosts may have one of those ingenious projectors that enable the speaker to put charts, graphs or maps on to a platform and have them projected on to a screen. Discuss your visual aids with your hosts and make sure you obtain and use the best that the equipment available will justify.

Remember, too, that if you do not have your own slides or photographs or film strips, there are various firms that hire projection equipment and machinery. Maybe your hosts will be able to help. Alternatively, some government departments and local authorities are extremely co-operative. If you can get hold of visual aids, then you should certainly do so. An uninterrupted lecture of considerable length may hold an audience if the speaker is sufficiently experienced, witty and wise and if his material is really of absorbing interest to his audience. But – as any recipient of lectures, university or other, knows to his cost – the chances of a lengthy lecture proving pleasurable as well as instructive are not great, in the absence of visual aids.

45 On radio – and TV

To the performer who makes his living on radio or TV, a 'fluff' may mean disaster. In a television studio, in particular, the moment before the cameras are turned on is fraught with tension. If the show is 'canned' – that is, pre-recorded – then a disaster may be cut out. Or if the radio programme is on tape, mistakes can be erased or re-recorded. But the 'live' show never loses its expectancy. 'Good luck, darling', say the experts, and then compliment the visiting celebrity, the amateur speaker, the non-professional guest, on his calm. He is probably thoroughly enjoying the experience. He should be. At worst, he will not be asked back. At best, he talks to the camera, the microphone, the technicians behind the glass screen – and forgets about the thousands (or even millions) who will see his performance when it eventually 'goes out'. But his path will be smoother and his calm as real as it is apparent if he knows a few of the basic techniques.

*   *   *

As a speaker, you will appear in one of two ways. Either you will be interviewed or you will deliver a set talk.

The interview lives on its informality. The interviewer may take you through in advance some of the questions he will ask. But seldom all of them. When the show is on, they will in any event take a different form, if only in their wording.

The interviewer's job is to encourage you to talk. The chances are that the questions he will ask will be pointed but either non-committal or friendly. But they may be hostile. Forget about the microphones, the cameras with their green eyes glinting when they are 'live', the studio audience. Chat with the interviewer as if the two of you were on your own. Choose your words with care, especially if you are criticising others. A defamatory statement made on television is a libel and not a slander (see Chapter 14). Do not be rushed or bullied. Relax and be yourself.

If yours is a set speech, then the chances are that you will have to provide a copy in advance. This will then probably be put on to an ingenious machine which sets your words on to a large, paper tape and runs them across your vision, just above the camera. The operator ensures that the words match the speed at which you speak. You will be reading – but your audience will be admiring your fluency and powers of memory. All you must remember is to read as if you were talking. Once again, be natural and conversational and you have nothing to fear.

For a sound broadcast, the chances are that you will have a script. This will probably have been retyped for you on to special paper that does not 'rattle'. If the pages are stapled together, remove the clip. Underline in black, red or green, so as to help you to remember what to emphasise. Above all, do as the producer tells you.

He will run through your script with you, and you may well have had to attend the studio for a rehearsal or two beforehand. Your voice will be tested, if you have not broadcast before. The object is not to remove any regional accent or spoken peculiarities but to ensure that your words will come through clearly and understandably.

The producer will give you your directions. Normally, he will operate a green cue-light, to tell you when to start. If you slow down too much, then you may receive a flashing signal to speed up. But if you have included a penultimate paragraph which can be cut out without adversely affecting the sense, he may not trouble. If you go too fast, you will probably receive the equivalent of a slow handclap on the green light. But, as in bridge, you and your partner (in this case, the producer) will arrange your signals in advance.

You may also have to co-operate with an announcer. He will give you your cue, and its nature will be agreed at rehearsal.

Common troubles? Dry throat. Stop and sip your glass of water. The urge to cough. Give way to it, if necessary – but turn your head away from the microphone. Loose dentures. Make sure that they are firmly in place before your talk begins or you may produce whistling sibilance, reminiscent of 'interference' from nearby stations.

When preparing your script, you can probably reckon on about 125 words a minute. As in the case of a lecture (Chapter 43), count your words and then declaim them to a stop-watch. If in doubt, add a few words to the minute. You can cut them out later, if the producer so directs. But remember that the chances of your being allowed to overrun are remote. Every second of radio time is allotted in advance.

You will probably speak a little slower on television. Once again, the producer will help you. Your talk will probably be directed straight at the lens of the 'live' camera and you may never have to look away. But you may be told to move around . . . to pick up some exhibit or to point to a visual aid . . . to speak to your announcer or to a fellow guest or to an interviewer. Do as you are told. When you do move, do not rush. And use as few gestures as possible. The camera tends to exaggerate the false and the unnatural. So be yourself. Talk as if you were at home, and you will not be returned there uncomplimented.

Postscript

The smallest mistake or the most apparently innocuous remark made in the most obscure radio or TV programme may let loose shoals of protests. Mistakes in print may sometimes be ignored and forgotten. But heaven help the man who broadcasts without due care. He may not lose his licence, but it may be a long time before he gets back on the air. So be extra careful to get your facts right if you do not want to regret your words for long afterwards.

46 *Titles*

If in doubt as to how to address a particular person, check with a reference book, telephone an information service (in London, *The*

Daily Telegraph service is excellent), or get your secretary to check with the guest's office to find out. If there is a toast-master, he will soon put you right. If you have an experienced chairman, follow his lead. Here, in any event, are some common examples. The lower you go down their scale, the more likely you are to meet them. Still, you may be privileged to start a speech with: 'Your Majesty' (for a king or queen); 'Your Royal Highness' for a royal prince, princess or duke; 'Your Grace' for an archbishop, a duke or a duchess; or 'My Lord' or 'My Lady' for members of the peerage below the rank of duke or duchess, children of peers who bear courtesy titles, the Lord Chancellor, Lord Chief Justice and Lords of Appeal and all bishops.

If there is only one bishop present, you may say 'My Lord Bishop'. The Lord Mayor (any lord mayor) is usually referred to as 'My Lord Mayor'. Reference to a particular honoured guest by name is generally appreciated, provided you get the name right (see Chapter 80). The word 'honourable' should be left together with 'right honourable' to those addressing their Parliamentary colleagues. 'Brothers' and 'comrades' have their place. But 'Ladies and Gentlemen' will usually do, even when you consider that your audience are nothing of the sort.

47   *A postscript – pastimes whilst others speak*

Part of the price of the pleasure of hearing your own voice is the necessity to endure the speeches of others. You may, of course, be lucky. The sole guest speaker of an evening only has the introduction and vote of thanks to sit through. During the former, he will be thinking of his speech – and, if he takes the advice given in this book to heart, trying to find something in the words of his introducer to quote, adapt or answer, and so establish a *rapport* with his audience. During the vote of thanks, he must simply try to believe that the words spoken of him are true. And no one need exhibit false modesty to himself.

But inevitably unlucky is the after-dinner speaker, no matter what his place in the toast list. The chairman of a committee may be able to regulate the speeches of others, but the rest must put up with them. If you happen to be a Member of Parliament, you may be able to escape from the function after you have spoken, perhaps alleging a three-line whip. ('Mr Jones must now return to his Parliamentary duties, I'm afraid. But we appreciate all the more that he has spared us some of his most valuable time to be with us.') But heaven help anyone else who leaves before the other speeches are complete.

So the art of listening is worth some cultivation.

In private, the good listener is generally credited with great powers of perception, intelligence and even eloquence. In public, to fall asleep whilst others speak is the height of bad manners. But how can you avoid it?

Every practised speaker is, of course, a skilled doodler. So much so that there is one handwriting expert who is alleged to make his living largely by interpreting the doodles of famous men. But much more constructive is the writing of those neglected letters.

The dinner is dull? Too bad. You must try to get your neighbour to talk about his speciality and, with a little luck, you may find that he is more interesting than you had realised. The after-dinner speeches are a misery? Then use the back of the menu or toast list or guest list or brochure. Take out your pen and write your correspondence. Look up every now and again at the speaker. And no one – least of all the speaker himself – will suspect that you are doing anything other than paying him the compliment of noting his words. My relatives in Australia always know when I have been cursed with dull speeches to hear. They receive missives on agendas, minutes, jotting-pads . . . anything that happens to be handy.

Of course, you could instead be jotting down notes for the current work which you have on hand. In the unlikely event of the speaker sparking off a constructive chain of thought, make a note of the idea before it flees for ever. If he happens to tell a good story, write it down. It may come in handy one day. If all else fails, and you can fight off slumber no longer, then you must do your best to organise your forty winks so as to attract the least possible suspicion. An acquaintance has, through long years of experience, learned how to sleep whilst sitting bolt upright and with his eyes open. Most of us must be content with the head rested on the hand, the elbow on the table. Alternatively, the head droops forward and the notes or brochure or agenda are in front of you so that it may (with luck) appear that you are reading – or at least engaged in deep thought.

It has been said that women knit to give themselves something to think about whilst they are talking. Every speaker should learn to amuse himself during the unamusing speeches of others. What matters is to do so without any appearance of flagging attention or concentration. Spare a thought for the diplomats who must do it all the time.

Part 4

In Courts and Tribunals

48 Introduction

Courts and Tribunals provide a highly refined and specialised area for speech-making. You may be lucky and only forced into the witness box or (woe is you) into the dock, on rare and isolated occasions. However, those occasions are likely to be of supreme importance – if not to you then to those on whose behalf you testify.

Today, though, businessmen are stepping into the legal arena with increasing frequency, not only to give evidence but also as advocates.

Industrial Tribunals now have vast powers. They may award over £16,000 to the employee who is unfairly dismissed – and you may need their help in your capacity as employer or as employee (however mighty). They rule over redundancy disputes and battles over equal pay, sex discrimination, race discrimination, notification to trade unions of intended redundancies and most areas of employment protection. In addition, they are the proper forum for appeals against improvement or prohibition notices, served under the Health and Safety at Work Act.

Now, you will employ a lawyer (through necessity or wisdom) to represent your interests or those of your business, in civil courts (County Courts – with jurisdiction, in general, up to £2,000; the High Court – above that sum); or Criminal Courts (Magistrates' Courts or Crown Courts). But you may prefer to represent yourself or your business in an Industrial Tribunal. There is no legal aid and (for all practical purposes) no provision for the recovery of costs from the loser, in any Industrial Tribunal.

So this Part of the book is designed to help you and those at your command, if and (as is likely) when you are faced with the miseries of court or tribunal proceedings. I offer: A guide to Courts and Tribunals and checklists for those who must appear as witnesses, as advocates – or both. I hope that these guides will be needed as little as possible.

As some of the rules for advocates are the same as those for witnesses – and as the checklists and guides and comprehensive – some repetition is inevitable in the chapters that follow. Never mind. If you remember a rule when you meet it again, you will have learned doubly well.

As the famous Rabbi in *Fiddler on the Roof* said of the man who controlled the temporal destinies on his flock: 'God bless the Tsar – and keep him as far away from us as possible'. The best view of the Courts is from a distance – but if you come close to the flames, these guides should help to keep you intact.

49 Courts and Tribunals – the legal framework

The law – civil and criminal

The *civil law* is designed to provide remedies for citizens (or their companies, firms or other organisations) – one against the other. The *criminal law* sets minimum standards, demanded by the community.

Some wrongful acts have both civil and criminal consequences, e.g. negligence on the road or at work – the guilty party may be prosecuted; and/or sued by the injured party. But civil courts seldom apply criminal sanctions – nor do criminal courts often give remedies to sufferers.

Powers of the courts

Civil courts generally award *damages*, as compensation. They may also make *declarations*, setting out the rights of the parties; grant *injunctions* – orders, restraining the continuation of wrongful acts, e.g. nuisances; and orders for the *specific performance* of contracts, where damages would not be an adequate remedy, e.g. contracts for the sale of land.

A *civil court* may imprison for contempt of court. It is a criminal offence to flout the orders of a civil court.

A *criminal court* may fine, imprison, bind over, grant discharges (conditional or absolute) – and occasionally, e.g. to compensate sufferers with up to £400 (in a Magistrates Court), under the Trade Descriptions Act, order those convicted to pay compensation.

The courts

The High Court – with unlimited civil jurisdiction – is divided into the *Queen's Bench Division* (general, common law jurisdiction) – as opposed to the *Chancery Division*, which has a so-called 'equitable' jurisdiction (deriving from the authority of the Lord Chancellor to supplement the ordinary powers of the common law courts, and now dealing with disputes regarding companies, overlaps that of the Queen's Bench Division). *The Family Division* deals with matrimonial disputes and their ramifications.

112

The County Courts have jurisdiction up to £2,000 – although sometimes smaller claims go to the High Court, e.g. under special procedures seeking swift, summary judgments.

Appeals from both County Courts and High Court go to the *Court of Appeal* and thence (with leave from the Court of Appeal or from the House of Lords) to the House of Lords (judicial committee).

Criminal Courts – All criminal cases commence in the Magistrates' Court – although the more serious ones (from theft to murder) may (and in some cases, must) be tried by the *Crown Court*. The accused may have a right to elect for trial (and will have in the most serious cases). Advantage of trial by jury: much greater prospect of acquittal; disadvantages – extra delay and cost. Where cases are committed by Magistrates to a higher court, the 'committal proceedings' are usually formal – but may be detailed and lengthy. Magistrates must find that there is *prima facie* case to proceed.

Appeals from Magistrates' Courts on points of law go to a special criminal division of the High Court (three Judges); but for rehearing on the facts before a jury, to Crown Court.

Industrial tribunals

Industrial tribunals exercise primarily a civil jurisdiction, including disputes about: redundancy pay; unfair dismissals; equal pay and sex discrimination; and under the Employment Protection (Consolidation) Act. But they also (and rarely) consider appeals against improvement and prohibition orders under the Health and Safety at Work Act (essentially a criminal statute, providing penalties for unsafe practices at work, etc.). Appeals from industrial tribunals go to the Employment Appeals Tribunal.

Who judges?

High Court Judges (all) and Circuit Judges (most) are ex-barristers – ex-solicitors may sit in some Crown Courts. Magistrates' Courts are staffed either by lay Justices (usually – but not always – legally unqualified – and assisted by a clerk) – or by 'stipendiaries', who are paid a stipend and are qualified lawyers.

Industrial tribunals have legally qualified chairmen, accompanied by two lay members, usually one nominated by the CBI (with management experience) and one by the TUC (with shop-floor background).

Appointments of Judges are by the Lord Chancellor and of industrial tribunal members by the Secretary for Employment.

Procedures

These range from the highly formal, jargon-ridden (House of Lords, High Court, County Court, Crown Court), through the comparative discipline of Magistrates' Courts to the informality of tribunals (no robes; everyone sits; members hunt for truth with varying regard for rules of evidence). In general, laymen may cope with procedures of tribunals but anywhere else they should recall the old adage: 'The man who is his own lawyer has a fool for a client'.

Scotland: civil courts

The equivalent of the English and Welsh County Court is the Sheriff's Court, with wide jurisdiction. The Court deals with actions of debt or damages with no upper limit.

Where a claim is for damages in excess of 500 these may (with certain exceptions) be remitted to the equivalent of the High Court – the Court of Session in Edinburgh – for a jury trial.

The Sheriff's Court also deals with landlord and tenant and rent restriction cases; with separation actions; with petitions for the adoption of children; with bankruptcy cases and with ordinary cases of contract and tort.

Where the value of the case does not exceed £500, the sheriff's decision is final. And in the civil sphere, the Sheriff's Court also incorporates a Court of Appeal – cases first heard by a sheriff may be appealed to the sheriff-principal. So this curious appeal from one single judge to another may be anomalous but it does enable people to appeal locally and without undue pressure.

The equivalent of the High Court is the Court of Session – the superior civil court. This is also both a court of first instance and a Court of Appeal. It sits in Parliament House, in Edinburgh.

The Court of Session deals with all actions concerning status (marriage, nullity, divorce, legitimacy); and with petitions for the winding-up of companies whose paid-up capital exceeds £120,000. And it shares jurisdiction with the Sheriff's Court in actions for damages, debt, etc., normally dealing with those involving the largest sums.

Scotland: crime

The Scottish equivalent of the Magistrates' Court is the Sheriff's Court (criminal). Minor prosecutions may also be brought in District

Courts before a stipendiary magistrate (in Glasgow) or justices of the peace – but the bulk of cases come before the sheriff. There is no appeal to the sheriff-principal.

About 90 per cent of prosecutions on indictment and more than 50 per cent of prosecutions on complaint, i.e. a summary prosecution, are dealt with in the Sheriff's Court. The prosecutor decides which mode of trial is appropriate and the accused has no right to elect for trial by jury.

Appeal in criminal matters goes to the High Court of Justiciary – made up of judges of the Court of Session. Apart from hearing appeals, it tries all serious crimes – including murder and rape and goes on circuit for the purpose.

50 Witness-boxing

One of the potentially most uncomfortable audiences for any speaker: is the court of law. With a bit of luck, you will avoid appearing in the dock. But the day is almost bound to come when you find yourself in the witness-box. With reasonable good fortune, you will be there as a witness for or against someone else. But you may be a defendant. Still worse, you might be an accused. Or you could be a plaintiff. In any event – whatever the capacity in which you appear – you must know the basic rules of successful witness-boxing. It is said that a judge must ensure not only that justice is done but that it is manifestly seen to be done. It is equally true that a witness must not only tell the truth but make it manifestly apparent that he is doing so. After all, it is no use being accurate and precise, is it, if nobody believes your story?

Your ordeal generally begins by the taking of the oath. Assuming that you have religious beliefs, you will be able to swear on the Holy Book of your choice. Every witness-box has an Old Testament as well as a New – and a Jewish witness would be well advised to bring a hat with him and make sure that his head is covered. Judges, who have no conception of the different rituals of the various Jewish sects, look askance at a Jewish witness whose head is not covered when he takes the oath. He may be relieved if a Chinese witness dispenses with the traditional ceremony of smashing a saucer to seal his promise to tell 'the truth, the whole truth and nothing but the truth'. But he tends to be baffled by a Jew who swears hatless or covering his head with hand or handkerchief*.

If you have no religious beliefs or your religion forbids the taking of oaths, you will be allowed to affirm. This simply amounts to a declaration that you will tell the truth to the court – a declaration that is intended to be binding upon your conscience.

When you take the oath, do not rely on your memory. The usher will hand you a card. Read from it. It is extraordinary how many intelligent people misread the oath. This may be due either to nervousness or overconfidence – or perhaps a state of partial shock induced by the usher's loud roar of 'Silence' just as you are about to intone the formula. But you need not have worried – no one is allowed to talk other than the oath-taker, and you were therefore the only person to whom the usher's injunction was not addressed.

'And now, Mr Jones', your counsel will say, 'will you kindly address your remarks to the learned judge and do please remember to keep your voice up'. Better advice you could not be given. Do not talk to counsel. One of them is already sufficiently or at least apparently convinced (even if only temporarily) that you are right and the other that you are wrong. It is the judge – or magistrate or magistrates or jury, as the case may be – who will need the convincing. So speak to them. This applies whether you are being examined by your own counsel or cross-examined by counsel on the other side. And in the latter case, it will save you from being put off by a favourite trick of some barristers – attempting to unnerve witnesses by asking them questions while looking in a completely different direction. Talk to the judge and you won't notice it.

'But how does one address a judge?' you ask. If it is a justice in a Magistrates' Court, he is called 'Sir' (or, on occasion, 'Madam'). If it is a judge in a County Court, he is 'Your Honour'. And if it is a judge of the High Court, you address him as 'My Lord'. If you call a magistrate, 'Your Honour' or 'My Lord', he will be flattered. But don't call a County Court judge 'Sir' or a High Court judge, 'Your Honour' – that is almost insulting.

You are now speaking to the judge and calling him by his correct name. Now is the time to remember to 'speak up'. Nothing irritates a judge more than not being able to hear what a witness is saying – and this is particularly important if the judge is elderly and possibly a little deaf. If you have a case, tell the world. If you have something to say, say it so that the world – including counsel, the jury (if any), the shorthand-writers, in fact, everyone in the court – can hear without straining.

*See also Chapter 50

'What is your full name?' your counsel goes on. 'And where do you live?' So starts the 'examination in chief'. Your barrister will do his best to prompt you and to help you along, but he cannot ask you 'leading questions'. A leading question is simply one which suggests the answer. For example, take an ordinary car accident. You are describing how it occurred. Your counsel cannot say to you, 'The van crossed against a red light, didn't it?' That is leading you to say yes. What he will ask is, 'What happened?' Then it is for you to explain, in your own words, the facts about the case. (Incidentally, 'That's a leading question', is one of the legal phrases most misused by laymen. 'And with whom did you spend last night?' is not a leading question, so do not try to hedge by telling your interrogator that it is!)

When your 'examination in chief' is finished, opposing counsel will weigh in with his questions. And he can ask as many leading ones as he wishes. He will try to needle you, to irritate you, to provoke you. Be not provoked, irritated or needled. Remember that he is only doing his job and he is not being nasty because he has any personal feeling against you.

Equally, if he treats you to a charming smile and asks you his questions in a respectful or a kindly tone of voice, do not be fooled. He is not doing it because he likes or respects you, but because he thinks it the best way to get you to drop into his little trap or to give your evidence in the way most favourable to his client.

So listen to counsel's questions. If you do not understand them, ask that they be repeated. And then reply, calmly and carefully. Don't lose your temper. That's what the other side wants you to do. And don't be afraid that counsel will take an unfair advantage of you – if he tries to do that, your own counsel will leap to his feet, objecting vigorously. But by then, if counsel really has been unfair, the chances are that the judge will already have choked him off.

When you are asked a question, answer it – do not reply by asking another one. You are not there to ask questions. 'What is your full name?' begins the classic examination in chief. 'What's my name?' replies the witness. 'Yes. What's your name'. 'Dai Jones', says the witness, 'and what might your name be, pray?' It may get a giggle from the back of the court – but it will not please the judge.

Of course, there are exceptions to every rule. We remember with affection a Dutch gentleman who was claiming commission as agent for a chocolate firm. He told Judge Block, of the Mayor's and City of London Court, of the excellence of the firm and its prospects – but continued with a sad tale of woe, ending with his leaving the employment. 'But if the job was such a good one', queried the counsel on the other side, 'why did you leave?' The witness turned round to the judge, spreading his arms out wide. 'My Lord', he cried appealingly 'if you were treated like that, would you stay on as judge?'. His question was never answered – but he won his case.

Another good rule is – do not make jokes. Leave that to counsel and to the judge. If you try to be facetious or funny, you are asking for trouble. And if the court or counsel do laugh about matters which you consider terribly serious, forgive them – if they were to become emotionally involved in the troubles that surround their lives, they would be sad folk indeed. So do not let their jokes upset you.

Not long ago, a small boy appeared before Mr Justice Stable in the High Court, claiming damages from a shopkeeper who he claimed had sold him a firework with which he had seriously injured one eye. When his mother came to give evidence, counsel cross-examined her, suggesting that she had put words into her little boy's mouth.

'Have you discussed this case with your son?', he inquired.

'Naturally', she replied.

'Often?'

'Not too often – I didn't want to remind him about his bad eye.'

'But I suppose you did discuss it with him when you knew that he was coming to court?'

'I did.'

'And I suppose you discussed his evidence with him?'

'Yes.'

'So you told him . . .'

'I told him to tell the truth, and that if he didn't there'd be one man who'd know – and that would be God.'

The judge turned round to her, wagging his finger, and beaming from ear to ear. 'And what about me, Madam?' he asked, amidst roars of laughter.

The lady was greatly discomfited. She need not have been. The judge had already made up his mind that her son was telling the truth –and in due course, he gave judgment to that effect.

Which brings us to one of the most common questions put to a witness – and one which upsets them the most. 'Have you discussed this case with anyone recently?' counsel asks. 'If I say yes', the witness says to to himself, 'then he'll suggest that I'm party to a cooking of the evidence. But if I say no, then he'll say I'm lying.' Quite right. But the answer is still, yes. First, you will undoubtedly have discussed the case with your solicitor. It is extremely doubtful whether you will have kept it back from your wife, your secretary . . . in fact, you'll probably have been dining out on it for months. So reply, 'Certainly I've discussed it – but what I've told the court is what I saw – and it's true'.

Do that, and you will have edged around yet another trap laid for the unwary and the liar.

Always remember, too, to treat the judge with tact. The witness who says, 'The man I'm talking about was really very old and decrepit', when the man referred to was sixty and the judge is over sixty-five, is hardly out to make friends and influence the court in his favour. Equally, it is rude and discourteous to talk to the court with your hands in your pockets, still less rattling coins in them. But it is not impolite to take your time before replying to a question. A very self-confident businessman came a cropper recently simply because he took no time to think. He was asked to mark on a map the place where a collision happened – and counsel passed him the document. With a slash of his red pencil, the witness marked the spot. But he only made one little mistake. Counsel had handed him the map upside-down; he failed to check that it was the right way up; and as a result he marked the spot exactly – on what everyone agreed was the wrong side of the crossroads. After that, it will hardly surprise you to hear that his evidence was completely disregarded by the court.

Do not take anything for granted. Your counsel will do his best to prompt you – but he cannot lead you. So do make sure that you tell your own story – and do not be one of those who says to himself, when the case is over and he has lost it, 'If only I'd said. . .'.

And now a last word about your relationship with solicitors and counsel. If you are yourself instructing solicitors, they will instruct a barrister on your behalf. You can pick your own counsel if you want to, but a solicitor prefers to do the choosing for you. If you make your own choice, then you will have to bear the responsibility. The normal rule is, you instruct a solicitor and he briefs counsel.

The story is told by a distinguished colleague of an occasion when he was called upon at the last minute to rush off to do a case in the Magistrates Courts. It seems that the counsel whom the accused businessman had asked for was not available and, as a personal favour to the solicitor concerned, our friend filled the gap.

He arrived at the court and won the case. Then, for the first time, he met his client outside. 'Thank you so much, Mr Jones', the man effused.

'Oh, you're quite welcome', counsel replied. 'But I'm afraid Mr Jones was in another court, I'm Mr Brown.'

'Mr Brown?' snorted the client. 'Who asked for you? What are you doing here? How dare you conduct my case when I didn't ask for you?'

The question was obviously rhetorical – but it does make it clear why counsel is happy that professional etiquette will not permit him to interview his lay client when a solicitor is not present. So you must not telephone up your barrister for a private chat. Nor must you try to see him without its being in a proper conference, arranged by the solicitor. Just as you cannot go direct to a specialist in medicine – you have to arrange it through your GP – so counsel must be approached through the proper channels.

Mind you, if you are only a witness, counsel will not talk to you at all before the case – unless, that is, you are an expert. Once again, etiquette permits him to discuss the evidence only with experts and clients. The interviewing of other witnesses is done entirely by solicitors.

And now, knowing the ropes and the rules, advised by solicitor and counsel, you sally forth to the witness-box. May the best man win. And may you be the best man!

51   *A witness's checklist*

Before giving evidence in any court or tribunal, check the following:

1   Do you know your case? Work out in advance what questions you are likely to be asked and ensure that you either know the answers or are prepared to say that you do not know. Therefore

2   Have you prepared (and preferably had typed out) a proper 'proof of evidence' – that is, a statement concerning all relevant facts? Read it through carefully before you give your evidence. You may not take it into the witness box with you (unless it is 'a contemporaneous document' – see below). But you are fully entitled to absorb and re-absorb its contents.

3   Can you get a colleague or friend to cross-examine you – to test and to probe your evidence, so as to prepare you for the cross-examination you will probably face? The better prepared the witness, the greater his prospect of being believed.

4   Are you satisfied that your evidence is correct? Check it out with any documents (those in the possession of your own side or those revealed by your opponents) – with special reference to dates, names, time, places, etc., which can be ascertained with certainty.

5   Have you prepared all contemporaneous documents (notes, letters, etc.) which you will need with you – not only at the hearing but also in the witness box? Remember that (like the policeman's note book) these documents may be referred to while you are giving evidence – although they will have to be shown in that case to the other side.

6   Are you dressed for the occasion? Respect for the court or tribunal – together with recognition that those who sit in judgment are likely to have to rely on first impressions – should encourage you to dress smartly and conservatively. (A young accused who declined to have his hair cut was warned by his lawyer that the result might be an even shorter crop, in one of Her Majesty's institutions. Unfortunately, appearance counts here – as elsewhere in life.)

7   Are you afraid of the witness box? If so, spare time to visit the scene of your future ordeal. Courts and tribunals are nearly always open to the public and you may sit in on someone else's troubles and imbibe the atmosphere and observe the procedures. Watch in particular:

   a   Usually, the witness may say what he has himself seen or heard – but not what someone else said that he (the other person) heard or said. This is known as 'the hearsay rule'.

   b   Watch how advocates 'cross-examine' witnesses on the other side, asking 'leading questions' (that is, questions which suggest the answer) to their heart's content – but how they avoid 'leading' their own witnesses. Your advocate will not be able to put the words into your mouth, nor suggest the answers to the questions which he asks you.

   c   Note with care the idiosyncracies of the court or tribunal – or, if you happen to know the individual judge, magistrate or Tribunal before whom you will appear, then those of the individual or individuals concerned. Judges decide cases – and each has his own ways. Also: The lower down the scale (especially at tribunal level) procedures are less rigid, more varied and are frequently decided by the presiding chairman.

8   Have you watched other witnesses and their mistakes – so as to avoid them: Examples: Unpleasant mannerisms of speech ('To tell the truth . . .') or of manners (picking noses, rattling coins); rudeness to court or counsel; speaking too fast, so that court cannot write down replies (most judges, etc., have to keep longhand notes); speaking so that they cannot be heard; and above all, failing (or refusing) to answer the questions asked.

9   Are you aware that you will be watched when you are not giving

evidence? The demeanour of witnesses when sitting in court or tribunal and not realising that they are being observed is highly revealing to any experienced judge, etc.

10 Have you checked on the time when you will probably be needed at the court or tribunal? Although there are occasions when witnesses (like litigants) have to hang around and wait their turn, courts and tribunals do try to oblige by hearing witnesses when they are available (sometimes even slotting in at convenient hours – perhaps at the start or end of a day or after the luncheon break). If in doubt or difficulty, ask your lawyer. He may, if necessary, make application to the court.

11 Recognising that (unless you are an expert witness – and hopefully, well paid) you will waste a good deal of time and cash through the proceedings, are you satisfied that your evidence is really necessary? If not, can you convince whoever is trying to call you that you are dispensable?

12 Have you received a *subpoena* or witness summons – which requires you to attend? Or a *subpoena duces decum* – one requiring you to bring with you the documents named? If so, then you must turn up. But if you do not want to come, do not hesitate to tell those who have seen fit to require your presence that they may regret putting you into the witness box. Every witness is a hostage to the other side – which (unlike the side which called him) may submit him to cross-examination.

13 If you are prepared to give evidence but do not wish to testify voluntarily against the other side, why not ask for a *subpoena* or witness summons? Then you can say to any objector, 'I couldn't help myself . . . I was subpoenaed. . .'.

14 If lawyers are involved, have you discussed your evidence with them? Unless you are an expert, you will not be able to talk to your barrister – but it is part of the solicitor's job to 'take proofs of evidence' from witnesses and to discuss cases with them.

*   *   *

Remember that in a criminal case, no witness is allowed into the court after the trial has begun, until he gives his own evidence – after which, he may remain. In civil actions, unless the court otherwise orders, witnesses may (and should) listen to all the evidence which precedes theirs.

The more important the case; the longer it is since the incidents you will describe; the more time you will have to invest in the hearing – the more important it is to check this list and to follow the rules.

Witnesses may discredit themselves as well as the side on whose behalf they are called.

52 An advocate's checklist

In the High Court, the County Court or the Crown Court, the company will inevitably be represented by solicitor or counsel (that is, by a barrister). The solicitor (roughly, the general practitioner of the legal world) has limited right of audience, mainly in lower courts and in tribunals; counsel (barrister) may appear in any court, up to the House of Lords. There are two ranks of barrister: 'Junior' (who may, in experience, knowledge and technique be very senior – but who has not 'taken silk') – and 'Queen's Counsel' (sometimes called 'Leading Counsel' or 'Silks', because they wear silk gowns). You will choose your solicitor (preferably, by recommendation) and he will select counsel, when he needs a consultant or an advocate or an expert with time to look up the law.

Lawyers are, of course, trained and experienced advocates (although most solicitors do little advocacy and not all barristers are at the top of their profession).

In the past, executives and managers seldom appeared as advocates – either for themselves or, still less, for their business organisations. With the advent of the Industrial Tribunal, though, managers and other more ordinary folk have taken to advocacy:

1 When the sum at stake is small and legal costs are high, tribunal advocacy becomes worthwhile.
2 You are usually better off in a Tribunal to represent yourself or your company than to employ anything other than an experienced (and hence, expensive) lawyer. And
3 While top people bring their own claims – with potentially £16,000 plus (at least £10,000 thereof tax-free) as the top prize of an unfair dismissal, claims are not solely for lesser business mortals. But as such claims are brought by people who are (by definition) 'dismissed' – and frequently, still out of work – and as legal aid is not available for representation in Industrial Tribunals and executives and managers are seldom members of trade unions (which supply representation) – they represent themselves.

Happily for the advocate, Industrial Tribunal chairmen invariably attempt to help those who are not good at helping themselves (or their companies or firms). But there are certain basic rules to follow. Here is a list of some of the most important:

1 Do your homework. Know your case. Be prepared to answer questions about it.

2 Know what is contained in your own documents.

3 Find out what documents the other side intends to produce. Ask for them and if they are either not produced or you think that there are others which are being hidden from you, go to the Tribunal in advance and seek an order for the production of these documents. An order for 'discovery' and 'inspection' is almost invariable in civil actions – too few industrial tribunal litigants realise that the same order can be obtained there. Do not be taken by surprise by documents produced in court by the other side.

4 Prepare your documents in proper (which usually means date) order. Make them into a bundle and number the pages. Then make copies – three for the tribunal; one for your witness; at least one for the other side.

5 Obtain statements (technically called 'proofs' of evidence) from potential witnesses. Remembering that each witness is a hostage to the other side – and likely to contradict himself under cross-examination – keep the list as short as possible. Call those who are essential; bring second liners to the tribunal, prepared to give evidence if necessary. You do not have to decide in advance.

6 Ensure that all witnesses who can produce 'contemporaneous documents' – that is, file notes, records or letters, made at the time of the occurrence – have the original available in order to refer to them in the witness box.

7 Take all witnesses through their 'proofs'; discuss their evidence – and ensure that they know their case and are prepared to answer questions about it. Naturally, you must not tell them what to say – but you are entitled to ensure that they know what they are about.

8 Decide whether you wish yourself to testify. In tribunals, you may both present the case and give evidence.

9 If possible, attend the tribunal in advance so as to study the procedures and the atmosphere. If in doubt, ask the clerk or the usher – enquire, especially, about any idiosyncracies of the individual chairman. (You will probably not know the composi-

tion of your own tribunal until a few minutes before the hearing.) The normal routine in a case is:

a   The party on whom the burden of proof falls 'opens' the case, explaining the facts and calling evidence. In dismissal cases, if the employer admits that he 'dismissed', then the burden falls on him to show the reason for the dismissal and that he acted 'reasonably' in treating that reason as sufficient to warrant depriving the employee of his livelihood. Therefore he will usually kick off. But in 'constructive dismissal' cases, where the employee must prove that he was 'dismissed', he will start.

b   The other party will then call his evidence – and address the tribunal. The claimant will then make his submissions.

c   The person who calls the witness may not 'lead' him – but only ask questions which do not suggest the answers. The other advocate then 'cross-examines' – asking any questions that are relevant. Then the witness's advocate may 're-examine' – that is, ask further questions arising out of the cross-examination.

10   In their presentation and manner, advocates should follow the same rules as those for witnesses (see witness's checklist). In particular, they should speak clearly; be concise; answer directly any questions asked of them by the tribunal; and always remain calm and courteous. He who panics or gives way to anger loses his temper and his case at the same time.

11   Finally: Arrive early; prepare yourself, your evidence, your witnesses with time on your side; do not be afraid to ask for a few minutes' grace, if your preparations are not completed – or (especially) if you are trying to negotiate a settlement with the other side. Just as litigation is an expensive luxury, to be avoided by potential litigants whenever reasonably possible, so members of tribunals are happy to have cases disposed of by agreement, rather than by argument.

The good advocate is frequently the man who can win the best settlement – which requires that skill in negotiation for which the businessman ought in any event to be prepared.

53 Winning cases – in Courts and Tribunals

The businessman who can avoid ever appearing before a court or (today, more likely) an industrial tribunal is indeed fortunate. This checklist should help ensure that your trials (in both senses of that word) are as few as possible – and their outcome as favourable as you would wish.

Prepare for battle

Documents

1 Documents win cases. Is your system of documentation professionally prepared and properly used? Check especially: contracts of employment or written particulars of terms of service; written statements under the Health and Safety at Work Act; written warnings of intended dismissal – and letters of dismissal; safety systems – including reproofs and warnings to employees who do not follow your systems; and requests to mothers that they give notice *in writing* of their intention to return.

2 All the above documents – and almost any other relevant document which is not specifically prepared for the purpose of litigation (and which is 'privileged' from disclosure) will have to be produced if trouble arises. Beware of carelessly phrased inter-office memos and notes scrawled on files. Conversely:

3 If you have a whiff of legal trouble, remember: documents avoid litigation – the other side can see your strength; they win cases – because they are more reliable than memory; and – if made at the time – they may be referred to while in the witness box.

Other preparations for trial

Other preparations for trial include:

1 Take careful statements from all potential witnesses, before you see your solicitors. You will save their time and (hence) your money.
2 If you make statements to anyone else (including the police or

other people's lawyers) say as little as possible. Most litigants lose cases out of their own mouths.

3 Instruct your lawyers early – when they still have time to guide and help you. Even if you decide to 'go it alone' before a tribunal, your lawyers should help you prepare your case – including your documents.

4 Put all documents into date order and make them into a bundle. Make at least five copies of the bundle for a court and seven for a tribunal, (one for each judge or tribunal member; two for your side; two for your opponents – witnesses may need copies while giving evidence).

5 If you are not satisfied that the other side is producing its documents in advance of the hearing, you may apply for 'discovery' – even industrial tribunals have the power to order disclosure.

Finally: ask your solicitors to give an estimate as best they can of the likely costs involves; weigh up your chances of success or failure; never despise a sensible compromise; and settle the case if you can because you will, in any event:

a Spend your time and that of your staff in the preparation of the case and at the hearing.

b Never recover all your costs, even if you win (from a tribunal, you will get none). And

c You are likely to suffer anxiety and adverse publicity.

Trial tactics

If the case must be heard, then check the following:

1 Do you need solicitors or counsel to represent you? In court, the answer is almost always: Yes (a company, in any event, cannot represent itself). Before a tribunal, the answer is probably: No – unless the sum involved is great and/or a difficult part of law is involved.

2 Choose the right lawyers when you need them: horses for courses and lawyers for cases. Recommendation is your best guide.

3 At the trial, dress conventionally – reckon that those who judge your case are likely to be middle-class and middle-aged.

4 When giving your evidence:

a Speak up – reckon that those who listen to you are deaf – they probably are.

b Answer the questions you are asked – as briefly as possible; if you wish to add a rider or some additional comment, say so.

c   Tell the truth – however unlikely it may sound.

d   Look at the judge, magistrate or chairman – and not at the person who is asking you the questions. And if the chairman or judge is writing down your answers, give him time to do so. Watch his pen.

e   Avoid unpleasant mannerisms of conduct (rattling of coins; picking of teeth, etc.) and of speech ('To tell the truth. . .', 'To be frank with you. . .').

f   Laugh at the jokes of others; make none yourself.

g   Finally: Watch your behaviour when you are not in the witness box. Wise observers (including experienced judges, etc.) watch the demeanour of witnesses when they (the witnesses) do not realise that they are being watched.

*   *   *

If you have to appear in a Tribunal or Court – in any capacity – familiarise yourself as best you can with its style, procedures and atmosphere. Take time to sit in on someone else's troubles before your own are reached. And if in doubt about the ways and customs of the court or the idiosyncracies of the Bench – ask the usher or the clerk. The more humble the official and the more distinguished the questioner, the more flattered he is likely to be.

*   *   *

The basic rule remains, of course: Let someone else be the test case. Only the lawyers are bound to win legal battles. Keep away from them if you can. But if you can't – then at least follow the above rules and you stand a good chance of winning – particularly if you happen to have truth and justice on your side.

54   *Guide to legal costs*

The costs of the law are mighty – but knowing their outline may save you much money. So here is your guide to legal costs – and how to avoid or to reduce them.

Industrial Tribunals

Tribunals may award costs to the successful party if the loser behaved in a way that is 'frivolous' or 'vexatious'. But successful employers rarely receive costs. And tribunal orders for costs rarely reach three figures. So if you are taken to a tribunal by an ex-employee reckon on paying your own costs in any event – but none of those of the employee, if he chooses to engage lawyers. (Note – legal aid is not available for tribunals, although help with preparation may be given under the Legal Aid and Advice Act.)

When considering settlement of Industrial Tribunal claims, then, take into account your own time and that of colleagues or employees; potential bad publicity; and inevitable legal cost if you employ lawyers.

If the sum demanded by the claimant is too high – or you feel that you must set an example to others by fighting, then consider whether you should not keep the legal costs down by representing your own firm or company or getting a manager or executive to do so for you. If you do decide to employ a lawyer (perhaps because the sum claimed is high or the legal points involved are intricate) spend enough to get one experienced in tribunal battles.

Costs without litigation

If you use lawyers to negotiate the settlement of a dispute (perhaps over alleged defects in machinery or in your repair service), you will probably have to pay the costs yourself unless: *(a)* payment of your costs by the other party is made part of the settlement; or *(b)* you start proceedings and win them.

The costs of a law suit

The costs of litigation in the County Court (usually, claims of up to £2,000) or in the High Court (usually, above £2,000) depend upon all the circumstances of the case, including: *(a)* the number of documents to be examined, copied and produced; *(b)* the complication and length of any pre-trial ('interlocutory') sommonses or appeals; *(c)* the length of the hearing; and *(d)* the stature and fees of the lawyers employed by the parties.

Ask your lawyer how much he thinks the costs of an anticipated law suit are likely to be. Then put a limit on your expenditure (actual – on your own costs; potential – on those of the other side) – and tell him to report back when that figure is reached – if the case is not settled in the meantime.

The winner's costs

In a civil action, normally 'costs go with the event' – in other words, the winner is entitled to an order that the loser pay his costs. But these will normally be payable only on a so-called 'party and party' basis – that is, the loser will only have to pay those costs which are assessed (or 'taxed') by a court official or agreed as having been necessarily incurred in order to achieve the victory. Other (less important but still properly incurred) costs will be payable by the client to his solicitor (hence called 'solicitor and client' costs).

Because of 'solicitor and client' costs – or, if you prefer, because costs are seldom awarded on an 'indemnity basis' – even if you win a case, you are unlikely to emerge scot free.

Legally aided opponents

In general, a litigant who receives legal aid will only be ordered to pay costs equal to the amount of his legal aid contribution – and by the same instalments – even if he loses. So if you are sued by a legally aided plaintiff, enquire what is his contribution to the legal aid fund – and you will then know what amount of your costs he will pay if you win. Result: It may be cheaper to pay the whole of the claim than to fight the case and to win it.

Criminal costs

Legal aid apart, if you are prosecuted, e.g. under the Health and Safety at Work Act, you must expect to pay your own costs – although criminal courts do have power to award costs to innocent defendants (power normally only exercised when the prosecution should not have been brought).

However, if you bring a private prosecution with the co-operation of the police, you are likely to get your costs awarded out of public funds. A similar award (paid by the public) is available to those (rare) civil cases in which hardship is caused to the opponent of the legally aided litigant who cannot pay his costs.

Insurance

Where insurers step into the litigious shoes of their assured, e.g. in personal injury claims by employees, cover includes legal costs. So it also does under many road traffic policies. Insurance against the legal costs of industrial safety prosecutions is also available.

Payments into court

In civil cases, it is usually possible for the defendant to pay money into court with a denial of liability. The plaintiff may then take out the money paid in – and recover his costs up to that date. But if he decided not to accept the sum paid in, he takes a chance – because even if he wins his case and is awarded no more than the sum paid in, he will have to pay his costs and those of the other side, from the date of the payment in.

Conveyancing and other non-litigious costs

To find out how much your solicitor will charge to execute the conveyance of your property; to make your will; to draw up standard terms and conditions; to prepare contracts of employment for your staff – ask him. Sometimes there are fixed scales based on the sum involved. Usually, you are back in the market place, finding the best lawyer at the most reasonable price – in the same way as your customers must search for the best bargains in your line of trade.

Relief against forfeiture

Where a tenant fails to pay his rent and is sued for possession, he can normally apply for 'relief against forfeiture'. At any time before he is actually put out of the property, he may pay the rent properly due – and escape from having to forfeit his tenancy. But it will almost always be a term of the Court's grant of relief that he pays all of the landlord's cost on an indemnity basis.

Scales

In both the County Court and the High Court, scales of costs are frequently laid down, setting out the maximum payable to solicitor and/or to Counsel (barrister – 'junior' or Q.C.) – in return for the work stated. Details from your lawyer.

Beware

So take care over costs – they often amount to more than the sum in dispute between the parties to a legal battle. If you are going to settle your case, try to do so early – the longer you wait, the higher the costs . . . the higher the costs, the more difficult it becomes to reach a compromise . . . the harder the compromise, the longer the battle and the greater the costs . . . which can only (and properly) benefit the men and women of the law.

55 *Settling legal cases – a checklist*

Any legal dispute that is settled on reasonable terms should be regarded as a victory. Rare indeed is the winner of any legal battle because:

1 In any court case, the winner is normally entitled to his costs. But normally the loser will only be ordered to pay those costs which were regarded as essential for the winning of the case – the winner is likely to find a balance which was properly incurred and which he must pay to his solicitor out of his own pocket (or out of the winnings).

2 If faced with a legally aided plaintiff, e.g. in an industrial injuries case, even if you win, the plaintiff will only be ordered to pay a sum towards your costs equal to his contribution to the Legal Aid Fund (and by the same instalments). This means that you will probably have to pay the bulk of your costs out of your own pocket.

3 Industrial tribunals only order the loser to pay costs in very exceptional cases (i.e. where the other party has behaved 'frivolously', 'vexatiously', or 'unreasonably' – see Chapter 54). In practice, regard money spent on industrial tribunal proceedings as an investment in success. Do not expect its return.

4 Proceedings take time – hours and days and sometimes weeks, spent in preparing for trial; waiting for cases to be called or heard; enduring the trial.

5 Law suits – civil and especially criminal – are 'trials', in all senses of that word. Anxiety . . . the possible bad publicity . . . possible bad effects on industrial relations. . . .

The lawyer who advises you to accept a sensible compromise is not a coward – nor is he saving money for himself, because most lawyers who take on litigation make far more from the trial than from the preliminaries. A lawyer's advice to 'settle' should be as welcome as that of a surgeon to avoid the knife, treating an ailment with drugs. So here is a checklist of some of the essential rules for settling.

* * *

1 Regard the settlement of a legal claim in the same way as any other business transaction. Exclude emotion and 'principles' – you are engaged in a commercial battle. Balance the probable cost of proceeding (estimates from your lawyers) against the probable loss involved in a settlement. Remember to include allowance for time, anxiety, etc. (see above). If the balance is in favour of settlement, then write off the loss and cut clear.

2 Everything has its price – even a law suit. So even if you did originally intend to fight (perhaps to show others that you are not prepared to be beaten down or ill treated), then prepare yourself for battle – but do remember that litigation is a most chancy affair and even the best cases are sometimes lost and the most unlikely ones are won. First by all means – but recognise that you are involved in a gamble.

3 If you are a defendant in a civil action, you can normally reduce the odds by making a payment into court. If the plaintiff takes the money paid in (with denial of liability), then that is the end of the case. He gets the payment in plus his costs to that date. If he does not accept the money paid in, then if he wins his case and recovers no more than that sum, he will have to pay most of your costs from the date of payment in – even though he got judgment. So if you have nicely judged that payment, you put him on the spot. You should pay in as much as you are willing to lose, to get rid of the case – although you may pay in a smaller amount first, then add to it later if necessary. If the sum paid in is not taken out, the judge will not know of its existence – still less of its amount. So remind your lawyer of the possibility of a payment in, at an early date.

4 Efforts to settle a case may begin with the threat of litigation and end at the door of the court – or even when the case is under way. Some 95 per cent of all cases are settled before judgment.

5 About 50 per cent of all unfair dismissal claims are either withdrawn or settled before they reach the tribunals. Remember that claimants cannot normally contract out of their right to take a case to the tribunal. Exception: Where an agreement is approved by the

conciliation officer. The Advisory, Conciliation and Arbitration Service (ACAS) provides conciliators who can frequently bring parties to terms. Use them – their advice is free and often as well informed as that of any lawyer except those specialising in employment work.

6   Use 'without prejudice' conversations and correspondence whenever you are negotiating and do not wish to risk any offer being treated by a court as a sign of weakness. Once a letter is marked 'without prejudice' it cannot be produced in any legal proceedings without your consent – unless it leads to a settlement, in which case it may provide evidence of that 'accord and satisfaction'.

7   The art of negotiating a settlement is (again, like all business transactions) one requiring experienced and delicate handling. If you negotiate on your own behalf, good luck – but once you have placed the negotiations in your lawyer's hands, let them get on with it. Do not 'keep a dog and do your own barking', otherwise you will inevitably get the worst of all worlds.

8   If you do reach a settlement, make sure that the terms are clear. Even if you have done your own bargaining, have those terms checked by your lawyer, if you have any doubt as to their precision or enforceability. Once you have reached an agreement to settle, it (like any contract) is enforceable through the courts. The original dispute has then been overtaken by the agreement and a dispute over that agreement becomes a new battle, on revised territory.

9   Once you have settled a case, have no regrets. Do not complain: 'If only we had fought, then. . .'. After all, you might have lost – far more than the compromise cost you. And the earlier you settle, the less you will have to pay in legal costs. Conversely, once you reach the door of the court (where so many cases are compromised because the parties become reasonable when in sight and fear of the witness box), the costs may (and in many cases do) equal or even exceed the amount in dispute between the parties.

Part 5

The chairman – and chairmanship

56 The company chairman

There are certain duties of a chairman which are prescribed by law. Section 134 of *The Companies Act, 1948*, provides: 'Any member elected by the members present at a meeting may be chairman thereof'. That is all the Act has to say about the chairman, whose duties are usually set out in the company's Articles. Table A, which most companies adopt, provides (in Article 55) as follows: 'The chairman, if any, of the Board of Directors shall preside as chairman at every general meeting of the company, or if there is no such chairman, or if he shall not be present within 15 minutes after the time appointed for the holding of the meeting or is unwilling to act, the directors present shall elect one of their number to be chairman of the meeting. If at any meeting no director is willing to act as chairman' (Article 56 adds) 'or if no director is present within 15 minutes after the time appointed for holding the meeting, the members present shall choose one of their own number to be chairman of the meeting.'

So the company need not have a chairman at all. If the Board of Directors appoints a chairman, he presides over general meetings of the company, as well as over those of the Board itself.

At a directors' meeting, democracy prevails – 'questions arising . . . shall be decided by a majority of votes'. But if the scales are evenly balanced, 'the chairman shall have a second or casting vote'. But note: A chairman is not entitled to a casting vote unless the Articles say so. And as the principle of 'one man, one vote' is intended to rule supreme . . . and as in any event a casting vote must not be used unless there is 'an equality of valid votes' – it is obvious that (the law apart) this chairman's bludgeon should be used as rarely as possible. The chairman, after all, is (in theory at least) an impartial creature.

Once ensconced in the chair, it is the chairman's job to keep order, to conduct the meeting in a proper and regular manner, and (as was decided in an 1894 case) to be careful to see that 'the sense of the meeting is properly ascertained' in connection with any matter under discussion.

Articles may give a chairman the right to order a poll. Such power must be used with discretion. Accusations of prejudice or bias are to be avoided.

Both sides are entitled to be heard – but not indefinitely. When opposing views have been given a fair airing, the chairman is entitled to accept a motion for the closure. A small minority need not be allowed 'to tyrannise over the majority' (said Lord Justice Chitty), by being able to prevent the meeting from coming to a decision.

On the other hand, a chairman must not only allow resolutions to be put and to be argued. If an amendment is moved and seconded but the chairman refuses to put it to the meeting, the unamended resolution, if passed, will be a nullity. He must allow amendments to be put.

'At any meeting at which an extraordinary resolution or a special resolution is submitted to be passed', says Section 141 of the Companies Act, 'a declaration of the chairman that the resolution is carried, shall, unless a poll is demanded, be conclusive evidence of the fact without proof of the number or the proportion of the votes recorded in favour of or against the resolution'. So when it comes to special or extraordinary resolutions, in the absence of a poll, the chairman's arithmetic is taken as final. And the same rule is usually put into Articles of Association, with regard to ordinary resolutions.

So the chairman has a casting vote in a deadlock – the right to conduct meetings and to declare conclusively the results of votes. Apart from deciding 'incidental questions' which come up during the meeting, that is normally the quota of required power. Unless there is some disorder, he cannot adjourn a meeting at his own behest. And if he purports to do so, the meeting may elect someone to act as chairman in his place, so that the business can go on. On the other hand, he is not bound to adjourn a meeting. 'The chairman may, with the consent of any meeting at which a quorum is present (and shall if so directed by the meeting), adjourn the meeting from time to time and from place to place, but no business shall be transacted at any adjourned meeting other than the business left over from the meeting from which the adjournment took place. When a meeting is adjourned for 30 days or more, notice of the adjourned meeting shall be given as in the case of an original meeting. Save as aforesaid, it shall not be necessary to give any notice of an adjournment or of the business to be transacted at an adjourned meeting.' So says Article 57 of Table A – which, once again, is commonly incorporated in a company's Articles.

As to the actual conduct of the meeting, to some extent this is laid down by the 1948 Act and by the Articles of Association. But otherwise, consider the words of Lord Russell (pronounced in 1937):

'There are many matters relating to the conduct of a meeting which lie entirely in the hands of those people who are present and constitute the meeting. . . . It rests with the meeting to decide whether accounts, resolutions, minutes or notices and such like shall be read to the meeting or be taken as read; and when discussion shall be terminated and a vote taken; whether representatives of the Press, or any other persons not qualified to be summoned to the meeting, shall be permitted to be present, or if present, shall be permitted to remain; and whether the meeting shall be adjourned. In all these matters, and they are only instances, the meeting decides, and if necessary a vote must be taken to ascertain the wishes of the majority. If no objection is taken by any constituent of the meeting, the meeting must be taken to be assenting to the course adopted.'

So what does the law lay down about the conduct of a meeting?

First, resolutions (unless the Articles otherwise provide) are decided by a show of hands. One person, one hand. One hand, one vote. But then may come the poll. This is a formal vote. Those present in person or by proxy (see Chapter 51) will probably be asked to sign a paper headed *'For'* or *'Against'* the motion. The poll is taken by counting these votes.

According to Article 58, a poll may be demanded in any general meeting either by the chairman or by at least three members present in person or by proxy or by any member or members present in person or by proxy and representing not less than one-tenth of the total voting rights of all the members having the right to vote at the meeting. A member or members holding shares in the company conferring a right to vote at the meeting on which an aggregate sum has been paid up equal to not less than one-tenth of the total sums paid on all the shares conferring that right may also demand a poll. The demand for a poll may 'be withdrawn'.

If a poll is demanded (and not withdrawn) on the election of a chairman or on a question of adjournment, Article 61 says that 'it shall be taken forthwith'. Where a poll is demanded on any other question, it shall be taken 'at such time as the chairman of the meeting directs, and any business other than that upon which a poll has been demanded may be proceeded with pending the taking of the poll'. Note: 'On a poll, votes may be given either personally or by proxy' (Article 67).

What of the man who comes to break up your meeting? The chairman has the right to order his immediate removal. Alternatively, he may adjourn the meeting for long enough to remove 'the disorderly element'.

Naturally, the chairman will generally have the company secretary at his side – and he, one hopes, is a wise and experienced man who can advise on points of order and procedure. Like the Clerk to the Justices, if he knows his job, he is indispensable. Meanwhile, the above are the rules from the 1948 Act and Table A of the rules that the chairman needs to know. If the situation gets out of hand so that the chairman needs more detailed information, he should first consult the Articles of the company – and then a solicitor.

57   *The chairman as compère*

The chairman of a meeting – any meeting – sets the tone. If he is a dull dog, the meeting will be a bore. If he is in gay mood, the meeting will be of good cheer. If he is long-winded, any members of his audience not bound to stay will disappear. If he is angry, aggravated, tactless or unkind, this will soon be reflected in the atmosphere. Not for one moment dare he be off his guard. He is the compère . . . the life and soul of the gathering – or its death and decay.

Consider the ordinary variety programme. The compère is the link man. He holds the show together. If he fails, then it falls apart. The same applies to the chairman.

To keep a meeting in good humour, here are some suggestions:

Do not allow yourself to get aggravated. The more difficult the gathering, the more important it is for you to keep your self-control and your pleasant manner.

Set the tone before the meeting begins. Try to do your colleagues or your audience the compliment of arriving on time. Spare a few minutes beforehand, if you can, to iron out difficulties and to prevent personal affronts (see Chapter 44).

If the meeting is a small one, try not to ignore people who come in late. 'Good evening. It's nice to see you.' Worthwhile words to make a guilty latecomer feel at ease – and obliged to you.

There is no need to take too literally the old, chairman's warning: 'Stand up, speak up and shut up'. But do try to let others do as much of the talking as you can. Time them beforehand, if possible. Introduce them . . . invite them to have their say . . . ask what they think. Link the speakers together and provide the channel through which they speak. But yourself – talk only when you must.

Let your audience feel that they have had their say. In the case of a large meeting, do your best to allow as adequate a question time as possible. Cajole your speakers into brevity and into agreeing to answer questions at the end. The audience that has its questions answered is almost always satisfied. Question Time in the House of Commons is easily the most interesting period of the day. And so it is with most meetings. But where the session is a small one – a committee or Board meeting, for instance – the same principle is even more vital. Let the others put their views before the gathering. Try not to choke off discussion before it comes to an end. Wait until you get the feeling of the meeting that time has come for the particular debate or argument to be wound up.

Let everyone feel that his presence is appreciated. One way is by saying so: 'We are delighted to have you all with us'. When the meeting is small enough, make sure that everyone has said something. 'What are your views about this?' The quiet man may have more valuable advice to give than the garrulous soul who monopolises the discussion. The timid participant may be more expert than the exhibitionist. If talent is available, make sure it gets used.

Do not be afraid to season the proceedings with laughter. A few moments spent on a friendly joke may be more worthwhile than ten times as long devoted to argument. (But try to avoid the unkind cut – see Chapter 5). Round the meeting off with appropriate words of thanks – and set the atmosphere right for the next time.

*   *   *

Most of these suggestions could be brought under one word: tact. You are running the meeting. But (except in case of disorder) you should try not to let it be too obvious. The horse knows when it is mounted by a skilled rider who does not have to keep tugging at the reins or hurting the animal's mouth. The best leaders give their followers the maximum feeling that they (the followers) are running their own show. The top compères keep the programme going and ensure that everyone stays contented and awake. The finest chairmen are those who rule through good humour, quiet tact and gentle persuasion.

58   Chairing a safety committee

Since 1 October 1978 employers have not only had to recognise and consult with safety representatives appointed by recognised independent trade unions. If two or more such representatives require the setting up of a safety committee, employers are bound to comply.

Naturally, a safety committee (like any other) needs a chairman. He may be a manager – the managing director, perhaps, or the personnel chief or the company doctor. Or one of the safety representatives may himself be a capable chairman – perhaps with experience drawn from work for the local authority. The law prescribes neither the identity of the chairman of a safety committee nor how he should do his job. But the success of the committee's work will depend on how he carries out his function. So here are some hints to help him (or you) to do this vital job.

*   *   *

1   Do your homework. This means:

a   Read and understand the new Regulations, Code and Guidance Notes. They are all neatly set out in a small pamphlet available from the Health and Safety Commission (Baynards House, 1 Chepstow Place, London, W2 4DF. Telephone: 01-229 3456).

b   Read the Minutes of previous meetings, so that you know what has been discussed and decided in the past – otherwise you are bound to forget to check on implementation of decisions and/or to waste time re-covering old territory.

c   Study the safety set-up, organisation and problems within the unit concerned – if necessary, taking guidance from representatives or other committee members – so that you can guide the discussion in an informed and helpful way.

2   Prepare your agenda in advance. As in the case of all other meetings, you must know what is to be discussed. A typical agenda might read:

a   Apologies for non-attendance.

b   Minutes of last meeting.

c Matters arising from Minutes, not included elsewhere.

d Correspondence.

e Reports of safety representatives on incidents – including accidents or hazards occurring on inspections carried out since last meeting.

f Report of safety officer.

g Report of medical officer/nurse.

h Recommendations for action.

i Any other business.

3 Ensure that someone on the committee is capable of taking careful Minutes; that he in fact does so; and that the Minutes are circularised to all members before the meeting – so that at the start you can say: 'Minutes have been circularised. May I sign these as a correct record of what occurred at the last meeting?' If there are any alleged inaccuracies, these should be sorted out. Remember: the Minutes are neither more nor less than a record. They set out what happened – not what you or anyone else would have preferred to have happened.

4 Prepare the rest of the meeting in advance, in so far as you reasonably can. Help the safety representatives to have their reports ready and encourage them to discuss with you beforehand any queries on presentation. You may also find items which it would be better for the safety representative (at least initially) to deal with behind the scenes rather than in public. The job of the chairman is to get results and to encourage discussion – not disputes. Conversely: the more harmony he can achieve, the better.

5 Take special care to bring into the full discussion those whose views may be valuable but who may be reticent or inarticulate. Particularly when dealing with people who have practical safety experience or interest but who are not used to committee work, it is the chairman who can make them feel valuable – and so encouraged in their efforts.

6 Guide the discussion so that it stays within the intended limits – of health, safety and welfare. Do not allow the meeting to turn into a battleground, with discussion or argument raging over other areas. If a safety committee trespasses into the arena of (for instance) collective bargaining, union and management are likely to move back to their own sides of the table – whereas in a safety committee they should be brought and kept together.

7 The safety committee chairman's job is to focus attention all the

time on the united purpose of management and unions – to preserve life and limb. There should not be two sides. If you are successful in bringing and keeping people happily together for this purpose, then you may indeed improve the atmosphere for all other purposes. But if management and unions cannot combine successfully for safety purposes, what hope can there be for industrial peace?

8   If disputes arise over the composition of the committee, check back to the Commission's Guidance Notes. Remember that management should certainly not constitute more than 50 per cent of the membership – and there is no reason why it should not be less. Yours is a practical committee with one, sole, crucial job – to reduce the risks of accidents. Keep your mind concentrated on that task – and ensure that the discussion does not drift away from it.

9   As in the case of all chairmen, keep cool; retain your good humour; and use tact, courtesy – and flattery – rather than sarcasm or the stick. A firm appraisal (especially when dealing with deviations from the health and safety area) should be fully acceptable.

10   Always try to achieve a consensus of opinion. But do not be afraid to call for a vote. Votes are rare on boards of directors but frequent at trade union meetings. Directors who chair safety committees are often too chary of calling for a vote where clarification of views becomes necessary. You will sometimes find that the vote brings results which are quite different from those that you would have expected from the discussion.

11   Always fix the date of the next meeting – and make sure it is one that is suitable for yourself. The Commission stresses that meetings should only be cancelled or postponed in the most rare emergencies. If you expect others to give priority to your committee and to its decisions and deliberations, you must do so yourself. A chairman's job is to lead. Chairmen of safety committees are leading the way into a safer industrial world.

59 Controlling the audience

Whether you are dealing with a committee of three or a crowd of three thousand, as chairman you must be in control. Except in the rare cases of people who have deliberately arrived with the intention of breaking up the proceedings, your audience have given up their time for a purpose. It may be the wish to advance the company's business and hence their own prospects. They may be seeking knowledge or entertainment. They may wish to extend the work of the trade charity. Whatever the reason, they wish the business to be done. And then they will want to get back to their offices or, at the end of the day and with even more fervour, to their homes. A chairman who controls his audience and hence the business of the meeting is appreciated.

So do not be afraid to put your foot down (metaphorically) or (literally) to tap with the gavel. You were elected or appointed chairman to keep order and if you do so, you will have the meeting behind you. This does not mean that you should shout. A firm: 'Order please, gentlemen'; 'Will you please give Mr Black a fair hearing'; or 'I must insist on quiet for our speaker, please' – these are the courteous and successful gambits. Occasionally you may need: 'I'm afraid that if those who are attempting to break up the meeting will not desist, I shall have to ask the stewards to have them evicted' (see Chapter 60). But much more common is the 'Thank you, gentlemen', addressed to those of your colleagues whom you hope to thank for their future silence.

Of course, it is essential for you to know precisely what you are doing. You must understand the basic rules of procedure (see, in particular, Chapter 61 on resolutions and amendments). But if you do make a mistake, then you have two alternatives, and one or other must be grasped as firmly as possible. Either you stand by your mistake or you smile and apologise.

In general, even when a chairman is wrong, the law will if necessary uphold his decisions. In one case, for instance, it was decided that a chairman who had incorrectly counted the votes on a show of hands could not be overruled because, in the absence of fraud or bad faith, the Court would not interfere with his decisions. So if you have chosen the wrong procedure or decided to rule that an intervention is

147

out of order or have declined to allow a resolution to be put to the meeting, and you regret that decision, it may still be best to stand by it.

Alternative: 'It is clear that the meeting would, in fact, like to discuss this matter. So be it.' Or: 'You are quite right, Mr Jones. I should have allowed the discussion to go further. Please do carry on.' A graceful retreat. As the French put it: '*Se reculer pour mieux sauter*' – you recoil so as the better to jump forward. You are being decisive even about your indecision.

Still, it is 'the sense of the meeting' that usually matters. The chairman needs antennae. He must be able to judge what people want. He must employ his tact so as not to override the wishes of those who have seen fit to put him in charge of their proceedings. Whilst not pandering to the inevitable mischief-maker, abrasive irritant and aggravating nuisance who nearly every organisation or body or community seems to throw up, he must nevertheless give even such persons (who may be right on occasion and have a certain acid usefulness) the opportunity to let off steam. When the meeting has had enough of them, you will know. And so will the aggravators. Sense your meeting – and run it. That is your job as chairman.

60   Order – and disorder

To some extent, a speaker can and must control his own audience. He must command attention. He must know how to deal with his own hecklers (see Chapter 26). And, if necessary, he must be prepared to tongue-lash those who will not pay heed to his words. But if the speaker fails, the chairman must step in. Indeed, it is part of the chairman's task to ensure that the speaker gets a hearing (literally as well as metaphorically).

In most cases, a smart rap with the gavel and a command of 'Order' should suffice. (If you have no gavel, a smart rap on the table with a coin, pen-knife or lighter, will probably do the trick. It is also both more effective and more dignified than a pounding of the fist which may, in any event, prove painful.) But if disorder does break out, the chairman must know precisely how to handle it.

The main rule, of course, is to handle himself with restraint, calm and dignity. He must never lose his head, or he will have failed. With luck, he will have the secretary sitting beside him, to guide him on procedure. But to know the rules in advance breeds the confidence he needs. (And the secretary should know them, too). So here they are.

61 Debates and procedure

The chairman must know the rules of debate. His duty is to enforce them. Speakers must know the rules either to follow them or attempt to evade them.

*   *   *

The chairman is in charge. He has been elected or appointed to his position and is expected to guide and control the meeting. He is in charge of proceedings.

When the chairman stands, everyone else is expected to sit and to be silent. If the chairman cannot obtain order by rapping his gavel and demanding silence, he may have to adjourn the meeting. Unless the meeting is closed, the chairman is entitled to speak whenever he wishes – and to prevent anyone else from doing so unless he wishes. He decides the order of speeches. He will have the agenda but may vary it (see Chapter 66). He is in charge.

But, of course, he should rule by consent. For instance, if he decides to change the order of business, he should explain his reasons. If the bulk of the meeting objects to the change, then he should normally revert to the original order. He is not a dictator.

Normally, each item of business should be discussed separately. If there are steps to be taken – or even if it is to be resolved that there be no action on the matter – a resolution or motion will be 'put'. This can be done quite informally, where there is either no opposition or a general consensus. But if after discussion has taken place there is no agreement, there should be a vote (see Chapter 66).

Where the formalities are being preserved, a motion will be proposed and seconded. It will then be thrown open to the meeting for discussion – and the chairman will attempt to call upon someone who will oppose the motion. After the matter has been sufficiently ventilated, the proposer will normally exercise his right of reply (see Chapter 24). Then a vote may have to be taken.

If the motion or resolution is not on the agenda, the proposer should be asked to phrase it as concisely and clearly as possible. The chairman who has to put a resolution which even the proposer has not put into sensible English (and into words which can be put into the minute book) is in a bad way. The motion should be clearly stated either by the proposer or by the chairman before it goes forward for debate.

The length and number of speeches will depend upon the chairman. But anyone may 'move the closure'. Or it may be resolved that 'the question be now put'. A show of hands will indicate whether those present have had enough of the subject or whether they wish to debate the matter further. If a chairman is in doubt as to whether or not the debate should be closed – or if he feels that it would appear partisan for him to terminate it – then he can easily test the feeling of the meeting, if necessary by asking whether anyone wishes 'to move the closure'.

If it is agreed that the question 'be now put' – then that is what happens. The motion is voted upon. If a motion is carried that the meeting move on to 'next business', then no vote is taken on the motion. It is often better not to reveal the split in the ranks. Or all sides may prefer to avoid a vote which no one is really confident of winning.

Some organisations allow the moving of 'the previous question'. The effect of this being passed is that the discussion on the current topic terminates and all reference to it is expunged from the minutes. No vote is, of course, taken on the matter in question. There are times when people feel that it would have been better for the organisation or meeting had the discussion not taken place at all. 'The previous question' is a useful procedure.

Again, someone may move that the entire meeting be adjourned. It is not only the chairman who can terminate the proceedings. If those present at the meeting wish to put an end to it, they may normally do so. But, of course, there may be a lengthy debate 'on the adjournment'.

Whilst the debate goes on, there may be interruptions (see Chapter 26). One common device is a 'point of order'. Anyone is entitled to raise any point he wishes concerning the order of the meeting, at any time. In theory, he is only free to query as to whether the procedure in hand . . . what the speaker is saying . . . the chairman's ruling . . . is 'in order'. He should not stray away to deal with side issues or to use the occasion to deal with the substantive issues. But skilled interrupters can often disguise their disruptive attacks in the form of 'points of order', and so insinuate extra speeches where none would otherwise be allowed.

In some meetings, the custom is for speakers to give way on 'points of information' – but generally, it is a matter for them (the speakers themselves) to decide. The chairman cannot force them to give way, or take any step if they decline to do so. But if the chairman himself addresses the speaker, the latter may remain standing but (like anyone else at the meeting) must accord the chairman the right to speak – and whilst he does so, must remain silent.

The speaker, then, must 'obey the chairman's ruling'. The fact that he 'has the floor' does not mean that he is entitled to occupy it in the teeth of objection from the chair.

If all motions were proposed, seconded, opposed and voted upon as they stood, a chairman's life would be moderately easy. But there are always amendments to be considered. In general, motions to amend a resolution must (if seconded) be allowed. They should be considered individually and voted upon if necessary. If accepted (whether or not after a vote) they become incorporated into the original motion, which must then be put, as amended. If rejected, they die. An amended motion, once put, can then be the subject of further amendment, with the procedure as before.

Often a skilled chairman can manage to induce the mover of a resolution to vary or extend its terms so as to incorporate the amendment. A peaceful meeting is a chairman's delight. But equally, if an amendment is really no more than an attempt to kill the resolution, he may rule it out of order and require the proposer of the amendment to put forward his views in opposition to the substantive motion. The chairman's job is to ensure that everyone is given a reasonable opportunity to express his views. But he is not bound to allow a minority to dominate. He is entitled not only to select the speakers (in the fairest possible way), but also to sort out the resolutions and the amendments, so that the feelings of the meeting may be tested in the fairest way.

Note, then, that once the meeting has a reasonable opportunity to express its view, the chairman himself may – with the consent of the meeting – close the debate and put the motion to the vote.

Some additional points:

Unless a company's Articles (or the constitution of the organisation in question) require motions to be seconded and/or submitted in writing, neither will be strictly necessary.

No one has any right to speak more than once on any motion or amendment – although the proposer of an original motion (but not usually of an amendment) will generally be given the right to reply.

Once a motion has been defeated, it should not be allowed back into the meeting under some other guise.

No amendment can be proposed after the original motion has been passed or rejected.

Amendments cannot be proposed or seconded by those who performed that service for the original motion; but they can, of course, accept (or speak on) the amendments proposed by others.

If you wish to frame an amendment, the best way is usually to do so by moving that the words you have in mind be added to or omitted from or inserted into (as the case may be) the motion or resolution.

*   *   *

Meetings are usually governed by consent and common sense. The chairman must keep his head and never panic. Speakers should help the chair in every case except that in which the chairman has shown himself to be unwilling to act impartially. In that case, the battle is on.

62   Trespass – and who may be present

The occupier of premises has the sole right to decide who may – and hence, who may not – be upon them. Anyone who enters or remains upon premises without the occupier's consent (express or implied) – or, of course, against the occupier's wishes – is a trespasser. And proper steps may be taken to eject him.

The organisers of a meeting occupy the meeting-place. It may be your company, welcoming its members to a general meeting. It may be a trade organisation, using a room in a local hotel. Or perhaps it is a political or charitable organisation, which has hired a hall. Wherever the gathering, the organisers are (for the time being at least) the occupiers. They are entitled to decide who may or may not be present.

Now, if the meeting is advertised as open to the public, anyone is entitled to turn up and to take part. If special invitations are sent out (as to a company meeting) then the recipients are expressly invited. If people simply wander in to a gathering (perhaps one organised by a charity) they may well have an implied invitation to attend. They will be present as lawful members of the assembly.

But the fact that someone arrives lawfully does not mean that he is entitled to remain for ever. You are free to ask anyone to leave the premises over which you have control. He is then bound to go. If he fails to do so, he becomes a trespasser – just as effectively as if his initial arrival had been unlawful. You may start your visit as a welcome guest. The moment you become unwelcome and are asked to leave, the law requires you to comply. If you do not, you are a trespasser.

Take the ordinary case of the shopkeeper. He may specifically invite a particular customer to come to buy from him. That customer is no trespasser when he arrives. Nor is the potential buyer who comes in off the street. But then there is a dispute. The customer is asked to leave. He must do so.

Or a representative comes to your office. He probably had an implied invitation to display his wares. If you ask him to go and he stages a sit-down demonstration, he is a trespasser. He has no more right to be there than the man who gate-crashes a private meeting, breaks into a factory or home or trespasses upon someone else's land.

Trespassers cannot normally be prosecuted. Only military establishments, certain government departments and others with special statutory powers can bring criminal proceedings against those who set unlawful foot on their property. But – the Englishman's home being, in theory at least, his castle – anyone can sue a trespasser for damages. And the Court may award him an injunction – that is, an Order, forbidding any repetition of the wrongful behaviour. So you and your colleagues may have to consider taking that sort of action against the people who attempt to break up your meeting.

But there is one much more important, practical, immediate and valuable remedy given by the law to those who trespass against you. You may eject the unwanted guest. If necessary, you may employ 'reasonable force' to do so.

How much force is 'reasonable'? That depends on all the circumstances. You should employ no force at all until you have asked the trespasser to leave and he has refused. Then a polite frog-march will normally suffice. Anything more desperate (which goes beyond that which is reasonably necessary to get rid of the individual) would be frowned upon. A refusal to leave is not a licence to inflict actual or grievous bodily harm on the offender.

In the unlikely event of your being threatened with some weapon, you are entitled to defend yourself. The man who offers force whilst engaged in trespassing is likely to have little luck if he complains that too much force was used against him. But generally speaking, your stewards – or some of the younger and more powerful members of your audience – should have no difficulty in hustling the intruder out of the room or hall. Actions in law taken by ousted trespassers, alleging that unreasonable force was used against them, are almost unknown.

The chairman, then, should not descend into the arena of physical force. He should direct that the stewards or others do the ejecting. But he should not hesitate. He must be firm – make his decision and stick to it.

Of course, the decision may be wrong. It may prove to be a tactical error. But dither and all is lost. You are far more likely to make the wrong decision effective if you move with determination and due speed than to achieve the correct results by acting with perfect moderation, when your indecision becomes apparent to the meeting. Act – and act swiftly.

Suppose, though, that in fact the alleged trespasser had every right to be present and that you, as chairman, make a mistake in having him ejected. Suppose, for instance, that you take umbrage at something said by a member of staff at an employees' meeting and you require him to leave the premises. You may have been quite wrong. He may have been wrongfully dismissed and entitled to claim damages against the company. But that still gave him no right whatsoever to remain, contrary to your wishes. You were entitled to eject him. His remedy lay elsewhere.

In a small meeting, there should be no difficulty in getting trespassers to leave. Indicate the nearest convenient route and they act unlawfully if they do not make use of it. If the meeting is a larger one, then stewards should have been appointed beforehand. They are under the authority of the chairman. He may require them to take any necessary measures to deal with disorder. They act on his instructions. If he tells them to eject a trespasser, they may do so.

Incidentally, even the stewards have no right to require trespassers to identify themselves. By all means let names and addresses be asked for. But if they are refused, no offence is committed. The chairman appoints the stewards and they have considerable powers. But they are not the police.

The police should be called in as the ultimate resort. If the police have reasonable grounds for believing that there is likely to be a breach of the peace or that such a breach is 'imminent', they may enter the meeting even without your consent. If you genuinely believe that a breach of the peace may result, you may call them in and they are bound to come to your assistance. And it is statute – as well as 'common law' rules, built up through centuries of usage – which lends weight to the arm of the law, where there is likely to be disorder at a public meeting.

63 Public order

'Any person who in any public place or in any public meeting uses threatening, abusive or insulting words or behaviour with intent to provoke a breach of the peace or whereby a breach of the peace is likely to be occasioned, shall be guilty of an offence.' (Section 5 of *The Public Order Act, 1936.*) Penalty? Up to three months' imprisonment or a £50 fine or both. And 'a constable may without warrant arrest any person reasonably suspected by him to be committing an offence under Section 5 . . . of this Act.'

* * *

So if you are chairing a public meeting, the police have a good deal more power than yourself. Those who break up your proceedings are not only offending against good taste and good manners and destroying your goodwill, but they may well be committing a criminal offence which is regarded more seriously by the law than many people realise.

Note in particular: 'Threatening, abusive or insulting words or behaviour' is a very broad phrase. But it does not cover the case of the firm, straightforward, and outspoken dissenter, who causes chaos by using words which stir up trouble but which are not 'threatening, abusive or insulting' in the ordinary meaning of those words;

The trouble-maker may be guilty of the offence either where he intends to create or provoke a breach of the peace or where such is the likely result of his words or behaviour – either will do;

'Public meeting' is defined as including 'any meeting in a public place and any meeting which the public or any section thereof are permitted to attend, whether on payment or otherwise';

'Public place' is defined as meaning 'any highway, public park or garden, any sea beach, and any public bridge, road, footway, lane, court, square, passage or alley, whether a thoroughfare or not; and includes any open space to which, for the time being, the public have or are permitted to have access, whether on payment or otherwise;

It follows that these rules are most likely to apply to you in respect of a meeting in a private place to which the public or any section of it are invited or permitted to attend. Your shareholders are a section of the public.

For amusement, note that it has been held that these rules are 'not designed to create a new offence as between neighbours engaged in abusing each other'. They are, however, directed at those who abuse (amongst others) the chairman.

*   *   *

Any person who in a public place or at any public meeting uses threatening, abusive or insulting words or behaviour or distributes or displays any writing, sign or visible representation which is threatening insulting or abusive, with intent to provoke a breach of the peace or whereby a breach of the peace is likely to be occasioned, is guilty of an offence. (Section 5 of *The Public Order Act, 1936* – as amended by *The Public Order Act, 1963*, and *The Race Relations Act, 1965*).

Any person who at a lawful public meeting acts in a disorderly manner for the purpose of preventing the transaction of the business for which the meeting was called together shall be guilty of an offence. And so is any person who incites another to commit the offence (*The Public Meeting Act, 1908*).

If any constable reasonably suspects any person of attempting to break up a public meeting, he may – at the request of the chairman of that meeting – require the interrupter immediately to give his name and address. If he refuses or fails to do so or gives a false name and address, then he commits an offence. If the constable reasonably suspects him of giving false particulars – or if he refuses to give any particulars at all – he may be arrested without a warrant. (Section 6 of *The Public Order Act, 1936*.)

*   *   *

Finally, remember a few more rules on police powers.

They are not entitled to enter private premises without either the invitation of the occupiers or a warrant.

They are not bound to eject trespassers from private premises (but see Chapter 62). However, if there is an actual breach of the peace, they are bound to take action.

When the police have reasonable grounds for believing that a breach of the peace is likely to be committed, they may enter a meeting held on private premises, even without a warrant. But in practice, the odds against this happening are considerable. When you need the help of the police, ask for it – and do not wait until things get desperate. As we have seen, they have enough power, if they need it. But the mere knowledge of their presence usually obviates the need.

64 *Introducing the guest*

However well you know the person you are about to introduce, have his name written down in front of you. The chances of your mind going blank are remote. But it happens. The most famous occasion? During the 1966 Election when a local Conservative party chairman was introducing Mr Edward Heath. 'In the short time since our guest of honour has become leader of the party', he thundered, 'his name has become a household word. I am proud, honoured and delighted to introduce to you our future Prime Minister, Mr . . . er . . . er . . . er. . . .' Calamity.

Or: 'The name of our guest is a household word in the trade. Ladies and Gentlemen, Mr . . . er . . . er . . . er. . .'.

'Our guest needs no introduction . . . without further ado, I am pleased to introduce to you Sir Robert . . . er . . . er . . . er. . . .'

This sort of gaffe can never be undone. And it is possible even when you have done your homework. But it is far more likely without preparation. This business of 'the speaker needs no introduction' generally implies that the chairman has not bothered to find out anything about the speaker. Let your secretary dip into *Who's Who* . . . *The Wine Producers' Year Book* . . . *The International Dictionary of Great Millionaires* . . . or whatever the appropriate reference work happens to be. Alternatively, get someone to phone up the man's assistant or secretary or manager and get some details of his doings. Even better, hunt around for a personal and friendly anecdote. The less it appears that you had to do research, the better – but the more research you do, the more effective your introduction is likely to be.

If the speaker arrives and you have no information about him, do not despair. Speakers appreciate being asked. Take the man on one side and say to him quietly, with your pencil in one hand: 'I am to have the pleasure of introducing you to our audience. Which of your many offices would you like me to mention? How would you like to be introduced?'

Every speaker has his foibles. He may not want you to say that he is an ex-president of the Undertakers' Society – he may have been defeated in a recent and bitter election contest. He may prefer to forget that he was the author of a book which resulted in a libel action. On the other hand, he may especially want you to remind his audience that he is an ex-president of the Oxford Union . . . former secretary to Sir James Director . . . a champion golfer, as well as a prominent industrialist or trade union leader.

Or suppose that you are introducing a man who has really fought his way up the ladder. Maybe he would like you to refer to his humble origins. Or perhaps he would prefer to forget them. Unless someone has given you the tip off, you cannot know. The number of potential bricks to be dropped is immense.

At a recent dinner, a famous, generous and charitable businessman was introduced to his audience as the man who 'not only conceived the idea of the . . . Girls Boarding School but had personally raised the very large sum needed to establish it.' Unfortunately, the chairman had omitted to check on how the school was going. Had he done so, he would have discovered that there were only eight applicants for the 120 places and that the entire venture was a flop which the guest of honour was not anxious to recall. The mixture of embarrassed silence and delighted laughter which greeted this *faux pas* reflected in no way upon the affection which the audience had for the gentleman concerned, whom everyone knew to be a first-class man. But it made the audience feel sorry for him – and for the chairman. The fact that the chairman was another voluntary worker in good causes and a popular man of business in no way excused an error which could so easily have been avoided.

If you are too busy to prepare your introduction, then get someone else to do it (either the preparation or, if necessary, the introduction itself) for you. There is no law to prevent a chairman from saying: 'I shall now ask his ex-mentor/disciple/managing director (or as the case may be) to introduce our guest to you'. It does not happen very often – which makes it all the more delightful when it does.

So speak of your guest's known achievements. By all means couple this with friendly or flattering references to his firm or his forebears. But the following are to be avoided:

'We are very pleased to have Mr Jackson with us tonight. His father is a very famous figure in the industry and we know that, in listening to his son, we shall have a treat awaiting us. . .'. Little better is: 'Mr Bloggs is the distinguished son of famous parents. . .'.

Much worse (but often happening in practice): 'Lord Bloggs is unfortunately unable to be with us tonight. But we are pleased that Lady Bloggs has consented to speak to us. Without further ado, I introduce Lady Bloggs.'

This is not to say that a word could not have been introduced to compliment Lord and Lady Bloggs on their splendid and happy partnership. But the disappointment at the absence of the original guest must not be made apparent. Anyway, has Lady Bloggs herself nothing to commend her other than her good taste in husbands? The Honourable James Bloggs inherited his courtesy title. But surely he has done something with his life which the chairman ought to explain? The guests will be curious to hear something of the background of their speaker. Heredity is not all.

Try this: 'This is an industry which is proud of its family connections. Many of us are old colleagues and friends of William Harness. We have been delighted to see the active part taken by his son, Roger, in our great charity. Naturally, we honour him because he is the son of our old and distinguished friend. But it is in his own right that he is invited to speak to us tonight. His achievements are many. He is . . . he was . . . and we are confident that he will be a leader in our industry for many years to come. Ladies and Gentlemen, Mr Roger Harness. . . .'

Or: 'Tonight, we are honoured by Lady Bloggs. It is true that her husband was to have addressed us. I will not repeat the gaffe of the chairman who once introduced the wife in circumstances such as these by saying: "Sir William's misfortune in being ill is our good luck. We are indeed happy to welcome his wife in his place." We are delighted that the reason for Lord Bloggs' absence is that he is busy selling his goods overseas and hence keeping up his company's magnificent record in the field. We are fortunate that he has been good enough to leave his wife behind, in England – and to trust her in our company this evening. He is. . . .'

If (as so often happens) the speaker is a last-minute substitute, do not apologise for the fact. 'We were to have had Mr Hodge to speak to us, but he has let us down at the last minute. We are grateful to Mr Black, his assistant, for stepping into the breach. Ladies and Gentlemen, Mr Black.' That just will not do. There are two decent alternatives. Either ignore altogether the fact that Mr Hodge has let you down. Everyone will know it. The word will have gone around.

And it may be much less embarrassing if nothing is said. Alternatively, make a virtue out of necessity. Thus:

'Ladies and Gentlemen. I know that you will all have been very sorry to have heard that our proposed guest, Mr Arthur Hodge, has been struck down by the 'flu. But equally, you will be pleased to learn that he is making a good recovery. He sends his greetings to us all – I have a telegram from him here.' (That was intelligent of Mr Hodge, incidentally.) 'It wishes us every good fortune. And I know that you will want me to reply, on behalf of us all, wishing him the most speedy recovery.

'I cannot tell Mr Black how grateful we are to him for having agreed to come to us as such very short notice. His readiness to step into the breach is just one indication of his loyalty to our organisation . . . of one reason at least why he has earned the affection of all of his colleagues. . . . He is . . . he was . . . he will be. . . .'

Or: 'Our good friend and proposed guest, Mr Arthur Hodge has, alas, been called abroad on urgent business. We know that he would never have let us down had there been any possible alternative. We wish him success in his venture – may he bring home the bacon – or, to be more precise, may he have every success in exporting his prize pigs. And we are very much obliged to him for having on our behalf asked Mr Robert Rook to address us in his place.

'Mr Rook is already well known to us. He is . . . he was . . . he will be. . . . We know the pressure of work upon Mr Rook and we are extremely grateful to him for honouring us by joining us this evening. Ladies and Gentlemen, Mr Rook. . . .'

There are, of course, occasions when the speaker should not be introduced. For instance: 'I shall ask our chairman, Edward Smith, to propose the loyal toast'. Or: 'Thank you, Mr Hodge. I am pleased to ask our treasurer, Richard Bright, to propose the vote of thanks.'

The chairman, then, sets the tone and calls the tune. He has many important duties, one of the most vital of which is the introduction of the speakers. He should treat his job seriously. He should apply the same rules to the brief speeches of introduction as he would to longer efforts. Introduction needs a beginning, a body, an end. The opening and closing sentences matter. Careful preparation (which, as usual must be as unobtrusive as possible when the speech is in fact made) is important. A bad introduction can ruin a good speech – and a potentially fine meeting.

65   Handling the speaker

No area of a chairman's duties is so potentially hazardous as handling the guest speaker. Here are a few hints:

As we saw in the last chapter, the importance of remembering his name can scarcely be exaggerated. And if you are not quite sure how to pronounce it, ask him. If his name is to be put in a programme, toast list, brochure or other document, check that the spelling is correct. People are very touchy about their names.

Ascertain in advance as much as you can about the speaker. Several members of the Royal Family are renowned for their splendid memories. They come into a room and promptly recognise people and even remember where they last met. This is partly because they have good memories, but mainly because they do their homework. The best way to flatter your speaker is to remember all about him. The surest way to antagonise him is to be indifferent to him and to his past achievements.

If he has incurred expenses, remember to invite him to let you know (see Chapter 41).

Remember to say thank you – and to write and repeat your thanks afterwards. You can never express gratitude too often.

Whilst trying to ensure that the speaker gets a fair hearing, be careful not to interrupt him too often. Competent speakers can handle their own audiences and prefer, where possible, to do so. The chairman should exercise his authority with moderation.

Prime the speaker in advance as to the length of time you want him to speak, and ask him whether he would like to be reminded when he is a few minutes away from the appointed end. Most speakers will gladly agree, and will not then resent a reminder. If necessary, push a note in front of the speaker, with: '*Five minutes to go*' in large letters. But to do this without pre-arrangement can upset the speaker and your friendship with him.

*   *   *

Much of the chairman's job is done before the meeting actually begins. If he reads this book beforehand, he should do better at the time. Otherwise, he can bring it with him . . . in a plain, white cover if he prefers. . . .

So all that remains is to wish you – in the role of speaker or the chairman – the very best of luck. However experienced and able you may be . . . however carefully you follow the rules we have given . . . whatever the occasion . . . there is no substitute for good fortune. Whether you are on your feet or in the chair, may you be blessed with success.

Book Two

DRAFT SPEECHES

Introduction

Oscar Wilde once remarked that the joy of making a mistake is that you can recognise it when you make it again. Learning speech-making by your own mistakes is no problem for you, but it is scarcely likely to increase the size or enthusiasm of your audiences. So why not follow the same course with speeches as lawyers and businessmen do with letters – which means: Use precedents . . . drafts . . . models. . . .

First, I offer some draft speeches, as examples and as precedents . . . and again to illustrate lessons learned from Book One. Of course you must change them to suit your own scene and style. You may even hook on to them some of the stories in Book Three.

Then relax and read a selection of great and memorable speeches. Note how each orator moulds the rules on speech-making into his own idiosyncracy. Imagine the style and the poise . . . the modulation and the pause . . . the matching of word by gesture. . . .

165

Part Two

DRAMATHERAPY

Part 6

Model speeches for varying occasions

66 Opening speeches

Prominent people are frequently invited to declare functions or occasions duly open – from trade exhibitions or fairs to sales conferences, from new premises to the same old annual garden fete run by the local church or by the trade benevolent society.

The opening pronouncement may be one of two varieties, which must be carefully distinguished from each other – the formal opening and the keynote speech. Either way, you may be asked to speak because of your eminence; because of past usefulness or benevolence; in hope of future service or cash – or a mixture of all of them. If you want to be asked again, though, you must do a good job this time.

The following are examples of brief openers plus skeletons of keynote speeches (which, by their nature, are expected to be longer, fuller and likely to provoke thought or action, rather than an atmosphere of generalised goodwill).

Opening a trade fair

Mr Chairman, Ladies and Gentlemen,

Some ancient peoples had disgusting habits – like examining the entrails of animals to see whether the auguries were satisfactory for some proposed enterprise. I have taken a much shorter and pleasanter route – to the great oracle of this organisation – Mr. . . . He tells me that the preparations for today's gathering have been carried out swiftly, in harmony and without a whiff of industrial ill-will; that advance orders already total half as much again as those received at this stage last year; that we are expecting one of the biggest gatherings in the history of the trade.

What a delight it is, then, for me to sound the tocsin and to proclaim in advance the value, the importance and the success of this year's vital exhibition.

On your behalf as well as my own, I thank our organisers – Mr . . . and Mrs . . . and Miss . . . , as well as . . . Ltd and their staff. If the arrangements look smooth and simple, it is because the organisers have worked so hard.

And now – in anticipation of good companionship, top sales and a continuation and ending to the fair which will be as successful as its inception – I have the greatest pleasure in declaring the fair – open.

Opening an industrial exhibition

Mr Chairman, Ladies and Gentlemen,

We are not as wasteful in this industry as our colleagues who build ships. We will not smash and spill good champagne on the side of our machines (*or: furniture or equipment – or as the case may be*). Instead, we will use the wine to drink a series of toasts.

First, we drink to the prosperity of our trade/industry/company. Today's effort is of vast importance to it and so to us all.

Second, we toast the health of those whose efforts have created this exhibition – from our Chairman/chief executive/organiser (etc.) at the top of our tree, to the carpenters, the electricians and the cleaners who have damped down its roots. Our warmest thanks to them all.

Third, we drink to the future of our great new product, the . . . (*Here give details*).

This is an exhibition of machinery/equipment/furniture (*or as the case may be*). It is designed to exhibit products – and to help design exhibits. Its success depends on orders and cheques, not on words – however warm or well meant.

Symbolically only, then, I am proud to launch this exhibition. By its end, I hope that we shall drink a toast to the beginning of a new era of prosperity for our trade/industry/company.

Mr Chairman, Ladies and Gentlemen – I declare the exhibition open.

Opening a new building

Mr Chairman, Ladies and Gentlemen,

Like most of us here, I have survived many happy, successful but hideously cramped, cribbed, cabined and confined years in our old premises. It is therefore with delight that I can declare this new building open.

Think what we can now do. Each of us can swing as many cats as we wish; turn around in our chairs without being accused of indecent assault; drink a cup of coffee without worrying whether we have swallowed our neighbour's sustenance.

Seriously, we can now expand our business and, inevitably I hope, our profits – so bringing delight to our bank manager, our shareholders and to all of us who are a proud part of our enterprise. We hope that we will pack our custom-built building with more and more satisfied customers. Certainly we shall be able to do our work and not only with greater economy and speed but also in greater comfort – and that is important because the environment of our workforce has taken top priority in the plans for our new structure.

Mr Chairman, Ladies and Gentlemen – this is a time for building. The bricks, the mortar, the cement, the steel – all is in place. We must now build the business – and have done with the words – mine or anyone else's. I thank the architects, Messrs. . . . ; I thank all of you for putting up with the inevitable discomfort involved in the move; I thank those who have organised this reception and in particular, our own Miss. . . . I most happily declare the new building opened.

Opening an old people's home

Mr Chairman, Ladies and Gentlemen,

A sage once divided a charity into categories of merit. At the bottom came gifts where the donor was known to the recipient and the recipient to the donor. At the top were those where neither knew the other. This old people's home has been created by the generosity of the trade/industry – individuals, firms and companies – each giving so that others may enjoy their old age.

There is far too much clap-trap talked about old age, isn't there? Autumn years . . . senior citizens . . . well earned years of pleasurable rest. . . . Well, that's how they should be. But too often, they are nothing of the kind. They are years of loneliness and poverty.

But not for the residents of this home. Here they will have privacy in their own rooms . . . companionship in the communal rooms . . . relaxation in the gardens . . . peace when they want it but kindly supervision and help when they need it.

Your committee has had more trouble in selecting residents than it have even in the raising of the money for the building. With hundreds in need, how do we select the tens who get help? Who are we to select who shall live here in happiness and who shall die alone? All have served the trade/industry; all deserve service from us.

So my functions are twofold. First, I join you in looking back with pride and thankfulness to what has been achieved – and in thanking those responsible. Our special gratitude to . . . and . . . and. . . .

Second, we must now service and expand the home.

I once went to a very rich man and asked him for the money to create a building for a certain charity. He replied: 'How are you going to run it . . . to staff it . . . to pay for it once it is opened? I am tired of giving buildings and then having the same people come back to me and saying: "What's the good of giving the building without the running costs?" '

Well, we have the building – given not by one man but many – our thanks to them all. And we have enough to keep the place going for . .

months. Did you know that it costs about . . . to pay for each resident for each year?

So in thanking you all for your kindness and generosity . . . for your presence here today and for your presents to this home in the past – I ask for your support in the future. We close one era when we open another.

Mr Chairman, Ladies and Gentlemen – it is with the greatest of pride – and in the hope and confidence that this home will provide a great comfort and joy to its residents – that I declare the building open.

Keynote – sales conference

Mr Chairman, Colleagues and Friends,

This company lives through sales – and we all live through the company. It is by building the sales that we cannot only ensure a prosperous future for the organisation but also for each one of us here. We are part of the same team; we are part of the same family; we are working to the same end. This conference has been carefully designed to help us all in that work.

I am happy to introduce to you not only the conference but also our new season's range/tremendously successful line, to introduce our . . ./new equipment, specially designed for our market by . . . (*or as the case may be*).

(*Description and explanation of product/service, etc. follows*).

The key to this conference, then, lies in expanding our territory and our sales – but with the help of our new lines/products/equipment (*etc.*).

My introduction marks the beginning of two/three days/weeks of intensive discussion/instruction/conference – which I am confident will herald with a fanfare of trumpets, the start of a year of distinction and prosperity.

The conference will also enable us to get to know each other socially and to enjoy that good companionship which is so much part of the atmosphere of this organisation. On behalf of your Board/directors/chairman, I wish you good days and fruitful discussions – followed by brisk and burgeoning sales and continuing success for the company and for all of you. I am happy to declare this conference duly opened. Good luck to you all.

Opening an exhibition

Mr Chairman, Ladies and Gentlemen,

We are honoured to be holding in our shop/factory an exhibition of paintings by Martha Smith and of sculpture by Roger Jones, drawing their inspiration from our trade/industry.

You will all have seen the brochure/catalogue, designed by our own Walter Brown. One half, read from the top, sets out the work of Martha Smith; the other half, reading from the bottom of the page, lists the sculpture of Roger Jones.

I know that our two guest artists will not be offended if I say that the hanging committee felt a little like the brochure – not quite sure which way up to hang many of the pictures or to stand some of the sculptures. No matter. The shapes are glorious and the colour superb. And we can at least be grateful that we know in most cases which way up to stand our stock/machines.

You will, I am sure, be as delighted as I was to learn that each of the artists has offered to donate one work to our trade charity. This is immensely kind of them and we are very grateful.

I am told that it took Martha Smith about a week to create each painting and Roger Jones took nearly as long with his larger sculptures. But it is not the time and motion that matters but the spirit.

Many years ago, when a pound was twenty shillings and worth a sovereign of gold, the painter Rex Whistler claimed £500 for a portrait in oils, commissioned by a client. No price had been agreed and he sued on a *quantum meruit*, claiming that £500 was reasonable and right.

Counsel cross-examined him on behalf of the client. 'Mr Whistler', he said, 'how long did it take you to paint this portrait?'

'Three days', the artist replied.

'Then are you asking my client to pay £500 for three days' work?'

'No', retorted the painter. 'I am claiming £500 for a lifetime of work which enabled me to paint this portrait in three days.'

It was not the time that was taken by our generous artists which is the dominant matter – it is their lifetime of skill which has made each of them predominant in his own sphere. They are giving us of their own best work. I offer them on behalf of all of us our warmest thanks.

Industry and commerce take pride in design. Individually, we may not be able to be patrons of the arts. But an exhibition of this sort enables us to harmonise artistic forms with our working environments. It is an experiment that deserves success. It is a contribution that we can make to the artist's fame and which the artists make to our pleasure and understanding.

The time has now come, then, for each of us to browse, to look and to learn. There may be some of you who are capable artists – I have trouble in drawing a circle with the help of a compass. A cynic remarked: 'He who can, does; he who can't, teaches'. We might say: 'He who can't, visits exhibitions and admires those who can'.

We have an exhibition now on our doorstep. I thank the artists for bringing that collection together and enabling us to enjoy it at our leisure. I have much pleasure in declaring the exhibition – open.

67   Guests of honour

To the disabled

Mr Chairman, Ladies and Gentlemen,

Some people are obviously disabled because they are missing a limb . . . , because parts of their body do not work properly. But I know plenty of people whose bodies are in excellent shape, but who never use their heads. I congratulate this organisation on its work, because it helps disabled people to make the best possible use of their assets – and encourages people here, who have absolutely excellent heads, to use them, and to compensate for their physical disabilities.

We must each make use of the assets we have. This organisation helps its members to recognise and to exploit those assets to the full.

Far too many disabled folk are left vegetating at home. You help to get them out into society, so that they are part of the world, making their contribution and enjoying doing so.

Your committee are themselves disabled – but by their work they have not only bought new and vigorous life to others, but have – I know and they know – enriched their own lives in the process.

I congratulate the committee for their efforts; I welcome so many members here today; I am delighted to be your guest of honour – and to give any impetus I can to your efforts, today and every day – and I thank you very much for inviting me.

Now, my friends – on with the party. . . .

Note: This approach is, of course, designed for the physically handicapped. A variation for the mentally ill-equipped now follows.

For the mentally disabled

Mr Chairman, Ladies and Gentlemen,
Our object must be to enable each member of our society to make the best of his assets.

When I went into the Army, many long years ago, my closest friend was a postman's son. We had our aptitude test together. I found the verbal reasoning and intelligence test extremely easy. The first question sticks in my mind: 'The sun is blue, yellow, green – cross out the answers which do not apply'.

Dick managed the first couple of dozen questions without too much difficulty, but then came to a dead halt. His vocabulary was tiny.

Next came technical aptitudes. I spent the first half hour trying to assemble a lock and the second a bicycle pump. I failed totally on both. Dick performed all ten puzzles without the least difficulty.

We all have different talents and the handiwork done by members of this club and on exhibition here today shows how much pleasure they can give to others – and at the same time, to themselves. They have a right to develop their talents to the full – and I congratulate the committee and organisers of this club for the work they have done to enable the members to enjoy their lives.

This place is full of happiness, isn't it? People have the odd idea that where human beings are not blessed with the same degree of mental aptitude as themselves, they are necessarily less happy. Some of the most miserable people I have ever met were of genius level – and some of them were immensely wealthy into the bargain. I congratulate you all on the measure of happiness which this organisation brings not only to its members but also to those who love and care for them.

Thank you, then, for inviting me to be your guest of honour. You, the organisers and committee are of service to your members – and I am at your service and proud to be here amongst you. The very best of luck to you all.

Note: This speech is essentially aimed at the organisers – with the probability that the members will not understand. You must always decide whom you are going to speak to. If you are addressing a school audience – then never mind the parents, talk to the youngsters. Thus:

School celebration

Headmaster, Parents, Boys and Girls,
I am here as a Governor of the School – which is a pretty grand

word isn't it? The Governor of a prison is top boss. The Governor of this School is only one of a group – all of whom work together with the Head and his staff to help you, the pupils, to make the most of your time here.

Why, then, is this School different from others? Why should I and my fellow Governors be proud to be associated with it?

First, ...

Second, ...

Third, ...

Well, I expect you know the story of Henry VIII – and what a happy time he had didn't he? I say to you – as he said to each of his wives in turn: 'I shall not keep you long'.

Didn't he say that? Unfortunately many of the best historical tales are not necessarily accurate. Like the one about Oliver Cromwell. Charles II definitely did dig him up, lift off the lid of his coffin, chop off his head and put it on a pike for six years on the roof of Westminster Hall – that is the ancient Hall of the Palace of West-minsister – the only part of Parliament which is still standing almost as it was when it was first built.

What cannot be proved is the old story, that when the head was on the pike on the roof of the Hall, it dripped blood down onto the flag stones for six years. Then one night there was a terrible storm and the head blew down with a horrible thud. A huge cat ran out of the crypt, grabbed the head in its teeth and was rushing off towards the door when the Sargeant of Arms – sort of Head Prefect – drew his sword, speared the cat and grasped old Cromwell's head.

The next part is true. The head was then taken up to Sidney Sussex College in Cambridge and duly buried. It is there to this day.

I do not recommend that you use that story in your history essays – but I do hope that someone will take you to Westminister Hall one day. If you look carefully enough, you might even find Oliver Cromwell's blood still on the flag stones.

Anyway before my blood is spilled for taking up too much of your time, I will simply wish you well . . . congratulate you all on a tremendous year of success . . . wish you happiness for the holidays. . . (*or as the case may be*).

Good luck to you all.

Note: Personal reminiscence is essential – and can be achieved without being egocentric or modest. Otherwise, an imaginative tale enlivens any speech. Drawn from your own experience or from anyone else's – but do not talk down to your audience – whatever its age.

At prize-givings, avoid telling children how badly you did when you were young – even if it was true, they will not believe it. But do by all means remember the children who get no prizes. Skip the tale of how dreadfully Winston Churchill did as a boy – and try something like this:

Prize-giving

Headmistress, Parents, Boys and Girls,

Its marvellous being top of the class, head of the school, a prefect or a monitor, isn't it? Even being in the top form gives you status. You are a senior character, looked up to by the new boys.

Unfortunately, no sooner do we reach one pinnacle – no sooner do we get to the top of one mountain – than we slide right down again to the bottom and become new boys again.

All you leavers will be feeling a bit nostalgic today – when you start your new school, university or college – at your work – you will be back down at the bottom again.

Naturally, those of you who have won prizes today – and I congratulate you all – will treasure them as a memento of a happy and successful occasion. But you will be no higher on the ladder than those of your friends, who will be joining you at your work, without prizes. And next time, it may be their turn.

In many ways it is a pity that we have to have prizes at all isn't it? Many people here, I know, will have worked very hard and done extremely well but will not be getting rewarded. Never mind. Your turn will come.

Just think of all the successful politicians and scientists – teachers come to that – whom everybody congratulated and who won all the rich prizes in civilisation. Ten years later, where are they? Where is the businessman . . . the captain of industry . . . the big boss. . .? They retire and are forgotten about and that is the end of them.

Well, you are not retiring, any of you, are you?

Apart from presenting your prizes, which I shall look forward to doing, my task is simply to wish you all well – wherever you are going, whatever you do. I hope that your ambitions will be fulfilled.

As for those of you who remain – I hope that you will have very happy times ahead. Next year, some of you will reach the top. Enjoy it. Jimmy Durante, the famous American comedian, once remarked: 'You might as well be nice to people you pass on your way up because you will pass them again on your way down!'

To all of you who are going up or down – and even to a few who are staying still – the very best of luck to you – and thank you for inviting me to be with you today.

Note: Never mind the parents. They will enjoy your talking to the children. But adapt your words according to the age of the youngsters. Chat to them as if they were your own. A child can see through pomposity or insincerity far better than an adult. You may be elevated onto a platform – but pretend that you are in and amongst them. Indeed, it is sometimes possible to climb off the stage. On great, state occasions, the dignities and proprieties have to be maintained. But when talking to children, I try to perch on the edge of a table, to walk down among them – or even to remove my jacket and to hang it on the back of a chair – that almost always breaks the ice.

Once, I found myself the only white man in a sea of black children's faces in a school in Florida. Beside me there hung a cord – presumably attached to a rolled-up map, chart or screen. Before starting my speech I simply looked at the cord, shook it gently, looked at the audience in a worried way, looked upwards – they soon got the idea – and roared with laughter. This may not seem a particularly funny gimmick when reduced to cold print – but it is the original, topical, immediate and unexpected approach that breaks the ice. There should be no ice between children and adults.

Another beginning which I was taught by a member of the Magic Circle – and which requires a certain sleight of hand, which I have enjoyed acquiring – is like this:

Magic opening

Good Morning,

I am sorry that you are all looking so sad. I promise you that I am not going to bore you. So you can relax. There's a chap sleeping at the back – I can see you.

I know what you want, you would like to disappear out into the sunshine. Look. . . .

What's this . . . (*holding up a coin in left hand*).

It's an ordinary coin, isn't it? (*varnish coin*).

Now what is it? (*inevitable gasps and cries of; it's in your pocket . . . it's up your sleeve. . .*).

No, it's just gone, but you are not going until I have finished talking to you, so you might just as well relax. . . .

Note: At one famous school, there was a long pause before proceedings began. It was a small room, with about 50 restless youngsters in it. I said, 'I am sorry to keep you. We shall be starting soon.' 'I shall say when we begin', the Headmaster reproved me, publicly and rudely, in a way designed to remined me that he is the head of his organisation. This sort of treatment of a guest is unusual – but one reproof of that sort is enough. Always consult the organisers or chief citizens or bosses of the place or occasion, before opening your honoured mouth.

Equally you must choose your opening – and, for that matter, tailor your speech according to the nature and dignity of the occasion. If in doubt, relax. But there are those that regard too informal an approach as a slur – as not recognising the importance either of the occasion or (this is worst) of those present. And tread warily on the dignity of others.

For the homeless and unhoused

Ladies and Gentlemen,

Some regard homes as chattels to be bought and sold. Others – including everybody here – consider a home to be part of a man's entitlement. So is it not scandalous that so many people are so shockingly housed?

I am delighted to be with you today because you are working to provide roofs for the homeless – and more, to help those in homes to put down their roots and to cope.

Those are the twin challenges. First, there is the physical worry of providing a place for people to live in decent happiness and contentment. Second, there are many in our civilisation who cannot cope with life, even when they have a home to live in.

It is this last category that provides so many of our most under-privileged and deprived. They are inarticulate; they have no Members of Parliament, because they are on no register; they drift rootless through a world which prefers to disregard them.

Just as those who know no medicine tell the chronically depressed to 'snap out of it', making matters infinitely worse – so those who are able to cope with life tend not to understand the troubles of those who are inadequate.

This organisation . . . (*set out its objects*).

This organisation . . . (*set out its successes*).

This organisation . . . (*set out its remaining problems and how the person can help to solve them*).

To this organisation and all who struggle for it – and to those whom it seeks to help – my warm and affectionate greetings. If my colleagues and I can be of help to you, we shall be pleased – meanwhile, we are delighted to be associated your work.

Note: This sort of speech can easily be adapted for every industrial of benevolent association.

The magic of speech

Speechmakers are (or certainly should be) entertainers. And occasionally we politicians get invited into the entertainment world. The following speech was the first of the evening at a grand banquet held by the International Brotherhood of Magicians at the Hanover Grand Banqueting Suite, London. Guests included not only some of the world's outstanding men of magic but a star-studded array of show-business personalities.

Note the break towards the end where (with a borrowed touch of showman's flourish) I introduced a special presentation.

Mr President, Ladies and Gentlemen,

The toastmaster just whispered in my ear: 'Would you like to speak now, Mr Janner – or shall we let them go on enjoying themselves for just a little longer?' I think he had forgotten that politicians, like magicians, are part of the entertainment business. The main difference between us is that politicians do infinitely more harm.

I think that there are only two people that can make coins and notes disappear swifter than David Berglas – the Chancellor of the Exchequer – and my wife, Myra. Still, Myra and I are both delighted to be with you this evening.

The first time that I saw David Berglas working – perfectly, as always – was about 15 years ago. At that time, I was running a folk music group in the Brady Boys' Club, in a particularly tough part of London's East End. We were desperately short of funds so we decided to organise a public concert. I asked friends in the entertainment world who among the great and the famous were the most likely to help us if they could. They gave me three names – all of whom consented.

The first was that spirited and warm-hearted singer, Alma Cogan. The second was that prince of character actors, David Kossoff. And the third was our President, radio and TV's man of magic, David Berglas.

David not only took part in the concert but I remember particularly how he took under his wing a young and very under-privileged magician who specialised in the floating ball illusion, accompanied by music of my group. He encouraged and coaxed and baffled the lad – who adored him.

Since then, I have seen how David has with quiet and dignified reticence used the magic of magic to bring entertainment and happiness to people who have needed it badly.

Two years ago, David gave up his Christmas holiday. He came

with me to Leicester and he put on shows for old people, for children and for youngsters in a local borstal. Tonight I have a surprise for him. I wish to make him a small presentation. I have searched for a 'Berglas' – which I have always presumed was a sort of Holy Grail which casts no shadow. But instead I have found a Wedgwood parliamentary inscribed goblet – which I will now ask him to accept as a token of appreciation not merely from me but especially from those thousands of people whom he has so freely entertained and helped without any possibility of reward – and who do not enjoy my honour of paying tribute to him tonight.

* * *

Those who believe that politicians and magicians lead wholly glamorous and undemanding lives suffer from a very common and pernicious delusion. But few recognise the strains which these lives place upon our wives. Tonight we pay tribute not only to David but to that splendid lady who held tightly to him on his roller coaster of fortune for the past 20 years – to Ruth Berglas – and also to their children.

Just as our affection for David is a link between all of us, so the British Ring of the International Brotherhood of Magicians provides a link between men of magic of many lands – a link that holds far tighter than the classic Chinese rings – and the British Ring with over 1500 members is the largest in the entire chain.

I ask you to rise and to drink a toast – to the British Ring of the International Brotherhood of Magicians – to its President, David Berglas – and to Ruth, his wife. May they enjoy the magic of good health and happy fulfilment together, for very many years to come.

Benevolent or other trade association

Dear Friends,

We are all part of the same trade/industry aren't we? Some of us are more fortunate than others – and those of us who are here today are certainly very lucky.

It has not all been smooth sailing, has it? We can all remember difficult days when we might have been toppled into trouble.

I know some people here, who have fought their way back to the top, after slithering into great difficulty, usually by no fault of their own.

However, this benevolent association of ours is designed to help those who have not been fortunate enough to make success a permanence – who need a broad shoulder, to lean on.

The association has many achievements . . . (*outline them*). The association has great plans . . . (*outline them*).

This gathering today is designed to . . . (*set out objects of meeting*).

My colleagues and myself are honoured to be part of your work. I am delighted to be your guest/chairman – and I can assure you that I will do everything in my power to help. 'There but for the Grace of God' go any of us, in our great industry.

68 Introductions, greetings and thanks

To the Minister

Mr Chairman, Secretary of State, Ladies and Gentlemen,
We are all very grateful to the Minister for joining our family (*or: the family of our trade, industry or as the case may be*) when he could so easily and comfortably have been with his own. We appreciate not only what he has said, but the fact that he has snatched the time to be with us today.

I once asked a friend who is a safety officer how he defined his job. 'Oh', he replied, 'I'm in charge of accidents!' By that token, the Minister is in charge of illness, deprivation and disease (*or unemployment or as the case may be*). He deals with our problems and his own with admirable calm – and for the sake of us all, we wish him success.

For our part, we recognise the acute dangers created for our society by any condition of unrest. When people regard all politicians with equal distaste, democracy is in danger. A statesman was once defined as a dead politician. We are glad that there are live statesmen like our guest, concerned with the affairs of our land.

(*Then refer to one or two points made by the guest.*)

So once again I thank the Minister for giving this event the accolade of his lively presence – and I ask you to join me in expressing to him our warmest appreciation.

Apologies for a small audience

There is nothing in the speaker's world more embarrassing than bringing a prominent guest to speak to your organisation, membership or club and then to find that – for whatever reason – the audience is pathetically small. How do you handle the situation?

1   Make your apologies as best you can – relying on the foul weather, apparent trade disputes – or any other excuse that seems reasonable.

2   If possible, transfer to a smaller room – a few people in a small room make a fine audience – a large crowd is lost in a huge hall.

3   Adapt your introduction to the occasion. Thus:

Distinguished Guests, Ladies and Gentlemen,

I know that we will all be sorry that the weather (*the strike or as the case may be*) has kept so many people away. We are to have the treat. We are the fortunate few. I am reminded of a story:

Mr Brezhnev and Mr Kosygin were discussing the problems of the Jewish minority wanting to emigrate.

Mr Brezhnev said: 'Why don't we let them go?'. Mr Kosygin replied: 'Once you let them out, you will have to release the Ukranians, the Armenians, the Baptists, the Uzbeks . . . and after that, I will go. . . . You will be the only person left. . . .'

Mr Brezhnev replied: 'No I shall not be alone. The Soviet Union will be empty!'

We are far from empty this evening, we have here among the most distinguished members/some of our top industrialists/some of the most famous men in our trade.

We have gathered here because we know of the work of our guest – and on behalf of us all, I welcome him to. . . .

(*Then give details of the guest's work*).

Ladies and Gentlemen, I present Mr. . . .

Vote of thanks

The guests of honour could scarcely have been more disparate: Winston Churchill, MP; Colonel Nahum Alshansky; and the Lord Mayor of Westminster. The occasion: the annual rally of the Association of Jewish Ex-Servicemen and Women (AJEX). The venue: a London theatre holding about 2,500. The platform was military and distinguished. In the chair: Major Edmund Rothschild. Among the platform guests was my own father, Lord Janner.

The President introduced Winston Churchill in the usual manner – talking about his grandfather's footsteps. I had to deal with him in his own right. Alshansky was a much harassed Jewish Colonel from the Russian town of Minsk – allowed to leave eventually, but now campaigning on behalf of others, left behind because the Soviet authorities would not let them out.

The proceedings began with a flourish of trumpets; the arrival of the Standards of AJEX branches from various parts of the country; and the Chairman's speech. The audience was relaxed and extremely responsive. The evening needed a rousing end – and I decided to risk rhetorical questions – which brought loud and prompt responses. Their theme – the United Nations motion passed that week equating Zionism and racism – and, of course, absolute anathema to the anti-racist Jewish ex-servicemen.

*   *   *

Mr President, my Lord Mayor, my Lord (*pause to bow in the direction of father – affectionate laughter from audience*) – your Excellency; distinguished guests; Ladies and Gentlemen.

We salute Colonel Nahum Alshansky for his own personal courage and as a symbol of the courage of those he left behind in the USSR.

Colonel Lev Ovsisher; Colonel Yefim Davidovich; Academician Benjamin Levich; Professor Mark Azbel; Dr Michael Stern; Vladimir Slepak – we shall remember them and we shall meet them in freedom just as we have met Nahum Alshansky today.

At our parade, Colonel Alshansky told me that he was amazed that the police were there to protect us and not to arrest us. That, he said, could not happen where he came from.

Here we may protest in freedom at the slavery of others.

And we thank the police. Our freedom depends on them – and theirs on us.

And we say to Nahum Alshansky; we wish you health and happiness, good luck and prosperity, in freedom in your own land. Our freedom depends on our friends and on ourselves. A person and a people are both judged by their friends. To be judged by Winston Churchill is an honoured judgement indeed.

Friends are judged by their staunch help in rough times. It will not have escaped your notice, Ladies and Gentlemen, that Winston's speech – attacking recognition of the Palestine Liberation Organisation – came in a week when his own leaders said that we must recognise that terrorist body.

I hope that he will not regard it as interference in the internal affairs of the Conservative party if I say how much we hope that he will take over the foreign policy of that party as soon as possible.

Winston has been given one of the Association's ties. He has been made an honorary Jew. But I warn him – he must not take this as an invitation to introduce his children or his grandchildren to the descendants of Sir Adolf Tuck.*

Winston is always ready to help the oppressed. He is an excellent friend of the cause of Soviet Jewry – regarding it as he does as a humanitarian battle and not merely as a Jewish issue. We are delighted and honoured to welcome him and his wife among us this evening.

The Lord Mayor of Westminster symbolises the friendship of our civic leaders. It is a friendship that we need and we value. As the Standards proudly paraded onto this stage, I thought how fortunate

*A reference to the then current legal battle in which Sir Adolf's grandson unsuccessfully attempted to keep money left only to those of his descendants who married 'approved' Jewish brides.

we were that our communities are so happily embedded in our great cities. In thanking the Lord Mayor of Westminster, we pay tribute to his City – to the cities of Newcastle and Manchester, Liverpool and Leeds, Leicester and London – and to all those British centres where our branches work in freedom and in harmony.

Finally, I pay a tribute of thanks to an absent friend – to a hero and a saint – Doctor Andrei Sakharov. Winston was right. It is not just the Jews who are persecuted in the Soviet Union. And Sakharov who is a distinguished and brilliant non-Jew, battles for the rights of all minorities – not least that of the Jews.

Some of us at Westminster nominated Sakharov for the Nobel prize. We were delighted when he was awarded this vast honour. But we were appalled when he was refused permission to travel to Oslo to receive his award. I spoke to him, two weeks ago – but now his telephone is cut off. He is forbidden to collect his prize.

Yet in the midst of his own trouble, he raised his mighty voice in outcry at the United Nations resolution, so disgracefully equating Zionism with racism.

We Jews are not racist – are we? (*audience: No, No.*) We Jewish ex-servicemen fought racism, did we not? (*Yes. . . .*)

And we are all Zionists, aren't we? (*Yes. . . .*)

All Jews are Zionists. But, thank God, not all Zionists are Jews.

Tonight, we pay special tribute to those outstanding Zionists – Churchill and Sakharov.

They do not forget us. And we shall never forget them.

Thanks – surprise tale

Mr Chairman, Ladies and Gentlemen,

I am delighted to propose the vote of thanks to our guest speaker, Mr . . . . He is a man of enormous distinction and we are very grateful to him for visiting us tonight.

Perhaps one reason why Mr . . . has become so famous is, curiously, his unassuming and almost deceptive approach. He reminds me of the true story of a Member of Parliament driving home at 3 o'clock in the morning, after a particularly late sitting. He drew up outside the Member's entrance to see whether anyone wanted a lift home and a colleague asked him whether he would take a friend to North London. 'With pleasure' said the MP, and ushered the middle-aged, balding gentleman into the passenger seat.

It soon became clear that the guest had been taking advantage of the evening to enjoy the delights of the Strangers' Bar. After giving his instructions as to where he wanted to go, he started dozing off.

'Are you one of the new Members', asked the politician.
'No, I am a Union Official', the guest replied.
'Do you live in London?'
'No, in Scotland.'
The MP turned on the radio and a reader was giving some important Union news. 'You had better listen to this', he said to his guest.
'Oh, I have heard it all before', said the guest.
About fifteen minutes later, the MP asked the guest what his name was. The answer shook the politician rigid – his guest was one of the most famous trade union leaders in the land.
'I am very pleased to meet you', said the MP. 'I am Member of Parliament for . . .', and he named his seat.
'You are what?' retorted the guest, obviously startled. 'You are an MP? What the bloody hell are you doing driving a taxi around London at this time of night?'
Once the embarrassment of the misunderstanding had been cleared away, the two men became friends – and have remained friends ever since.
Ladies and Gentlemen, I was the MP – and our guest of honour tonight was that Union leader.
We salute him . . . we thank him . . . and we wish him great success and good fortune in the future.

Thanks to celebrity

Ladies and Gentlemen,
I regret that I have only got to know our guest speaker tonight – personally, that is. Like most of you, I have long admired him from afar – in the Press, on the radio, on television – for his devotion to the fate of others. The chance that has bought us together this evening is undramatic – but very welcome.
Mr . . . (*naming the speaker*) – we are very grateful to you – and hope that you will join us again often. We wish you well in your work and we thank you for telling us about it.

Retirement

Mr Chairman, Colleagues and Friends,
It will seem strange to attend a meeting of the . . . without Arthur Jones presiding over it. In the past . . . months/years, he has established himself as the epitome of all that is best in our trade/industry/organisation. There is much to thank him for.

First, I thank him for the kindly way in which he has referred to me. He has been warm, generous and extremely accurate. . . .

I can therefore say with equal accuracy that his qualities of . . . and . . . have enlightened his period of office and helped him to create a vibrant organisation.

Most of us here are forthright individualists – or we would not be doing this job. We may disagree as to the best way to serve our customers/clients/company/company's business interest. We argue, we debate and we dispute. But we are united in our admiration for Mr. . . .

Let me list some of his achievements during the past. . . :

1　. . . .
2　. . . .
3　. . . .

And now that his period of office is over, we know that we will receive the same, unassuming, and kindly and affectionate welcome – and the same help from him – as a fellow member of our . . . as we did when he held the highest office and honour which we could give him.

The Poet wrote:

'Sound, sound the clarion, fill the fife . . .
Let all the sensual world proclaim . . .
One crowded hour of glorious life . . .
Is worth an age without a name. . . .'

Our friend, and mentor, Arthur Jones, has enjoyed his very crowded hour – and he has put glorious life into our proceedings/company/ organisation. We thank him – and we wish him well.

Distinguished guests

Ladies and Gentlemen,

In the unavoidable absence of our President, I have been asked on behalf of the guest to thank our hosts for the splendid, austerity lunch – smoked salmon sandwiches? – I would wish this sort of austerity on all businessmen, everywhere.

In particular, I thank our two guests for being here – and for their enthusiastic words. How they adjust – physically and mentally – to their eternal round of the world is a mystery. Maybe it is due to the sustenance provided by the international smoked salmon sandwich.

One of our guests is a lawyer – the other is a financier. When justice and money come together on the same platform, then indeed we have found common cause.

We have listened with immense care to their speeches – and I can assure them that we are happy to associate ourselves with their work. (*Then a few sentences about that work.*)

We are involved – and we are all grateful to our guests for increasing that involvement. We look forward to seeing our guests back with us again – very soon and next time for a much longer stay.

69 Business speeches

Company meetings

The lengthier the company meeting, the greater its potential for conflict and harm. The Chairman's Report should set the tone; set out essential facts that shareholders need to know; and indicate future prospects.

Remembering that this report will often be published, it should be prepared with care and read with precision. It may be preceded or concluded with embellishments, naturally or apparently impromptu.

I am grateful to Lord Sieff of Brimpton for his permission to reproduce the following typically brisk example of a recent report that he gave to shareholders in Marks & Spencer.

Statement by the Chairman of Marks & Spencer, Lord Sieff of Brimpton

During the last six months economic recession has deepened, unemployment increased and inflation remained high. In these circumstances our sales are encouraging, particularly as there has been an improvement in August and September.

The recent improvement is largely due to better values in clothing and foodstuffs where, as a result of co-operation with our suppliers, we have substantially reduced the price of a number of major items. Our clothing prices are now only 2 per cent and our food prices 8 per cent higher than a year ago. These improved values have been achieved while maintaining St Michael high-quality standards.

If the present trend continues we expect the full year's profits to be satisfactory.

We have continued our long-term policy of 'Buying British'. In recent years a number of major suppliers have invested substantially in the most modern equipment. By working closely with them we have been able, in nearly all cases, successfully to meet the challenge of imported clothing.

On April 1st we awarded salary increases to our staff three months earlier than last year. As a result, compared with last year, the first six months' costs include an additional quarter's salary increase amounting to approximately £3¾ million. This now completes the rephasing of our salary reviews which we intend to take place at the beginning of April in future years.

Our Canadian operation is making progress. In Europe we face similar economic problems to the UK. A substantial proportion of the merchandise sold is manufactured in the UK and margins have suffered from the strength of sterling.

The Directors have declared an interim dividend of 1.5p per share, the same as last year, which will be paid on 16th January 1981 to shareholders whose names are on the Register of Members at the close of business on 14th November 1980.

* * *

State of the industry

I am happy to have this opportunity to review the state of our industry – and to appeal on behalf of all of us for government understanding and help. We have honourably adhered to governmental guidelines and advice. We have – as Ministers have sometimes unhappily put it – cut away the fat. But we are becoming extremely and dangerously lean. First, the dangers. They are many.

We face increased competition from countries where employees are paid miserably low wages. We contend with the dumping of goods by suppliers who – directly or indirectly – lawfully or otherwise – are heavily subsidised by their governments. And no government appears ready to help us to meet this unfair competition.

We are neither against competition nor imports. We recognise the needs of others to sell. And we must export to live. We know that if we place undue restriction on our imports, then we must expect the same treatment by others to whom we must export. We are against *unfair* competition . . . *unfair* imports . . . *improper* dumping . . . wilful subsidy by others, unmatched by governmental aid to our ailing industry.

Add to these overseas miseries over which we have no control whatever the results of our own recession . . . the strength of the pound . . . the weakness of our economy . . . the problems of overseas demand matched by the collapse of the UK market – and the reasons for my anxieties are clear.

So let us plan and plot . . . organise and lobby . . . work together for the preservation of our industry. Let us learn from the unions that individually we are weak, but if we fight and use our unity, then these times of trouble have brought great lessons for us all.

* * *

Remedies

The diagnosis for our trade is clear – cure the recessional misery. That cure requires capital and investment – but above all, hope and confidence.

The time for cut-throat competition in our industry has passed. We must now work together for the survival of . . . , recognising that collapse for one is a signal of tempest for all.

So my colleagues and I are proposing the following specific steps, to draw our plight to the government's attention and to take constructive help with our problems – not least in preserving employment in this key area of British industry.

First. . . .

Second. . . .

Third. . . .

I commend these proposals to you. I ask you to accept them unanimously. We need more confidence and you need leadership which we have now united together to provide.

70 *Unions and colleagues*

Never talk down to anyone – least of all to trade unions. I have watched speeches collapse into ruin at school prize-givings, company occasions, debates at universities and conferences of trade unions – nearly always because the speaker made it plain that he regarded his listeners as inferior, whether by reason of their youth, their education, their status or otherwise. Conversely, nearly all the most successful speeches shine because the listener is treated as a colleague, a partner, an equal.

Trade unions are especially sensitive to apparent condescension, even when it is in fact a mask for shyness or apprehension.

The younger and the less educated the audience, the greater its nose for the scent of insincerity. And you only fool your unions once. They will not trust you again. Nor will they accept your invitation to share with them the miseries of recession if you do not also let them benefit in times of profit. Provided that their accounts will not reach the eyes of their creditors, employers are always glad to show the miseries to their workforce. But in days of gloom, the accounts only emerge after due provision has been made for the pension reserve fund and other receptacles for profits that are better unseen.

So the key to a successful speech to employees – and especially to those with the combined strength provided by a well run union – is: the sharing of information, anxieties and hopes, with sincerity and frankness. Or to use a useful American phrase: 'Level with them. . .'.

Disclosure

Mr Chairman, Ladies and Gentlemen,

Thank you for agreeing to meet me today. I would like to explain to you very briefly the position of the company and our plans and hopes for the future. Then I shall be glad to answer your questions.

Our company secretary, Roger White – who is, of course, here with me – has just provided your Board with our latest figures. I have provided a summary for each of you – and when I have concluded this introduction, Roger will be glad to join me in answering your questions on these accounts. They provide management with a guide to liability and prospects. And they will give you an indication of the state of business which, of course, provides a livelihood for us all.

Remembering that the period covered is the year/six months/three months from . . . to . . . , let me summarise for you:

First: the turnover during this period increased/decreased from £ . . . to £. . . .

Second: our workforce grew/diminished from . . . to. . . .

Third: working days lost through absenteeism due to illness rose/fell from . . . to . . . ; and from industrial action rose/fell from . . . to. . . .

Fourth: and do please treat this information as entirely confidential – in broad terms, at the start of this period we had enough orders on our books to keep us busy/on full-time working for a period of . . . weeks/months. We can now see confidently ahead only until. . . .

Our plans for the future are as follows.

We shall make every effort to retain our present workforce. If unfortunately we do have to reduce numbers, we shall make every effort to do so through wastage – that is, through not replacing employees who leave us. But if redundancies do become inevitable – and I repeat that we hope and believe that this will not occur – we shall consult with your union/unions concerned; and we shall seek to achieve redundancies with the minimum of hardship – perhaps through making redundancies voluntary. If ultimately redundancies become inevitable and either or both of the above methods do not work out, then we shall of course follow the 'last in, first out' procedure provided for in our union agreements.

Anyway, I repeat that I hope that this situation will not arise. It is certainly the determination of your Board and of all the management team to scour the countryside/the world for orders and to take any steps within our power to keep our organisation – with all its skills, experience and comradeship – together. We know that you know the problems – and how much we appreciate your partnership and help. We believe that together – all of us together – we can survive this miserable recession. Thank you – and now please do ask your questions. We shall try to answer them all – frankly and in the confidence that you recognise that we are all working – together – for the future of this, our works/business/undertaking.

Note: The redundancy section of this speech sets the tone for misery and, of course, should not be used unless that misery is at least in prospect. If you have any alternative joy to offer, then by all means do so. Alternatively, you could use the redundancy section to form a major part of an even more unhappy speech, if redundancies really do become inevitable.

Similar principles apply to speeches to management, thus:

To management colleagues

I appreciate greatly your coming together today. I know how far some of you have had to travel and the difficulty which some of you have had in leaving your work/departments. But it is essential that we confer together so as to decide how to meet the current emergency/ how to make the best of the present opportunity/how to avoid (*or as the case may be*).

First let me refer to the background paper which has been provided to you all. I must emphasise the following points:

1 . . . .
2 . . . .

The Board consider that the following steps should now be taken – but before making any decision irrevocable, we are seeking your views. Our proposals are:

1   . . . .
2   . . . .
3   . . . .

I look forward to hearing your comments and any counter-proposals. We shall value your constructive criticism and your ideas – as we do your comradeship, your partnership and your assistance – without which this business could not be surviving in such excellent shape.

Note: Accounts (as in the previous precedent); a background paper (as in this) – or some other document – prepared carefully in advance will avoid waste of time; provide the basis for discussion; and reduce the length of your speech.

Sales team talk

I have asked you – our sales team – to join me today so that we can together plan for the future of the entire business. In the past, customers have come to us. In these troubled times, we must go to them – and arrive well ahead of our competitors.

I shall now ask our colleague, Bill Black, to present to you our new product – which will lie at the centre of our effort for the coming year. Bill. . . .

(Mr Black then introduces and explains the product – with appropriate diagrams, charts and/or visual aids.)

So now you have seen the product and you know the plans. So how do we beat the competition . . . sell well – and justify the skill, the brilliance and the enterprise of our colleagues in research and development? How do we make the most of this great new opportunity? If we succeed, then the company will flourish. Failure is unthinkable – for the company – and for us all.

Note: Visual aids are vital – as a supplement to speech (see Chapter 33). Visual aids are absolutely indispensable (a) to explain complicated ideas or machinery; (b) to punctuate a lengthy speech or to brighten a shorter one; or (c) to feed other people's talents into your talk.

Part 7

Classic speeches

71 Lloyd George: 'Limehouse Speech'

(Extract from Lloyd George's address to over 4,000 people at Limehouse in 1909.)

...Now unless I am wearying you, I have got just one other land tax, and that is a tax on royalties. The landlords are receiving eight million a year by way of royalties. What for? They never deposited the coal there. It was not they who planted these great granite rocks in Wales, who laid the foundations of the mountains. Was it the landlord? And yet he, by some divine right, demands – for merely the right for men to risk their lives in hewing these rocks – eight millions a year!

Take any coalfield. I went down to a coalfield the other day, and they pointed out to me many collieries there. They said: 'You see that colliery there. The first man who went there spent a quarter of a million in sinking shafts, in driving mains and levels. He never got coal. The second man who came spent £100,000 – and he failed. The third man came along, and he got the coal. But what was the landlord doing in the meantime? The first man failed; but the landlord got his royalties, the landlord got his dead-rents. The second man failed, but the landlord got his royalties. These capitalists put their money in. When the scheme failed, what did the landlord put in? He simply put in the bailiffs. The capitalist risks at any rate the whole of his money; the engineer puts his brains in, the miner risks his life. Have you been down a coal-mine? Then you know. I was telling you I went down the other day. We sank down into a pit half a mile deep. We then walked underneath the mountain, and we did about three-quarters of a mile with rock and shale above us. The earth seemed to be straining – around us and above us – to crush us in. You could see the pit-props bent and twisted and sundered until you saw their fibres split. Sometimes they give way, and then there is mutilation and death. Often a spark ignites, the whole pit is deluged in fire, and the breath of life is scorched out of hundreds of breasts by the consuming fire.

In the very next colliery to the one I descended, just three years ago, three hundred people lost their lives in that way; and yet when the Prime Minister and I knock at the door of these great landlords and say to them, 'Here, you know these poor fellows who have been digging up royalties at the risk of their lives, some of them are old, they have survived the perils of their trade, they are broken, they can earn no more. Won't you give something towards keeping them out of the workhouse?' they scowl at you. And we say, 'Only a ha'penny, just a copper!' They say, 'You thieves!' And they turn their dogs on to us, and every day you can hear their bark. If this is an indication of the view taken by these great landlords of their responsibility to the people who, at the risk of life, create their wealth, then I say their day of reckoning is at hand.

The other day, at the great Tory meeting held at the Cannon Street Hotel, they had blazoned on the walls, 'We protest against the Budget in the name of democracy, liberty, and justice.' Where does the democracy come in in this landed system? Where is the justice in all these transactions? We claim that the tax we impose on land is fair, just, and moderate. They go on threatening that if we proceed they will cut down their benefactions and discharge labour. What kind of labour? What is the labour they are going to choose for dismissal? Are they going to threaten to devastate rural England while feeding themselves and dressing themselves? Are they going to reduce their game-keepers? That would be sad! The agricultural labourer and the farmer might then have some part of the game which they fatten with their labour. But what would happen to you in the season? No week-end shooting with the Duke of Norfolk for any of us! But that is not the kind of labour that they are going to cut down. They are going to cut down productive labour – builders and gardeners – and they are going to ruin their property so that it shall not be taxed. All I can say is this – the ownership of land is not merely an enjoyment, it is a stewardship. It has been reckoned as such in the past, and if they cease to discharge their functions, the security and defence of the country, looking after the broken in their villages and neighbourhoods – then those functions which are part of the traditional duties attached to the ownership of land and which have given to it its title – if they cease to discharge those functions, the time will come to reconsider the conditions under which land is held in this country.

No country, however rich, can permanently afford to have quartered upon its revenue a class which declines to do the duty which it was called upon to perform. And, therefore, it is one of the prime duties of statesmanship to investigate those conditions. But I do not believe it. They have threatened and menaced like that before. They have seen it is not to their interest to carry out these futile menaces. They are now protesting against paying their fair share of the taxes of the land, and they are doing so by saying, 'You are burdening the community; you are putting burdens upon the people which they cannot bear.' Ah! they are not thinking of themselves. Noble souls! It is not the great dukes they are feeling for, it is the market-gardener, it is the builder, and it was, until recently, the smallholder.

In every debate in the House of Commons they said, 'We are not worrying for ourselves. We can afford it, with our broad acres; but just think of the little man who has only got a few acres'; and we were so very impressed with this tearful appeal that at last we said, 'We will leave him out.' And I almost expected to see Mr Pretyman jump over the table and say – 'Fall on my neck. and embrace me.' Instead of that, he stiffened up, his face wreathed with anger, and he said; 'The Budget is more unjust than ever.' Oh! no. We are placing the burdens on the broad shoulders. Why should I put burdens on the people? I am one of the children of the people. I was brought up amongst them. I know their trials; and God forbid that I should add one grain of trouble to the anxiety which they bear with such patience and fortitude. When the Prime Minister did me the honour of inviting me to take charge of the National Exchequer at a time of great difficulty, I made up my mind, in framing the Budget which was in front of me, that at any rate no cupboard should be barer, no lot should be harder. By that test, I challenge them to judge the Budget.

(Reprinted, by kind permission of Caxton Publishing Co. Ltd, from The Book of Public Speaking, *Volume 3, edited by C. Fox-Davies.)*

72 George Bernard Shaw: 'The Labour Party'

(Shaw's speech on his seventieth birthday; at a dinner in his honour given by the Parliamentary Labour Party in 1926.)

Of late years the public have been trying to tackle me in every way they possibly can, and failing to make anything of it they have turned to treating me as a great man. This is a dreadful fate to overtake anybody. There has been a distinct attempt to do it again now, and for that reason I absolutely decline to say anything about the celebration of my seventieth birthday. But when the Labour Party, my old friends the Labour Party, invited me here I knew that I should be all right. We have discovered the secret that there are no great men, and we have discovered the secret that there are no great nations or great States.

We leave that kind of thing to the nineteenth century, where they properly belong. Here you all know that I am extraordinarily clever fellow at my job. But I have not got the 'great-man feeling'. You have not got it either. My predecessor in my professional business, Shakespeare, lived in a middle-class set, but there was one person in that set who was not a middle-class man. He was a bricklayer, and when, after Shakespeare's death, the middle class generally started to celebrate Shakespeare by issuing a folio edition of his works (I haven't come to that yet, but I have no doubt some one will do it), all the middle class generally wrote magnificent songs about the greatness of Shakespeare. Curiously enough, the only tribute ever quoted or remembered today is the tribute of the bricklayer who said: 'I liked the man as well as anybody did this side of idolatry'.

When I began as a young man Labour was attached to Liberalism and to Radicalism. Now Liberalism had its traditions, the traditions of 1649, of 1798, of 1848, and those traditions are still rampant in what is called the Communist Party. What were those traditions? Those traditions were barricades, civil war and regicide. Those are the genuine Liberal traditions, and the only reason that we can't say they exist today is that the Liberal Party itself has ceased to exist.

The Radical Party was publican and atheist, and its great principle was in the great historical phrase, that the world would never be at peace until the last king was strangled in the entrails of the last priest. When asked to put it a little more explicitly, and to put it into practical politics, they said that the world was full of tribulation and injustice because the Archbishop of Canterbury got fifteen thousand a year and because perpetual pensions were enjoyed by the descendants of Charles II's mistresses.

Now, however, we have built up a Constitutional Party. We have built it up on a socialist basis. My friend, Mr Sidney Webb, Mr MacDonald and myself said definitely at the beginning that what we had got to do was to make the Socialist Party a constitutional party to which any respectable God-fearing man could belong without the slightest compromise of his respectability. We got rid of all those traditions; that is why Governments in the present day are more afraid of us than they were of any of the Radical people.

Our position is a perfectly simple one and we have the great advantage of understanding our position. We oppose socialism to capitalism, and our great difficulty is that capitalists have not the slightest notion of what capitalism means. Yet it is a very simple thing. It is a theory of the Socialist Party that if you will take care of private property and if you will make all the sources of production as private property and maintain them as private property, in so far as that is a contract made between persons on that basis, then production will take care of itself and distribution will take care of itself.

According to the capitalists, there will be a guarantee to the world that every man in the country would get a job. They didn't contend it would be a well-paid job, because if it was well paid a man would save up enough one week to stop working the next week, and they were determined to keep a man working the whole time on a bare subsistence wage – and, on the other hand, divide an accumulation of capital.

They said capitalism not only secured this for the working man, but, by insuring fabulous wealth in the hands of a small class of people, they would save money whether they liked it or not and would have to invest it. That is capitalism, and this Government is always interfering with capitalism. Instead of giving a man a job or letting him starve they are giving him doles – after making sure he has paid for them first. They are giving capitalists subsidies and making all sorts of regulations that are breaking up their own system. All the time they are doing it, and we are telling them it is breaking up, they don't understand.

We say in criticism of capitalism: Your system has never kept its promises for one single day since it was promulgated. Our production is ridiculous. We are producing eighty horsepower motors cars when many more houses should be built. We are producing most extravagant luxuries while children starve. You have stood production on its head. Instead of beginning with the things the nation needs most, you are beginning at just the opposite end. We say distribution has become so glaringly ridiculous that there are only two people out of the 47,000,000 people in this country who approve of the present system of distribution – one is the Duke of Northumberland and the other is Lord Banbury.

We are opposed to that theory. Socialism, which is perfectly clear and unmistakable, says the thing you have got to take care of is your distribution. We have to begin with that, and private property, if it stands in the way of good distribution, has got to go.

A man who holds public property must hold it on the public condition on which, for instance, I carry my walking stick. I am not allowed to do what I like with it. I must not knock you on the head with it. We say that if distribution goes wrong, everything else goes wrong – religion, morals, government. And we say, therefore (this is the whole meaning of our socialism), we must begin with distribution and take all the necessary steps.

I think we are keeping it in our minds because our business is to take care of the distribution of wealth in the world; and I tell you, as I have told you before, that I don't think there are two men, or perhaps one man, in our 47,000,000 who approves of the existing distribution of wealth. I will go even further and say that you will not find a single person in the whole of the civilized world who agrees with the existing system of the distribution of wealth. It has been reduced to a blank absurdity. You can prove that by asking any intelligent middle-class man if he thinks it right that he should go begging for a civil list pension while a baby in its cradle is being fought over in the law courts because it has only got six millions to be brought up on.

The first problem of distribution is distribution to the baby. It must have a food income and a better income than anybody else's income if the new generation is to be a first-class generation. Yet a baby has no morals, no character, no industry, and it hasn't even common decency. And it is to that abandoned person that the first duty of the Government is due. That is a telling example of this question of distribution. It reaches our question, which really is a question which is going to carry us to triumph.

I think the day will come when we will be able to make the distinction between us and the capitalists. We must get certain leading ideas before the people. We should announce that we are not going in for what was the old-fashioned idea of redistribution, but the redistribution of income. Let it always be a question of income.

I have been very happy here tonight. I entirely understand the distinction made by our chairman tonight when he said you hold me in social esteem and a certain amount of personal affection. I am not a sentimental man, but I am not insensible to all that. I know the value of all that, and it gives me, now that I have come to the age of seventy (it will not occur again and I am saying it for the last time), a great feeling of pleasure that I can say what a good many people can't say.

I know now that when I was a young man and took the turning that led me into the Labour Party, I took the right turning in every sense.

(Reprinted, by kind permission of Dover Publications, New York, from The World's Greatest Speeches *[second revised edition], edited by L. Copeland and L. Larner.)*

73 King Edward VIII: 'Abdication Address'

(Edward VIII's abdication address, which he broadcast to Britain and the world on 11 December 1936.)

At long last I am able to say a few words of my own. I have never wanted to withhold anything, but until now it has not been constitutionally possible for me to speak.

A few hours ago I discharged my last duty as King and Emperor, and now that I have been succeeded by my brother, the Duke of York, my first words must be to declare my allegiance to him. This I do with all my heart.

You all know the reasons which have impelled me to renounce the throne. But I want you to understand that in making up my mind I did not forget the country or the empire, which, as Prince of Wales and lately as King, I have for twenty-five years tried to serve.

But you must believe me when I tell you that I have found it impossible to carry the heavy burden of responsibility and to discharge my duties as King as I would wish to do without the help and support of the woman I love.

And I want you to know that the decision I have made has been mine and mine alone. This was a thing I had to judge entirely for myself. The other person most nearly concerned has tried up to the last to persuade me to take a different course.

I have made this, the most serious decision of my life, only upon the single thought of what would, in the end, be best for all.

This decision has been made less difficult to me by the sure knowledge that my brother, with his long training in the public affairs of this country and with his fine qualities, will be able to take my place forthwith without interruption or injury to the life and progress of the empire. And he has one matchless blessing, enjoyed by so many of you, and not bestowed on me – a happy home with his wife and children.

During these hard days I have been comforted by her majesty my mother and by my family. The ministers of the crown, and in particular, Mr Baldwin, the Prime Minister, have always treated me with full consideration. There has never been any constitutional difference between me and them, and between me and Parliament. Bred in the constitutional tradition by my father, I should never have allowed any such issue to arise.

Ever since I was Prince of Wales, and later on when I occupied the throne, I have been treated with the greatest kindness by all classes of the people wherever I have lived or journeyed throughout the empire. For that I am very grateful.

I now quit altogether public affairs and I lay down my burden. It may be some time before I return to my native land, but I shall always follow the fortunes of the British race and empire with profound interest, and if at any time in the future I can be found of service to his majesty in a private station, I shall not fail.

And now, we all have a new King. I wish him and you, his people, happiness and prosperity with all my heart. God bless you all! God save the King!

74 Winston Churchill: 'Blood, Toil, Sweat and Tears' – 1940

I beg to move,

'That this House welcomes the formation of a Government representing the united and inflexible resolve of the nation to prosecute the war with Germany to a victorious conclusion.'

On Friday evening last I received His Majesty's Commission to form a new Administration. It was the evident wish and will of Parliament and the nation that this should be conceived on the broadest possible basis and that it should include all parties, both those who supported the late Government and also the parties of the Opposition. I have completed the most important part of this task. A War Cabinet has been formed of five Members, representing, with the Opposition Liberals, the unity of the nation. The three party Leaders have agreed to serve, either in the War Cabinet or in high executive office. The three Fighting Services have been filled. It was necessary that this should be done in one single day, on account of the extreme urgency and rigour of events. A number of other positions, key positions, were filled yesterday, and I am submitting a further list to His Majesty tonight. I hope to complete the appointment of the principal Ministers during tomorrow. The appointment of the other Ministers usually takes a little longer, but I trust that, when Parliament meets again, this part of my task will be completed, and that the administration will be complete in all respects.

I considered it in the public interest to suggest that the House should be summoned to meet today. Mr Speaker agreed, and took the necessary steps, in accordance with the powers conferred upon him by the Resolution of the House. At the end of the proceedings today, the Adjournment of the House will be proposed until Tuesday, 21st May, with, of course, provision for earlier meeting, if need be. The business to be considered during that week will be notified to Members at the earliest opportunity. I now invite the House, by the Motion which stands in my name, to record its approval of the steps taken and to declare its confidence in the new Government.

To form an Administration of this scale and complexity is a serious undertaking in itself, but it must be remembered that we are in the preliminary stage of one of the greatest battles in history, that we are in action at many other points in Norway and in Holland, that we have to be prepared in the Mediterranean, that the air battle is continuous and that many preparations, such as have been indicated by my Hon. Friend below the Gangway, have to be made here at home. In this crisis I hope I may be pardoned if I do not address the House at any length today. I hope that any of my friends and colleagues, or former colleagues, who are affected by the political reconstruction, will make allowance, all allowance, for any lack of ceremony with which it has been necessary to act. I would say to the House, as I said to those who have joined this Government: 'I have nothing to offer but blood, toil, tears and sweat.'

We have before us an ordeal of the most grievous kind. We have before us many, many long months of struggle and of suffering. You ask, what is our policy? I will say: It is to wage war, by sea, land and air, with all our might and with all the strength that God can give us; to wage war against a monstrous tyranny, never surpassed in the dark, lamentable catalogue of human crime. That is our policy. You ask, what is our aim? I can answer in one word: It is victory, victory at all costs, victory in spite of all terror, victory, however long and hard the road may be; for without victory, there is no survival. Let that be realised; no survival for the British Empire, no survival for all that the British Empire has stood for, no survival for the urge and impulse of the ages, that mankind will move forward towards its goal. But I take up my task with buoyancy and hope. I feel sure that our cause will not be suffered to fail among men. At this time I feel entitled to claim the aid of all, and I say, 'Come then, let us go forward together with our united strength.'

(Reprinted, with kind permission of HMSO, from Hansard, *Fifth Series, issue No. 1096, volume 360, 13 May 1940, col. 1501 to col. 1502.)*

75 Jawaharlal Nehru: 'A Glory has Departed'

(Nehru, first Prime Minister of independent India, addressing the Constituent Assembly at New Delhi on 2 February 1948, three days after the assassination of Mahatma Ghandi.)

What then can we say about him except to feel humble on this occasion? To praise him we are not worthy – to praise him whom we could not follow adequately and sufficiently. It is almost doing him an injustice just to pass him by with words when he demanded work and labour and sacrifice from us; in a large measure he made this country, during the last thirty years or more, attain to heights of sacrifice which in that particular domain have never been equalled elsewhere. He succeeded in that. Yet ultimately things happened which no doubt made him suffer tremendously though his tender face never lost its smile and he never spoke a harsh word to anyone. Yet, he must have suffered – suffered for the failing of this generation whom he had trained, suffered because we went away from the path that he had shown us. And ultimately the hand of a child of his – for he after all is as much a child of his as any other Indian – a hand of the child of his struck him down.

Long ages afterwards history will judge of this period that we have passed through. It will judge of the successes and the failures – we are too near it to be proper judges and to understand what has happened and what has not happened. All we know is that there was a glory and that it is no more; all we know is that for the moment there is darkness, not so dark certainly because when we look into our hearts we still find the living flame which he lighted there. And if those living flames exist, there will not be darkness in this land and we shall be able, with our effort, remembering him and following his path, to illumine this land again, small as we are, but still with the fire that he instilled into us.

He was perhaps the greatest symbol of the India of the past, and may I say, of the India of the future, that we could have had. We stand on this perilous edge of the present between that past and the future to be and we face all manner of perils and the greatest peril is sometimes the lack of faith which comes to us, the sense of frustration that comes to us, the sinking of the heart and of the spirit that comes to us when we see ideals go overboard, when we see the great things that we talked about somehow pass into empty words and life taking a different course. Yet, I do believe that perhaps this period will pass soon enough.

He has gone, and all over India there is a feeling of having been left desolate and forlorn. All of us sense that feeling, and I do not know when we shall be able to get rid of it, and yet together with that feeling there is also a feeling of proud thankfulness that it has been given to us of this generation to be associated with this mighty person. In ages to come, centuries and maybe millenia after us, people will think of this generation when this man of God trod on earth and will think of us who, however small, could also follow his path and tread the holy ground where his feet had been. Let us be worthy of him.

A glory has departed and the sun that warmed and brightened our lives has set and we shiver in the cold and dark. Yet, he would not have us feel this way. After all, that glory that we saw for all these years, that man with the divine fire, changed us also – and such as we are, we have been moulded by him during these years; and out of that divine fire many of us also took a small spark which strengthened and made us work to some extent on the lines that he fashioned. And so if we praise him, our words seem rather small and if we praise him, to some extent we also praise ourselves. Great men and eminent men have monuments in bronze and marble set up for them, but this man of divine fire managed in his life-time to become enshrined in millions and millions of hearts so that all of us became somewhat of the stuff that he was made of, though to an infinitely lesser degree. He spread out in this way all over India not in palaces only, or in select places or in assemblies but in every hamlet and hut of the lowly and those who suffer. He lives in the hearts of millions and he will live for immemorial ages.

(Reprinted, by kind permission of Dover Publications, New York, from The World's Greatest Speeches [*second revised edition*], *edited by L. Copeland and L. Larner.)*

76 Harold Macmillan: 'The Winds of Change'

(Addressing the South African Parliament in 1960 on the theme of emerging third-world nationalism, Macmillan opened his speech as follows.)

Sir, as I have travelled round the Union I have found everywhere, as I expected, a deep preoccupation with what is happening in the rest of the African continent. I understand and sympathise with your interest in these events, and your anxiety about them. Ever since the break-up of the Roman Empire one of the constant facts of political life in Europe has been the emergence of independent nations. They have come into existence over the centuries in different forms, with different kinds of Government, but all have been inspired by a deep, keen feeling of nationalism, which has grown as the nations have grown.

In the twentieth century, and especially since the end of the war, the processes which gave birth to the nation states of Europe have been repeated all over the world. We have seen the awakening of national consciousness in peoples who have for centuries lived in dependence upon some other power. Fifteen years ago this movement spread through Asia. Many countries there of different races and civilisations pressed their claim to an independent national life. Today the same thing is happening in Africa, and the most striking of all the impressions I have formed since I left London a month ago is of the strength of this African national consciousness. In different places it takes different forms, but it is happening everywhere. The wind of change is blowing through this continent, and, whether we like it or not, this growth of national consciousness is a political fact. We must all accept it as a fact, and our national policies must take account of it. . . .

(Reprinted, by kind permission of Macmillan London Ltd, from Pointing the Way 1959–61, *Volume 5 of Macmillan's bibliography.)*

77 Martin Luther King: 'I Have a Dream'

(Martin Luther King's evocative black masterpiece of hope – 1963.)

I have a dream that my four little children will one day live in a nation where they will not be judged by the colour of their skin but by the content of their character.

I have a dream today.

I have a dream that one day the state of Alabama, whose governor's lips are presently dripping with the words of interposition and nullification, will be transformed into a situation where little black boys and black girls will be able to join hands with little white boys and white girls and walk together as sisters and brothers.

I have a dream today.

I have a dream that one day every valley shall be exalted, every hill and mountain shall be made low, the rough places will be made plain, and the crooked places will be made straight, and the glory of the Lord shall be revealed, and all flesh shall see it together.

This is our hope. This is the faith with which I return to the South. With this faith we will be able to hew out of the mountain of despair a stone of hope. With this faith we will be able to transform the jangling discords of our nation into a beautiful symphony of brotherhood. With this faith we will be able to work together, to pray together, to struggle together, to go to jail together, to stand up for freedom together, knowing that we will be free one day.

This will be the day when all of God's children will be able to sing with new meaning 'My country 'tis of thee, sweet land of liberty, of thee I sing. Land where my fathers died, land of the pilgrim's pride, from every mountainside, let freedom ring.'

And if America is to be a great nation this must become true. So let freedom ring from the prodigious hilltops of New Hampshire! Let freedom ring from the mighty mountains of New York! Let freedom ring from the heightening Alleghenies of Pennsylvania!

Let freedom ring from the snowcapped Rockies of Colorado!

Let freedom ring from the curvaceous peaks of California!

But not only that; let freedom ring from Stone Mountain of Georgia!

Let freedom ring from every hill and mole hill of Mississippi. From every mountainside, let freedom ring.

When we let freedom ring, when we let it ring from every village and every hamlet, from every state and every city, we will be able to speed up that day when all of God's children, black men and white men, Jews and Gentiles, Protestants and Catholics, will be able to join hands and sing in the words of that old Negro spiritual, 'Free at last! Free at last! Thank God almighty, we are free at last!'

(Reprinted, by kind permission of George Allen & Unwin Ltd, from What Manner of Man: a Biography of Martin Luther King *by L. Bennett.)*

78 Enoch Powell: 'Rivers of Blood'

(An extract from the speech of Enoch Powell, MP, to the West Midlands Area Conservative Political Centre in 1968 on the Race Relations Bill.)

. . .The other dangerous delusion from which those who are wilfully or otherwise blind to realities suffer, is summed up in the word 'integration'. To be integrated into a population means to become for all practical purposes indistinguishable from its other members. Now, at all times, where there are marked physical differences, especially of colour, integration is difficult though, over a period, not impossible. There are among the Commonwealth immigrants who have come to live here in the last fifteen years or so, many thousands whose wish and purpose is to be integrated and whose every thought and endeavour is bent in that direction. But to imagine that such a thing enters the heads of a great and growing majority of immigrants and their descendents is a ludicrous misconception and a dangerous one to boot.

We are on the verge here of a change. Hitherto it has been force of circumstance and of background which has rendered the very idea of integration inaccessible to the greater part of the immigrant population – that they never conceived or intended such a thing, and that their numbers and physical concentration meant the pressures towards integration which normally bear upon any small minority did not operate. Now we are seeing the growth of positive forces acting against integration, of vested interests in the preservation and sharpening of racial and religious differences, with a view to the exercise of actual domination, first over fellow-immigrants and then over the rest of the population. The cloud no bigger than a man's hand, that can so rapidly overcast the sky, has been visible recently in Wolverhampton and has shown signs of spreading quickly. The words I am about to use, verbatim as they appeared in the local press on 17 February, are not mine, but those of a Labour Member of Parliament who is a Minister in the present Government. 'The Sikh community's campaign to maintain customs inappropriate in Britain is much to be regretted. Working in Britain, particularly in the public services, they should be prepared to accept the terms and conditions of their employment. To claim special communal rights (or should one say rites?) leads to a dangerous fragmentation within society. This communalism is a canker; whether practised by one colour or another it is to be strongly condemned.' All credit to John Stonehouse for having had the insight to perceive that, and the courage to say it.

For these dangerous and divisive elements the legislation proposed in the Race Relations Bill is the very pabulum they need to flourish. Here is the means of showing that the immigrant communities can organise to consolidate their members, to agitate and campaign against their fellow citizens, and to overawe and dominate the rest with the legal weapons which the ignorant and the ill-informed have provided. As I look ahead, I am filled with foreboding. Like the Roman, I seem to see 'The River Tiber foaming with much blood'. That tragic and intractable phenomenon which we watch with horror on the other side of the Atlantic but which there is interwoven with the history and existence of the States itself, is coming upon us here by our own volition and our own neglect. Indeed, it has all but come. In numerical terms, it will be of American proportions long before the end of the century. Only resolute and urgent action will avert it even now. Whether there will be the public will to demand and obtain that action, I do not know. All I know is that to see, and not to speak, would be the great betrayal.

*Commenting on this notorious speech, Bernard Levin (in *The Times*) compared him to the man who set light to seats in a cinema and rushed out, yelling: 'Fire!'. But a set of current examples of oratorical power would be incomplete without this influential and incendiary effort. Most parliamentarians agree that when on form, the most eloquent parliamentarians of recent years (filling the chamber when they are on their feet – as opposed to the 'chamber emptiers') were or are: Winston Churchill, Aneurin Bevan, Michael Foot and Enoch Powell – each of whom are represented in this collection.

79   *Axel Springer:*
'Nip it in the Bud'

(German publisher, Axel Springer, on the resurgence of right-wing terrorism – October 1980.)

There is no doubt: the signs of right-wing extremism are growing bloodier in Europe. The seed of violence is sprouting. Since the mid-sixties extreme-left terrorism has bombed itself irresistably into the underdeveloped consciousness of some of the marginal right-wing extremist groups in our society. A fatal reciprocal effect with exchangeable slogans but with the same blind and damnable brutality is taking shape. The track of insanity leads from the blood bath in Bologna railway station over the massacre at the Oktoberfest in Munich to the attack on the synagogue in Paris. Where will it end?

It would be premature to attribute to right-wing extremism a deadly peril to political morality in Europe. But it is imperative to nip the beginnings in the bud, with all our watchfulness and rigour. It is food for thought when in a country which was responsible for the holocaust, right-wing extremist elements ride the wave of hostility to foreigners, when the treacherous murder of two Vietnamese in a foreign workers' hostel in Hamburg releases no storm of public protest.

The writing is on the wall of more than the house of Germany. Heinz Galinski, the untiring chairman of the largest Jewish community in Germany, a man who survived Auschwitz, has therefore taken the right initiative at the right time. He addressed the passionate appeal to the President of the European Parliament, Simone Veil, to throw in the whole weight of her office to put the co-ordinated fight against right-wing extremism on the agenda of the European Parliament. Galinski is right when he points out that right-wing extremism is not a problem for this or that country but a European phenomenon.

Certainly there is not yet cause to dramatise and attribute to the extremists of the right a set of muscles which, thank God, they do not possess. The trammels of our free communal body still hold. Our political party landscape is still unstained by the entry of the incorrigibles as a political force. The German voter – up to and including the last elections to the Bundestag – still proves his maturity as a democrat. The crime of Auschwitz is not yet waste paper of history.

But the young German democracy has not yet been called upon to stand the ultimate test. If we were in misery, in a grave economic crisis, with millions of unemployed, crumbling internal security and under stress in our foreign politics – would we be proof against the slogans of yesteryear?

We are witnesses to the determination with which right-wing extremism tries to get on to the political stage via hostility to foreigners. Our sensitivity, sharpened by the tragedies and the guilt of our history, shows us that extremism of the right again feeds on anti-semitism.

Here we are immediately up against the unholy relation between anti-semitism and anti-zionism. It is not a polemic contrivance but provable that in every place where indifference to the fate of Israel guides the pen, or where even Israel's right to existence is questioned, anti-semitism raises its hideous head. A recent example:

With 20 adherents the 'Führer' of a right-wing extremist group is reported to have been trained early this year for two weeks in a Lebanese training camp of the terrorist organization 'El Fatah'.

We have, of course, enough to sweep at our own doorstep, but it is presumably no stupid coincidence that in France of all countries anti-semitism is stretching its muscles again – in a country which in the European Community in recent years has assumed a pro-Arab pilot function striking at Israel.

Just as left-wing extremism needed a mental field of trivialisation and sympathy which allowed the terrorists to move in it like fish in water, so must we take care that extremism of the right is deprived of its humus at the very beginning of thought on the subject. Nobody who utters reservations against Israeli policies or who gives equal weight to the interests of the Jewish state and to the Arab camp (if there is such a thing) must be assumed to be deliberately embracing the cause of right-wing extremism. But every responsible German politician should face the question of conscience as to whether, if he takes a critical attitude against Israel, he is not unwittingly encouraging those who say Israel but mean anti-semitism.

There is something wrong in a political landscape in which the Federal Chancellor's words calling Prime Minister Begin 'a danger to world peace' can circulate, at first without dementi, then only after protest by Israel followed by a dementi.

Government circles in Bonn were outraged when the Israeli press carried worried commentaries on the outcome of the Bundestag elections, which again brought in the social-democratic-liberal coalition. Was that really surprising? After all the West German Government is a partner in the EEC Venice resolution, which shamelessly favours Israel's enemies. After all Bonn unblushingly shares in raising Arafat's stock and that of his PLO, which is still proud of being a murder organisation. After all, the West German Government favours the establishment of an independent Palestinian state in which exactly those Arabs would rule who till this day have written on their flags the intention to annihilate the Jewish state.

Must not the insanity of people who hark back to Hitler feel strengthened when the West German Foreign Minister, Herr Genscher, as good as files away the 'special relations' between the Federal Republic and Israel, writing in large letters his sympathies for the Arab camp and favouring beleaguered Israel merely with statesmanlike coolness?

How shall a brain untrained in politics digest the Federal Chancellor's neutral declaration, given a few days before the Bundestag elections, that 'We are friends of Israel, but we are also friends of Saudi-Arabia, Jordan and Egypt'? How must one interpret the sad fact that during the entire election campaign no single responsible German politician uttered a word demonstratively for all to hear on the special German obligation towards Israel, especially in the present dangerous situation in the Middle East?

This indifference is a product of a false political and moral approach. The words slip with frightening ease from German lips, that a peace settlement in the Middle East can only be reached by stabilizing the Arab camp. Arab unity – this we know – has only existed, if at all, in the common fight against the Jewish state.

As things lie, anyone who calls for the amalgamation of Arabia forces the campaign against the Jewish state and against the Egyptian-Israeli peace settlement. We must be on the watch. We must not assume the disguise of statesmanship in order to steal away – in the dead of night – from Auschwitz.

(*Reprinted, by kind permission of Axel Springer Publishing Group, from* Die Welt, *October 1980.*)

80 Hugh Gaitskell: 'Fight and Fight and Fight Again'

(Speech delivered at the 57th Annual Conference of the Labour Party, Scarborough, 1960.)

. . .There is one other possibility to which I must make reference, because I have read so much about it – that the issue here is not really defence at all but the leadership of this Party. Let me repeat what Manny Shinwell said. The place to decide the leadership of this Party is not here but in the Parliamentary Party. I would not wish for one day to remain a Leader who had lost the confidence of his colleagues in Parliament. It is perfectly reasonable to try to get rid of somebody, to try to get rid of a man you do not agree with, who you think perhaps is not a good Leader. But there are ways of doing this. What would be wrong, in my opinion, and would not be forgiven, is if, in order to get rid of a man, you supported a policy in which you did not wholeheartedly believe, a policy which, as far as the resolution is concerned, is not clear.

Before you take the vote on this momentous occasion, allow me a last word. Frank Cousins has said this is not the end of the problem. I agree with him. It is not the end of the problem because Labour Members of Parliament will have to consider what they do in the House of Commons. What do you expect of them? You know how they voted in June overwhelmingly for the policy statement. It is not in dispute that the vast majority of Labour Members of Parliament are utterly opposed to unilateralism and neutralism. So what do you expect them to do? Change their minds overnight? To go back on the pledges they gave to the people who elected them from their constituencies? And supposing they did do that. Supposing all of us, like well-behaved sheep, were to follow the policies of unilateralism and neutralism, what kind of an impression would that make upon the British people? You do not seem to be clear in your minds about it, but I will tell you this. I do not believe that the Labour Members of Parliament are prepared to act as time servers. I do not believe they will do this, and I will tell you why – because they are men of conscience and honour. People of the so-called Right and so-called Centre have every justification for having a conscience, as well as people of the so-called Left. I do not think they will do this because they are honest men, loyal men, steadfast men, experienced men, with a lifetime of service to the Labour Movement.

There are other people too, not in Parliament, in the Party who share our convictions. What sort of people do you think they are? What sort of people do you think we are? Do you think we can simply accept a decision of this kind? Do you think that we can become overnight the pacifists, unilateralists and fellow travellers that other people are? How wrong can you be? As wrong as you are about the attitude of the British people.

In a few minutes the Conference will make its decision. Most of the votes, I know, are predetermined and we have been told what is likely to happen. We know how it comes about. I sometimes think, frankly, that the system we have, by which great unions decide their policy before even their conferences can consider the Executive recommendation, is not really a very wise one or a good one. Perhaps in a calmer moment this situation could be looked at.

I say this to you: we may lose the vote today and the result may deal this Party a grave blow. It may not be possible to prevent it, but I think there are many of us who will not accept that this blow need be mortal, who will not believe that such an end is inevitable. There are some of us, Mr Chairman, who will fight and fight and fight again to save the Party we love. We will fight and fight and fight again to bring back sanity and honesty and dignity, so that our Party with its great past may retain its glory and its greatness.

It is in that spirit that I ask delegates who are still free to decide how they vote, to support what I believe to be a realistic policy on defence, which yet could so easily have united the great Party of ours, and to reject what I regard as the suicidal path of unilateral disarmament which will leave our country defenceless and alone.

(Reprinted, by kind permission, from the Labour Party Report of the 57th Annual Conference.)

81 Aneurin Bevan: 'Socialism Unbeaten'

(Extract from Bevan's speech to the Labour Party Conference following Macmillan's General Election victory of 1959.)

What are we going to say, comrades? Are we going to accept the defeat? Are we going to say to India, where Socialism has been adopted as the official policy despite all the difficulties facing the Indian community, that the British Labour movement has dropped Socialism here? What are we going to say to the rest of the world? Are we going to send a message from this great Labour movement, which is the father and mother of modern democracy and modern Socialism, that we in Blackpool in 1959 have turned our backs on our principles because of a temporary unpopularity in a temporarily affluent society?

Let me give you a personal confession of faith. I have found in my life that the burdens of public life are too great to be borne for trivial ends. The sacrifices are too much, unless we have something really serious in mind; and therefore, I hope we are going to send from this Conference a message of hope, a message of encouragement, to the youth and to the rest of the world that is listening very carefully to what we are saying.

I was rather depressed by what Denis Healey said. I have a lot of respect for him; but you know, Denis, you are not going to be able to help the Africans if the levers of power are left in the hands of their enemies in Britain. You cannot do it! Nor can you inject the principles of ethical Socialism into an economy based upon private greed. You cannot do it! You cannot mix them, and therefore I beg and pray that we should wind this Conference up this time on a message of hope, and we should say to India and we should say to Africa and Indonesia, and not only to them, but we should say to China and we should say to Russia, that the principles of democratic Socialism have not been extinguished by a temporary defeat at the hands of the Tories a few weeks ago!

You know, comrades, parliamentary institutions have not been destroyed because the Left wing was too vigorous; they have been destroyed because the Left was too inert. You cannot give me a single illustration in the Western world where Fascism conquered because Socialism was too violent. You cannot give me a single illustration where representative government has been undermined because the representatives of the people asked for too much.

But I can give you instance after instance we are faced with today where representative government has been rendered helpless because the representatives of the people did not ask enough. We have never suffered from too much vitality; we have suffered from too little. That is why I say that we are going to go from this Conference a united Party. We are going to go back to the House of Commons, and we are going to fight the Tories. But we are not only going to fight them there; we are going to fight them in the constituencies and inside the trade unions. And we are going to get the youth! Let them start. Do not let them wait for the Executive, for God's sake! Start getting your youth clubs, go in and start now! Go back home and start them, and we will give all the help and encouragement that we can.

82   Michael Foot: 'Who Does that Leave?'

(Michael Foot savaging the Tory Cabinet. The House in uproar – and Foot in complete command. . . .)

The Foreign Secretary is an influential chap. I dare say that he is a bit persuaded by the Lord Privy Seal. In passing, there was a report the other day that one of the public expenditure cuts to be imposed tomorrow is a cut in the British Council.

The greatest possession of this country – more valuable than North Sea oil – is the English language, which is becoming the language of the world. At such a moment this penny-pinching Government are about to injure the processes whereby people throughout the world, can acquire the right and capacity to speak English. However, I believe that the Foreign Secretary can be persuaded on to the side of enlightenment in the discussions tomorrow.

Who does that leave? Where is the Home Secretary, the long-playing vice-captain? I suppose that we can add him to the list. I have a card here. I should like to add up the figures. It is a very close thing indeed. However, maybe that is another kind of election. I shall leave that for the moment. At any rate, it is very close indeed. We have a good chance of winning.

I am sorry that the Home Secretary is not here, because I should much rather say this to his face. He may consider that these financial questions are a bit beyond him now. If he has to listen to the Chancellor of the Exchequer at the peak of his form, as he was today, I am not surprised that he does. I have noted the right hon. and learned Gentleman's words carefully. He says that the high rate of the pound is not an objective of policy. Can he tell us whether anything that is happening in the country at present is an objective of policy? Unemployment has not been created on purpose. What about inflation? The Government are conquering inflation, but we should not know that if they did not tell us so. The right hon. Lady will not answer this question tonight, but perhaps she can think up an answer for tomorrow. How long does she believe it will be before she gets the inflation rate down to what it was before she started putting it up? I do not know whether the Government have an answer to that question.

The seriousness of the situation is that the Government, I believe, want to apply their minds to the problem. The Cabinet tomorrow will be quite a serious affair. I hope that I have contributed a little to its understanding. I hope that there will be people there to speak for Wales, Scotland, Northern Ireland, Merseyside, the North-East, the Midlands, London and Lancashire – to speak for Britain, for all the places that need a voice to speak for them.

The only people who seriously believe in the policy that the Government are pursuing is the diminishing little band headed by the right hon. Lady. I sometimes feel that, when the right hon. Lady stands on the burning deck all alone at the end, the only person who will be supporting her will be the Minister for Social Security. I have warned the right hon. Lady before. Does she not realise that we have put him here as an *agent provocateur* in order to test what damn fool statements can be made in Tory Governments? I warn the right hon. Lady that she needs a few better companions around her if she wants to deal with unemployment.

I realise that I have discriminated in favour of the wets. I have revealed to the House quite openly, as I would normally do, who are my favourites, but I should not like to miss out the Secretary of State for Industry, who has had a tremendous effect on the Government and our politics generally. As I see the right hon. Gentleman walking around the country, looking puzzled, forlorn and wondering what has happened, I try to remember what he reminds me of. The other day I hit on it. In my youth, quite a time ago, when I lived in Plymouth, every Saturday night I used to go to the Palace theatre. My favourite act was a magician-conjuror who used to have sitting at the back of the audience a man dressed as a prominent alderman. The magician-conjuror used to say that he wanted a beautiful watch from a member of the audience. He would go up to the alderman and eventually take from him a marvellous gold watch. He would bring it back to the stage, enfold it in a beautiful red handkerchief, place it on the table in front of us, take out his mallet, hit the watch and smash it to smithereens. Then on his countenance would come exactly the puzzled look of the Secretary of State for Industry! He would step to the front of the stage and say 'I am very sorry. I have forgotten the rest of the trick.' That is the situation of the Government. They have forgotten the rest of the trick. It does not work. Lest any objector should suggest that the act at the Palace theatre was only a trick, I should assure the House that the magician-conjuror used to come along at the end and say 'I am sorry. I have still forgotten the trick.'

We face a serious situation which, in some respects, is even worse than the 1930s and we have a Government who have learnt none of the lessons of the 1930s. We have to teach them. The way that our politics are to develop will depend first on what happens within the Cabinet and the Conservative Party. The troubled mind in the Conservative Party is widespread. Everyone who has listened to the speeches of Conservative Members can see that it is becoming very widespread. I am so generous that I will not even ask those Conservative Members who agree with the Government's policies to put up their hands. I do not believe that we would get even the few who enthusiastically obeyed on the previous occasion.

The disbelief does not exist only among trade unionists, Labour supporters and those in the sort of constituency that I represent. Throughout the country there is a rising disbelief in the policy that the Government are pursuing. If the right hon. Members that I have mentioned could capture a few more allies, it would be possible for them to change the situation, though that would not transform the whole industrial situation. The damage has gone so deep that it will be difficult to reverse it.

(Reprinted, by kind permission of HMSO, from Hansard, *issue No. 1184, Volume 991, Wednesday 29th October 1980, col. 605 to col. 608.)*

Book Three

COMPENDIUM OF
RETELLABLE TALES

Introduction

A live story is to a good speech as spice to a fine meal. A touch of wit
. . . a flash of humour . . . a shaft of laughter . . . each is appreciated by
every audience. Again: everyone likes a good story – whatever his or
its age. The best tales are like wine, they mature with the years.

As I have sat through millennial miseries of meetings and dinners,
many of them extremely boring, I have jotted down on menus,
notepads and scraps of assorted paper the cream of the story-teller's ·
crop. To create this section of the book, I have now raided piles of
files . . . deciphered scrawl and shorthand . . . rejected some tales, too
blue or too terrible to retell – and brought together the mixture which
now follows.

Each tale – be it a joke, an aphorism, an illustration, a wisecrack or
an unwise gaffe – has been well used and much appreciated. I have
sorted the accumulation into rough sections – although many stories
could fit just as well into several of my groupings. Anyway, if you
wish to pick out a story for a special purpose, the index should help.
Or maybe you will just enjoy browsing your way through a quarter
century of tales which – told or retold – have brought me much
pleasure. Use them in good health, in good voice – and with that good
fortune which is the essential prerequisite and precursor of every
standing ovation.

'Our next speaker needs no introduction from me. . . .'

83   Speeches and speakers

Opening gambits

As Henry VIII said to each of his wives in turn: 'I shall not keep you long. . .'. (*Lord Janner*)

Everything I know about this subject would fit into a nutshell and still leave plenty of room for the nut. (*Lord Mancroft*)

Your chairman has just said to me: 'Would you like to speak now – or shall we let them go on enjoying themselves a little longer?'

A woman said to the speaker at the end of his talk: 'You weren't on form tonight, were you, Mr Brown?'
Another woman who had been listening nearby sidled up to him. 'I am sorry about that', she said. 'Please take no notice of Mrs Green. She is a stupid woman. She hasn't a mind of her own. . . . She only repeats what she hears other people saying. . . .'

Like the time the toastmaster said: 'Ladies and gentlemen . . . pray for the silence of Mr. Greville Janner. . .'.

The last time the chairman introduced me and was told to be brief, he began: 'The less said about Mr Greville Janner, the better. . .'.

Brevity

I am sorry that I have had to write such a long letter. I did not have the time to write a short one. (*Horace Walpole*)

We no longer know how to be brief. For instance: the Lord's Prayer consists of 56 words; the Ten Commandments 297 words; the United States Declaration of Independence 300 words; and the EEC Convention on the importation of caramel – 26,911 words.

Former Israeli Prime Minister, Levi Eshkol, once chaired a meeting. A speaker, who was likely to be boring, asked him: 'How long shall I speak? There's so much to say, I don't know where to begin. . .'.
Eshkol replied: 'I suggest that you start at the end. . .'.

227

Error

As for the man who makes no mistakes, there is no such man. . . .

In conclusion

'Has he finished?'
'Yes, he finished a long time ago, but he is still going on.'

Jokes by numbers

At a jokesters' conference, everyone knew each other's stories so well that they simply used numbers. A man got on the stage and said: '75'. Silence – except for two men who were rolling in the aisles. When asked why they were laughing, one said: 'I like the way he tells it'; the other said: 'I haven't heard it before'.

Death after dinner

A guest for dinner who could no longer stand the eternal droning of the speaker passed a note to the chairman: 'Why not put an end to it by smashing him on the head with your gavel?'

The chairman picked up the gavel – but it slipped out of his hand and coshed the guest of honour, by his other side. As the poor man began slowly to sink out of sight under the table, he cried out: 'Hit me again. I can still hear him!'

Compliments

Mark Twain once remarked: 'I can live for two months on a good compliment'. You have given me enough compliments for several years. . . .

Timeless

The Vicar once remarked: 'I don't mind you looking at your watch during my sermon. But when you put your watch to your ear and shake it. . . .'

Shy?

I am a shy man and speech-making is very difficult. This problem is hereditary. When I was six years old, I asked my mother why I was still so young. She replied that if my father had not been so shy, I would now be at least eleven. . . .

Bars?

I have to make a great number of speeches and I am afraid that I have to use the same material on a number of occasions. The speech I am about to make to you is largely a repetition of a speech that I made last week in Sing Sing/Dartmoor/Wormwood Scrubs (*or the nearest prison to you*). I apologise to any of you who have heard it before. [*Careful – any ex-cons in your audience? GJ*]

Vote of thanks

At least Macbeth knew that when the dreadful banquet was over, he would not be the person required to return thanks.

Golden silence

A businessman must first learn when to make speeches. Then he gets wise and learns when not to make them.

Sleep

A new pastor arrived in a county parish. He noticed with dismay that each week during his sermon, the senior churchwarden dropped off to sleep. He put up with this until one week the man snored. After the service he went up to him and said, very gently: 'I am sorry to mention this, but it does set a very bad example when my senior churchwarden sleeps during the sermon'.

'Not at all', replied the Elder. 'It just shows that I trust you!'

Plagiarism

Copy from one book and that is 'plagiarism' . . . breach of copyright. . . . Copy from two or more books and that is 'research'.

'Just as the bee gathers honey from all flowers, so the wise man gathers knowledge from all men.' (*Indian proverb*)

Off the record?

'How did your speech go?'

'Marvellous. Even the journalists put down their pencils and listened. . . .'

Staying awake?

The cross-eyed javelin thrower does not break any records, but he certainly keeps his audience on its toes. . . .

Why me first?

I have been asked to speak before Mr . . . because I have several dates in (*naming two months hence*) which I wish to keep. (*Bob Monkhouse*)

After-dinner starter

There is nothing I like better than to eat with nice people, drink with nice people and sleep with a contented mind. . . .

The elderly

Toast at a pensioners' dinner: 'Now, will those who are able to, please rise. . .'.

'And before leaving I would like to express my thanks to all those at Fire Station 37, Beryl on the switchboard, Chief Officer Hargreaves, Driver Jenkins. . . .'

84 *Wit at work*

Supervisors

Supervisory staff can do no right. They can only mitigate their wrong. (*Lord Goddard*)

Whose trade?

Morgan and Dai went on safari. Suddenly, a woolly creature dropped from a tree onto Morgan's back. 'What is it? What is it?', he cried out.

'How should I know?', the other one replied. 'Am I a furrier?'

Partners?

The owner of a hotel quietly watched as his barman put 50p in his own pocket, out of every £1 he took from a customer. When he saw the barman putting an entire £1 note into his wallet, he pounced. 'What are you doing?', he asked. 'I thought we were partners!'

Risks

A 'calculated risk' was recently defined by an airline pilot as one 'when the engineers on the ground make the calculations and the pilots take the risk'.

Success

Mark Twain bemoaned that he had not seen the Niagara Falls, so they made up a special party to take him there. Afterwards his hosts said: 'What did you think of it?'

Mark Twain paused. 'It's certainly a success', he said.

Don't wait

Two men were due to fight a duel. One telephoned the other: 'Charlie, don't wait for me . . . if I'm not there within five minutes, please start without me!'

Insurance

Insurance people present plans to keep you poor while you are alive so that you may die rich.

Ideas

A friend once said to Einstein: 'When I have a good idea, I do not want to forget it. So I keep a notebook by my bed. What do you do?' Einstein replied: 'I do not understand your question. I have only had two or three good ideas in my life.'

Sailors

A sailor never wants to be where he is, but always longs to be where he is not. When a sailor stops complaining the time has come to start worrying. . . . (*Prince Charles*)

Insults

I always smile at Mr Smith's jokes. First at their elegant wit, and then again with nostalgia.

Mr Smith didn't say a word till he was ten. His mother didn't know whether he was dumb or just speaking his mind.

. . . we were all glad to hear his speech again.

Mr Smith has proven the theory that the brain is a wonderful organ that never stops functioning from the moment of birth until one rises to speak in public.

Mr Smith's speeches always do the audience some good; they either go away stimulated or wake up refreshed.

Working hours

Alistair Cooke passed a country station and found the station-master tending his roses. 'How many hours a day do you work?', he enquired.
    'Eight hours, sir. Five days a week.'
    'Always eight hours? Always five days a week?', said Mr Cooke.
    'Yes, always the same.'

'Why always the same?'
'Because if I worked less than eight hours, I wouldn't have enough money to buy roses. And if I worked more than eight hours, I would not have time to tend the roses. . . .'

Wanted

A Scot went up to the desk of his local Police Station. 'I have come for the job', he said.
'I am afraid there is no job here', replied the Sergeant.
'Oh yes there is. You've got a sign outside: "Scotsman wanted for rape", and I am applying for the job. . . .'

Compensation

Apprentice: 'What is a cubic foot?'
Foreman: 'I don't know – but I will make sure that you get full compensation.'

Warning

The managing director of a great engineering company invited school classes to see round the works. One of the teachers was overheard at the end of the morning saying to his class: 'There you are, lads and girls. You have now seen where *you* may end up, if you don't do well in your O-levels!'

Management – and industrial disputes

The latest argument at a works renowned for its management problems got senior executives so upset that they began to stab each other in the front.

A foreman at . . . (*use any topical reference*) was alleged to have molested a woman colleague on a workbench. Management were told that she had provoked him and she was then dismissed. The Transport and General Workers Union then brought everyone out on strike and immediately the management reinstated the woman and sacked the foreman. ASTMS then brought everyone out on strike, whereupon they reinstated the foreman and cut the bench in half.

Up yours

A worker removed the guard from a machine and lost two fingers on his right hand. He only noticed his loss when he said goodnight to the foreman!

Who dunnit?

A girl worker complained to her personnel manager that she had been raped. 'Who did it?', the manager asked. 'I don't know', replied the girl. 'I've never seen him before. But I think he must have been the foreman.'

'Why?'

'Because he was wearing a white coat and brown shoes – and I had to do all the work. . . .'

Self-service

Two foremen were arguing over whether or not sex was a pleasure or a chore. The first, a married man with eight children, regarded it as a chore. The second, a bachelor, thought it was the greatest delight in life. To settle their argument, they called over young Fred, the apprentice. 'So you tell us, Fred', they said. 'Is sex a chore or a pleasure?'

'It must be a pleasure', said the boy.

'Why?'

'Because if it was a chore, you fellows would make me do it for you!'

Salesmanship

A dealer in antiquities has what he regards as an infallible system. When a likely prospect enters his small and cluttered shop, he feigns deafness.

'How much is this object?', asks the customer.

'What did you say?', shouts the dealer, cupping his hand to his ear.

'How much? This object. . . ?'

'I can't hear you. I'll ask my wife.'

So he calls to his wife, who comes to the top of the stairs. 'What is it?'

The customer says: 'How much is this object?'

The wife replies: '£50.'

The dealer then says to the customer: 'She says it's fifteen pounds. . . .'
The customer shells out £15, as swiftly as he can, grabs the object and rushes to the door. . . .

Fringe benefits

On cabbage (*the rag trade term for material offcuts*).
'We usually sell cabbage to our staff – if they don't pinch it first. . . .'

Our staff reckon that they can only take the company's property off our premises at certain times. . . .

Bribery

When we know that one of our customers will not accept the whisky which we send him for Christmas, we send even more the following year – because then we know that it will be sent back and we can drink it ourselves. . . .

It's not bribery if you can eat it, drink it or sleep with it.

A well known company found difficulty in putting its 'commission' (*slush, payola or what-have-you*) through its books. But as it has a hunting lodge in Scotland, it listed the items as 'hunting expenses'.

A visiting customer from Nigeria was provided with a suite at Claridges and a girl in it. Unfortunately, he contracted a certain illness for which he had to be treated at the London Clinic. The cost of that treatment went into the books as: 'Repairs to gun. . .'.

Lord Goddard once remarked: 'Bribery is like a sausage – difficult to describe, but very easy to smell'.

Jewish business

Three Jewish men met for dinner.
The first one said: 'Oi!'
The second said: 'Oi yevay!'
The third said: 'If you boys are going to talk business, I'm off. . .'.

Liquidation

Noah was the bravest man in history. He floated his company when the rest of the world was in liquidation.

Accidents at work

There is no such thing as an Act of God when you are dealing with accidents in industry. The fact is that God has a down on inefficient managers . . . (*Bill Simpson*, Chairman, Health and Safety Commission)

Brains

Two army Captains were grousing about the stupidity of their respective batmen. They decided to have a bet on which one was more stupid. Captain X called for his batman and said: 'Take this £5 note and buy me a colour TV set down in the village'. 'Yes, sir. Certainly, sir.' He saluted and went out into the mess room.

Captain Y then rang for his batman and said: 'Go to the orderly room immediately and see whether I am there'. 'Yes, sir. Certainly, sir.' The batman saluted and left.

The two batmen met in the corridor outside and compared notes. 'Fancy asking me to buy a colour TV set on an early closing day', said the first. The second replied: 'Imagine making me walk half a mile when he could have used the telephone to see if he's in the orderly room!'

Men at work

A man applied for a job with a certain government department. 'I ought to tell you', he said, 'that I am war disabled . . . a German bullet went between my legs. . .'.

'We'll take you on', said the interviewer, 'but instead of starting at nine each morning, you can come in at eleven. . .'.

'Why is that?'

'Well, all the staff spend the first two hours of each day scratching their balls!'

Short-time?

Employer: 'Did you work a full week last week?'
Employee: 'Yes – but I don't want any publicity. . . .'

Three well known diseases:
'plumbi pendulosis' – swinging the lead;
'haemophraemia' – bloody mindedness; and
'non digitus extractus' – failure to pull out the finger. . . .

Patience – and head waiters

Description on head waiter's tombstone: God finally caught his eye.

Bright boy

A car dealer's son was trying to sell his own vehicle – but failing. His father told him to turn back the clock to 6000 miles. The following week, father asked his son whether he had sold the car. 'Certainly not.' 'Why not, then?' 'Well, it's only got 6000 miles on the clock so I decided to keep it. . . .'

Cash management

We have just created a new cash management programme. This means that we pay when we wish to. . . .

Non-contribution

He makes the same contribution to commerce (*or to the subject under discussion*) as Cyril Smith does to hang-gliding. . . .

Second chances

A man was dismissed because he nearly killed the foreman. The shop steward pleaded that he be given another chance.

'Differentials' and 'anomalies'

If I earn more than you do, that is a 'differential'. If you earn more than I do, that is an 'anomaly'.

AGM

Chairman: 'We now come to another annual meeting – after an interval of a year. . . .'.

Emergencies

An employee was lying on the operating table in the factory's sick bay, clenching his teeth while a doctor sewed up a large wound on his scalp. A pair of pliers had fallen from a scaffold and split open his head. I asked him: 'Haven't you got a hard hat?' 'Yes', he said. 'Where was it, then?' He replied, 'It's in my locker'. 'Why do you keep it in your locker?' 'It's there for emergencies', he answered.

Choice of language

A man could not get a good job because prospective employers kept finding out that his father had died in the electric chair. Eventually, he learned to reply to questions about his father thus: 'My father was at one of the great educational institutions in this country. He occupied the Chair of Applied Electricity.'

Mushroom management

UK business tends to be run through 'mushroom management', which means: keeping people below you perpetually in the dark and fertilising them from time to time from a great height.

Luck

A man convinced Rockefeller that he should take a lottery ticket. It won a hundred thousand dollars.

'You have done me a great favour,' said Rockefeller to the man. 'I offer you twenty thousand dollars or four thousand dollars a year for life.'

'I'll take the twenty thousand dollars', said the man, without hesitation.

'Are you sure?', asked the tycoon. 'You are a very young man. . . . Why have you made that decision?'

'Because with your damned luck, sir,' he replied, 'if I took the annuity, I would only live six months!'

Restaurants

A man complained that his 'chicken and camel stew' was 90 per cent camel.

'It's half and half', replied the restaurateur. 'Half a chicken to half a camel. . . .'

Passing the buck

An ordinary seaman was applying for promotion. He was asked to correct the following statement: 'It was me what done it'. He wrote: 'It was *not* me what done it'.

Bankruptcy

'Nothing in your deposit box? Nothing in your wife's name? Nothing dug into the ground? – You're not bankrupt, brother, you're skint!'

Jack went bankrupt so often that he even put his tombstone into his wife's name.

Invoice/free love?

'Do you believe in free love?'
'Have I ever sent you an invoice?'

Time and emotion study

A wealthy and charitable friend tells how emissaries from a religious seminary called on him regularly, year by year. He always gave them a cheque for £100.

Then one year when the collector called, my friend said to himself: 'I don't really know these people. And there are many calls upon me. So I think I'll give him £50.' Which he did.

The man thanked him gravely and turned to leave. My friend said: 'Why didn't you try to get the other £50, like I usually give you?'

The man smiled. 'I've a taxi waiting outside', he said. 'In the time that I spend arguing with you and trying to induce you to give me the balance, I could probably make another couple of calls. And anyway, I'm grateful for the £50 I've got and I don't want to upset you.'

My friend gave him the balance – and told him to call again next year.

How to become a millionaire

A bedraggled beggar wheeled a dollar out of Rockefeller, outside his Manhatten apartment block. After handing over the money, the millionaire enquired: 'Why don't you invest in some clean clothing, young man?'

'I appreciate the suggestion', the beggar replied. 'But if you don't mind my asking, do I try to teach *you* your business?'

Rubbish

To get rid of rubbish nowadays, all you have to do is to wrap it in silver paper, put it on the back seat of your car, and some silly sod will steal it. (*Bob Monkhouse*)

Staff training

Two waiters pass behind diner's chair. One says to the other: 'Look – she's eaten it – !'

Ethics

A son asks father at dinner: 'What are ethics?'

'Leave me alone to eat', father replies.

'But I must know. I have to write an essay tonight, which I must hand in tomorrow. Ethics is the title.'

'I see. Well, suppose I am closing the shop at night and I find a five pound note on the floor. I check the till and make sure that we are not five pounds light. Then, what do I do? I tell my partner, that's what. And I split it with him. That's ethics'.

Promotion refused

The Arab general who conquered Egypt some thirteen hundred years ago expected the Caliph of Arabia to appoint him governor of the country. In fact, the Caliph only offered him the command of the troops in Egypt, while another man became governor.

The general refused this command, with the memorable phrase: 'Why should I hold the cow's horns whilst someone else milks her?'

Sons

A son asked his father for a loan until pay day. His father asked: 'When is pay day?'

The son replied: 'I don't know. You tell me. You're the one who's working. . . .'

A wife in the business

I went into the beer business. My wife said: 'I'll drive the people to drink and you can sell it to them.'

Accountancy

If someone asks me: 'What is two and two?', I answer: 'Are you buying or selling?'. (*Lord Grade*)

Cheap is dear

A man came to buy a hearing aid. 'How much would it cost me?'
'You can have a gold one for £500. It has a gold button, a gold cord and a gold box.'
'Too expensive.'
'Well, you can have a silver one for £350 – silver button, silver cord and silver box.'
'Haven't you anything cheaper?'
'Yes, you can have a steel one for only £100 – steel button, steel cord and steel box.'
'I'm afraid it's still too much. Haven't you anything cheaper than that?'
'Yes. You can have a cardboard one for £5 – cardboard button, cardboard cord and cardboard box.'
'Would it help my hearing?'
'Certainly not. But at least everyone would know that you are deaf.'

Seagull management*

The European directors of a well known multinational described their head office people to me as 'seagulls'. 'They fly in . . . make loud noises as they land . . . and they fly off, fertilising all over you as they leave. . . .' [*Compare with 'Mushroom management'*]

Dismissal

The chairman of a large company called in his directors, one by one. Eventually, only the newest and most junior director was left outside the chairman's office. When his turn came, he found his colleagues sitting around a table.
Chairman: 'Bill, have you been having an affair with my secretary,

Miss Jones?'
    Bill: 'Certainly not'.
    'Are you sure?'
    'Absolutely. I've never laid a hand on her'.
    'Are you absolutely certain?'
    'Of course I am'.
    'Very well Bill, then *you* sack her'.

References

'I am pleased to recommend him for any other job . . .' or
'I am pleased to provide him with a reference for any other job. . . .'

Unanimity

Two directors were doing a crossword. One asked: 'How do you spell "unanimously"?'

The other: 'I am not surprised that you don't know. It's only a miracle that you can pronounce the word. . .'.

Whose worry?

A leading official asked Chief Rabbi Rosen of Rumania how Israel would cope with the large number of Rumanian Jews who would apparently leave if permitted to do so. He told them this story:

A Jewish man owed $100,000. The night before the sum fell due for payment, he could not sleep. He tossed and he turned and he strode up and down. Eventually, he walked around to his creditor's house and knocked on the window. 'What is it?' asked the man.

'I'm very sorry,' replied the debtor, 'but I shan't be able to pay what I owe you tomorrow morning. I've been so worried about it that I couldn't get to sleep. Anyway, I've decided to wake you so that you can now stay awake worrying, while I get some sleep!'

Explanations

A personnel director was having great trouble in inducing an employee to sign up under a non-contributory pension scheme – which was in fact far better for him than the current contributory pension scheme. But he refused to sign.

Eventually, the personnel manager sent the man to the managing director. 'Alex', said the M.D., 'you must sign. I know that you have been with us for thirty years without causing trouble, but that is no reason for not signing. . . .'

Alec: 'I refuse'.

Managing director: 'Alex, you must sign – or I will give you the sack'.

Alec signed.

The next time the personnel manager saw Alec, he said: 'Why did you sign when the managing director asked you to – but you always refused me?'

Alec: 'Well, no one explained it to me properly before. . .'.

Tell-tale twitch

A man applied for a job as a television announcer. Unfortunately, he suffered from a very severe twitch. His interviewer said: 'Wouldn't you be better off applying for a job with the radio?'

'No', the man replied. 'I take one of my special pills and I'm all right for a couple of hours.'

'In that case', said the interviewer, 'you'd better take one now and let me see how it works'.

The man fished in his pocket and pulled out a packet of contraceptives . . . then another . . . then a third . . . then a whole pile of them, before finally producing a bottle of aspirin.

'I understand the aspirin', he said. 'But why the contraceptives?'

The interviewee looked at him sceptically. 'Have you ever tried going into a chemist's shop and saying: 'I'd like a (*twitch*) bottle of (*twitch*) aspirin, please?'' ' [*This sure-fire story requires twitching-winks at appropriate places: GJ*]

Inspectors

People tend to approach a factory inspector gingerly – like the nudist approaches the holly hedge when trimming it.

Book review

An author wrote to the perpetrator of a fiercely offensive review: 'I am sitting in the smallest room in the house. Your review is before me. It will soon be behind me.'

Industrial peace

Peace at work – a period of cheating between strikes.

Energy

Britain is a lump of coal in a sea of oil on a bubble of gas. (*Clive Jenkins*)

Accountants

Three men apply for a job as an accountant. They are asked one question: 'What is two times two?'. The first two fellows got it right. The third one replies: 'What figure did you have in mind, sir?'. He got the job.

Deafness

Doctor to personnel manager at very noisy steel works: 'I don't know why you don't just hire deaf people in the first place and then you wouldn't have to worry. . .'.

When I asked a steel worker why he was not wearing his ear muffs, he replied: 'I'm already deaf!'

The gift of language

Sign on shop: '30 languages spoken here'. Customer comes in and tries to make herself understood in French, but nobody can manage. Another customer says to the shopkeeper: 'I thought you spoke 30 languages here?'.
Shopkeeper replies: 'That's the customers . . . not us. . .'.

Enterprise

Cohen owned a small tailor's shop and made a modest living. Then two firms of multiple-tailors opened on either side of him. 'What are you going to do now?' asked a friend.
'Don't worry,' said Cohen. 'Everything will be all right. I'll just change the name of my shop.'
'What good will that do you?'
'Plenty.'
'What will you call your shop?'
'I shall call it . . . "Main Entrance!" '

Debtors

If you owe £50, you are a 'shnorrer' (*a beggar, in Yiddish*). If you owe £500, you are a businessman. If you owe £5 million, you are a millionaire. If you owe £500 billion, then you are Chancellor of the Exchequer.

Permanent job

Teddy Kollek, Mayor of Jerusalem, kept seeing a man sitting on the roof of his house, looking up at the sky with binoculars. One day, he called out to him: 'What are you doing up there?'.
'Looking out for the Messiah,' came the reply.
'Why are you doing that?'
'I am being paid for it.'
'How much?'
'Not much. Just a few pence a day. . . .'
'That's pretty poor pay. . . .'
'I know. But at least the job is permanent!'

US petty cash slip

24 September – advert for typist	10 dollars
Violets for typist's desk	5.50 dollars
Week's salary for typist	120 dollars
Roses for typist	10 dollars
Candy for wife	75 cents
Lunch – typist and self	22.80 dollars
Typist's salary	190 dollars
Movies – wife and self	10 dollars
Theatre – typist and self	40 dollars
Candy for wife	75 cents
Lillian's salary	200 dollars
Theatre, dinner – Lillian and self	83 dollars
Doctor's bill – Lillian	780 dollars
Fur for wife (mink)	7,800 dollars
Advert for male typist	10 dollars

Connections

I recently complained to the manager of the Leicester branch of a major furniture retailers about the treatment of one of my constituents. I spoke to him by telephone; explained the circumstances and in particular that it was some six months since they collected a defective furniture suite from her, for replacement; and I asked him for immediate action.

The manager explained that he was having great trouble in getting delivery from the manufacturers and added: 'I am afraid, Mr Janner, that you don't know our trade. You are a very good MP, but if you had connections with the furniture business, then. . .'.

I stopped him and gently informed him that his company had been founded and owned by my grandfather and run by my uncles; that most of the major furniture retailers either were or had been directed by members of my family . . . and that I knew personally most of the members of his board.

The thud at the other end of the telephone was apparently caused by the man fainting.

Which goes to show that commercial ignorance on the part of an MP is only a rebuttable presumption.

Which leads us to. . . .

'The first part will drive everyone to drink – the second part
doubles the tax on liquor. . . .'

85 Politics and government

Recession

A deep sea diver feels tug on rope. Voice on intercom says: 'Come up quickly, the ship's sinking!'.

No confidence

Learie Constantine told how he was once walking down the steps of a pavilion on his way to bat when he heard the following telephone conversation:
'You want to speak to Learie Constantine? Oh, I'm sorry, he's just going into bat. Would you like to hold on?'

Chips with everything

A certain very disliked politician was once described as 'well balanced . . . he has a chip on each shoulder!'.

I object

A civil servant – one who has a valid objection to any possible solution.

Time

Captain of aircraft, about to land at Belfast Airport: 'The time locally is 16.00 hours. Kindly put your watches back 50 years. . .'.

Anger

My father told me never to argue with an angry man. . . . (*Nahum Goldmann*)

Sleep

MPs are people who talk in other people's sleep.

Corruption

Be especially careful not to bribe tax or factory inspectors or other public officials. 'Do not feed the hand that bites you. . . .'

Incipient modesty

Your first two weeks in Parliament, you wonder how you got there. Thereafter you wonder how the others got there.

So I said to myself: 'Self', I said. . . .

Time and tide

They believe in casting their bread on the waters – but only when the tide is coming in. (*Rt Hon. James Callaghan*)

Princely politics

It is very difficult to avoid making party political statements when you talk about almost anything. Sometimes, I fall into great elephant traps and no one notices. Other times, I trip into a very small trap – and all hell breaks loose. . . . (*Prince Charles*)

Self-fulfilling prophecy

Bernard Levin described Enoch Powell as being like the man who sets light to the seats in a cinema and then cries out: 'Fire!'.

The oldest profession?

Some say that gardening is the oldest profession – because Adam was the first man on earth. But the Bible tells us that before the world was created, all was chaos and confusion. And you all know who created that . . . politicians!

Presidents

What is the difference between a king and a president? A king is the son of his father.

Mania

Leonid Plyush told a group of MPs the sad story of his incarceration in Soviet mental institutions. When asked what diagnosis he had received from the Soviet psychiatric experts he replied: 'Reformist mania with messianic tendencies'. His listeners agreed that he would have made an excellent MP.

All change

Churchill once quarrelled with Lady Astor, the first woman MP.
'Nancy', said Winston, 'You are an ugly creature'.
'And you are drunk, Winston', she retorted.
'At least *my* condition will have changed by the morning', Churchill snapped back.

United Nations?

Former Secretary of State, Dean Acheson: 'When the United Nations is divided 50/50, then the decision does not represent "world conscience". But add Yemen, Haiti and Portugal and it becomes world conscience.'

Experience

Experience tells us that politicians do not *always* mean the opposite of what they say.

Lenin said. . . .

'War has devastating results', as Lenin said. And it would be true even had *he* not said it. . . . [*Translatable to, from or for anyone else. GJ*]

Sharing

A Soviet citizen who wished to join the Communist Party was interviewed by an official, who asked: 'If you are given two houses, what would you do?'.
He replied: 'Give one to the Party, comrade, and keep one for myself'.
'Now suppose that you are given two cars. What would you do?'
'Give one to the Party and keep one for myself.'

'Now suppose that you were given two shirts.'

'Oh, I'd keep both of them for myself.'

'Why would you give one of your houses and one of your cars to the Party and not one of your shirts?'

'You don't understand. I've already got two shirts.'

Equality?

Re: Israel and her Arab foes: 'They are many and we are one, but we represent 50 per cent of the conflict'. (*Yigal Allon*)

Gaol

Any eight-year-old child will tell you that a place from which you are forbidden to leave is a 'prison'. (*Tom Stoppard*)

Solution

Whenever the government thinks that it has solved the Irish question, the Irish change the question.

Tory advance

Conservative statesman: 'I see the *status quo* as the way forward. . .'

Ex

When you are a distinguished Ambassador, everyone wants you to make speeches and to be guest of honour. When you are an extinguished Ambassador, you have to look both for a platform and a livelihood. . . .

There is nothing so 'ex' as an ex-MP.

Dissidents

I was invited by the Prime Minister to an official lunch for Egyptian Vice-President Mubarak. Introducing me to the Guest of Honour, Mrs Thatcher said: 'Now, Greville Janner is one of my favourite dissidents. In the Soviet Union, of course, they lock up their dissidents. Here we invite them to lunch!'

Death wish

President Johnson attended the memorial service in Australia for a Prime Minister, recently drowned. He was asked by the press what he would do for peace. 'Anything', he replied.

'Mr President,' came a voice from the back. 'Would you take a swim?'

One all

For years, I had written to Ambassador Smirnowski, Head of the Russian delegation to the UK. My complaints about their treatment of Jews, dissidents, Baptists and other other minority groups were all ignored. Then, one day, he came to the Commons for tea, as guest of the Anglo-Soviet Parliamentary Group – of which I was and remain a member in good standing. The Chairman introduced us. I said: 'Your Excellency, I am very pleased to meet you. I did not believe that you really existed.'

'Why not?' he asked.

'How could I accept the existence of a person who fails to answer so many letters?'

Ambassador: 'Well, I am very pleased to meet you to. I did not believe that a man who wrote so many contentious letters could be so pleasant. . . .'

Democracy?

Ivor Richard, former British Ambassador to the UN, was asked by a southerner why the United Nations is so undemocratic.

'Undemocratic?' he replied. 'Why do you say that?'

'Because we keep getting out-voted!'

Opinions

A Russian Jew was asked whether he didn't have any mind of his own on political affairs. He replied: 'Yes, of course I do. I have my own opinions. But I don't agree with them.'

Russian elections

In the Soviet Union they have what are called 'Adam elections' – you have the same choice as he had.

Directions

A Cabinet Minister got lost, in a remote village. He lowered the window of his car and asked a passing villager: 'Where am I, please?'. The man replied: 'You are in your car, sir'.
'Thank you', replied the Cabinet Minister.
That reply is exactly like a Ministerial answer. It is brief; accurate; and adds nothing whatever to the sum total of human knowledge!

A man stopped his car in the village and asked the way to a local market town. The villager replied: 'If I were you, sir, I would not start from here. . .'.

Emigration

A Professor decided to emigrate. The Dean called him to his office: 'Why do you want to go?' he enquired. 'You have a very good job . . . an excellent home . . . splendid prospects. . .'.
'There are two reasons', the Professor replied. 'The first is that when I come home in the evenings, I usually find my neighbour outside my door, dead drunk. He keeps swearing at me: "Just wait till we get rid of this Tory government and then we'll slit the throats of all you useless academics!".'
'But the Tory government's in for years yet', replied the Dean.
'Precisely', said the Professor. 'That's my second reason.'

Rights

Here lies the body of William Jay
Who died defending his right of way
He was right – dead right – as he walked along
But he's just as dead as if he'd be wrong
(Epitaph on pedestrian's tombstone)

Patriotism

Kogan in Kiev applies for a visa for Israel. A few nights later, he hears loud banging on his door. He pulls the blankets over his head. The banging continues. Eventually, he calls out: 'Who is it?'.
'The postman.'
'Go away, please.'
The banging restarts. Eventually Kogan opens the door and five KGB men rush in, knocking him to the ground.

'Which is the best country in the world?', one of them asks, sitting on his head.

'The Soviet Union.'

'And where do children get the best education?', demands another, twisting his leg.

'The Soviet Union.'

A third twists his arm behind his back. 'Where is the best food, the best culture, the best of everything?'

'The Soviet Union.'

'In that case', enquires the man in charge, 'why do you want to leave for Israel?'.

'Because in Israel', said Kogan, 'the postman does not come at 2 o'clock in the morning'.

Divisions

Two lady tourists were standing in the central lobby in the House of Commons, when the division bell rang. 'What's that?' one of them asked the other. 'I don't know', she replied. 'I suppose one of them must have escaped. . . .'

Whipping

An MP complained that the 'whipping' had been so heavy that he could not even get out of the Commons to attend the christening of his son. His friend replied: 'You're lucky. You weren't there when your son was christened. I wasn't there when mine was conceived!'

Foreign Office

A tourist recently asked a policeman in Whitehall: 'Which side is the Foreign Office on?'. He replied: 'It's supposed to be on our side – but I sometimes wonder. . . .'.

On age

A distinguished US Senator was asked how he felt on his 80th birthday. 'Very well, thank you', he replied. 'Considering the alternative. . . .'

Freedom

It's a free country – you are entitled to be wrong!

Democracy

We cannot complain if a democracy exercises the rotatory principle and electors vote the wrong party into power. . . .

The right of citizens in a democracy is to make the wrong decision. That right is one which the British people have massively exercised.

Compromise

Compromise is when you do today that which you swore yesterday that you would not do – and while all politicians compromise, none of them like to be photographed doing so. . . .

Parliament

Parliamentary democracy is the worst form of government – until you look at all the others. (*Winston Churchill*)

Our parliamentary system is not good – but it's the best we've got. (*Winston Churchill*)

A communist economy

Why is the Soviet Union like an aeroplane in flight?
Because it's cold; it makes you feel slightly sick; and you cannot get out of it.

Illness – regretted

A Republican was elected for the first time in a Democratic stronghold. A few weeks later he fell ill and was hospitalised. The chairman of the local council visited him and addressed him thus:

Mr Jones,
Your colleagues and I were very sorry to learn of your illness. It was, indeed, my honour to propose a resolution at the last meeting of the Council and I have been asked to read it to you. It says: 'The Council conveys its greetings to Mr Jones; it expresses its regret at his illness and wishes him a speedy recovery'. I am happy to inform you that this resolution was passed by a majority of thirteen to twelve.

Death breeds hope

An MP died. Within a day, a young hopeful telephoned the national agent. 'I hope it's not too soon,' he said, 'but I'm wondering whether I might not take the place of the deceased . . .'

The national agent replied: 'Well, that's all right with me – provided the undertaker has no objection'.

Life after . . .

'The House of Lords? Life after death, my boy. . . .' (*Ex-cabinet Minister – now a Peer*)

Siberian parrot

A Russian dissident trained his parrot to say: Down with Brezhnev . . . Down with Marx . . . Down with Lenin. . . .

One day, the KGB called on the dissident. In panic, he shoved the parrot into his refrigerator.

The KGB men searched the house and eventually opened the refrigerator. The parrot emerged, shivering.

After an expectant pause, the parrot talked: 'I love Brezhnev . . . I love Marx . . . I love Lenin. . . .'

'Little bastard', snarled its master. 'After 5 minutes in Siberia, you join the Party. . . .'

Inflation

The Chancellor of the Exchequer is expecting to be immortalised by having his portrait, along with that of Her Majesty, on the first £1000 notes.

The Chancellor of the Exchequer went into a shop and said: 'I don't think inflation is that bad. Look at those handkerchieves – £1 each. And shirts for £10. And trousers for £15.'

His aide whispered quietly in his ear: 'I'm sorry, Minister. We're not in a man's shop. *This* is a laundry. . . .'

Open government

Sunlight is the most effective of all disinfectants. . . . (*US Supreme Court Justice Brandeis*)

Long distance?

When Kosygin died, he entered hell. He begged the devil to be allowed to keep in communication with friends on earth. 'Certainly', Satan replied. 'But you will need plenty of change for the telephone.'

'What do calls cost from here?'

'To the United States, 50 roubles; to South America, 40 roubles; to the United Kingdom, 50 roubles; to India, 55 roubles . . .' and so on, in a long list, ending with: 'and to the USSR, one rouble. . .'.

'Why is it so cheap to the USSR?'

'Because', replied Satan, 'it's only a local call. . .'.

Successors

After Mrs Thatcher took over from Mr Callaghan, she is reported to have said to him privately: 'You certainly left us a lot of problems'. Jim replied: 'I didn't ask you to take them on, did I?'.

Nothing succeeds like a successor.

EEC virtues

What we need are all the attributes of our colleagues in the Common Market. We should have the sovereignty of Luxembourg.. . . . the even temper of the Italians . . . the flexibility of the Dutch . . . the initiative of the Belgians . . . the good nature of the Germans . . . the reasonableness of the French . . . but we do have in any event the sheer hard work and culinary art of the British. . . .

No comment

Winston once tried unsuccessfully to get Lord Catto to make a statement on a particular issue. He got no results and complained: 'Alas – Lord Catto is lying doggo. . . .'

Committees

A Parliamentary committee is a cul-de-sac into which ideas are lured, there to be quietly strangled. . . .

If Moses had been a committee, then the Israelites would still be in Egypt.

A camel is a horse, invented by a committee.

Communist society

An East European was asked the following question by his eighteen-year-old son: 'Do you think that we already have 100 per cent Communism here, or is it going to get worse?'.

Who's the father?

Women in a Russian maternity ward were advised to call out the names of the child's father while in labour. When the pains came, the first woman yelled: 'Ivan, Ivan.' The second cried: 'Mikhail, Mikhail.' And the third – from a communal farm – cried: 'Comrades, comrades!'

Russian morale

A man phoned his friend in Moscow: 'How are you, Ivan?' he asked.

'Fantastic . . . marvellous . . . unbelievable . . . fabulous. . . .'

'OK', said his friend. 'I see you've got someone with you. I'll phone back later. . . .'

Withdraw, withdraw!

MP Willie Hamilton was criticising Harold Wilson for wanting to go into the Common Market . . . then out of the market . . . then into the market again. . . . He described such behaviour as: 'The politics of coitus interruptus.' The MP in front of him yelled: 'Withdraw . . . withdraw. . . .'.

Lobbying

As I was being wheeled on a trolley into the operating theatre at the Royal Free Hospital, the anaesthetist came up to me, green clad and masked, syringe in hand. He leaned forward and said: 'Mr Janner, I understand that you are a Member of Parliament.'

'Yes', I replied.

He paused, lifting his syringe: 'We anaesthetists', he said, ominously, 'are very badly paid!'.

'When my operation has been successfully performed', I replied, 'and I have recovered consciousness, do please come and discuss the matter with me!'

Plagues

I was recently at a charity dinner, with my wife on my right, and a very persistent lobbyist on my left. During the first three courses, he regaled me with horror stories of the way that politicians of all parties had ruined his business and how no country could really survive its treatment by those of us elected to office. Finally, my wife said to him: 'But surely you do make *some* distinction between the policies of the two parties?'.

'There's no difference between you', he retorted. 'I say: A plague on both your houses.'

My wife smiled across at him. 'When the plague comes to our house', she said, 'you must come and visit us!'.

Standard letters

I sometimes use standard letters for those of my constituents' queries which are identical. For instance, I at one time received a huge postbag, carefully organised and orchestrated by the League Against Cruel Sports. Letters flooded in from all over the country, asking me to support the Bill against hare coursing.

My assistants prepared a large pile of standard letters saying: 'Thank you for your letter. I have carefully considered your views and I appreciate your writing to me.' To each I added a note: 'I agree with you – I will do what I can'.

Unfortunately, I also received on the same day a letter from a gentleman of eccentric views, complaining about a television broadcast in which I had said that a person's background must be taken into account when considering the cause of his criminal tendencies – and in which I attacked the views of a judge who had declaimed to the contrary. The gentleman wrote: 'You are an idiot . . . you have no understanding of people . . . you and your kind are leading this country into decadent disaster. . . .'.

The man must have been somewhat surprised to receive a standard reply, sent off by an unthinking aide. It concluded: 'I agree with you – I will do what I can'.

Double crossing

I once travelled from Amman in Jordan to Damascus in Syria and back again in a day. I was somewhat surprised to find a large sign at the frontier: 'Double crossing only permitted for diplomats and for certain priests'. (*Rt Rev. Robert Runcie, Archbishop of Canterbury*)

Listen

God gave man two ears and one mouth so that he may listen twice as much as he speaks! (*King Faisal*)

Open secrets

A Russian spy came to Wales and was told to see their contact in Abergavenny, who lived at 25 Cwmbran Terrace. The password: 'The space ship is in orbit'.

By mistake, he called at number 5 Cwmbran Terrace. A woman opened the door. 'Yes?' she enquired.

'The space ship is in orbit', said the Russian.

'Oh', said the lady, 'you've come to the wrong address. You will be wanting number 25. That's where Dai the spy lives.'

Is there life on Mars?

Yugoslavia is full of delegations. Like Rumanians, Yugoslavs remain terrified by the memory of Chamberlain's infamous description of Czechoslovakia: 'That small, distant country, of which we know so little. . . .' So they welcome guests and their country is almost overrun by delegations, from East and West.

Three scientists were recently discussing whether or not there is life on Mars. The American said: 'We think, on the whole, that there probably is some form of primitive life on the planet. . .'. The Russian said: 'We are far more sceptical. On the whole, we think that there is probably no form of life, however primitive, on the red planet'. The Yugoslavs said: '*We* are absolutely *certain* that there is no life on Mars – otherwise we would certainly have had delegations from there by now'.

Good relations

A son asked his father whether in the 25 years of his marriage he had never thought of divorcing his mother. 'Never', said Dad.

'Never, ever?'

'No. I have never thought of divorcing her. Of course, there were many times when I wanted to murder her!' (*Jack Jones* – explaining the relationship between the TUC and the Labour Party)

Civic slip

I have to address a lot of these conferences. Indeed, last week somebody said: 'Would you please address a meeting of 150 cooperative women'. (*Mayor of Harrogate* addressing conference opening session)

Conferences

I suffer from a disease called conference syncopation – making irregular movements from bar to bar. . . . (*Bill Simpson*)

Misunderstanding

An Irishman answered an advertisement, offering £1,500 for a man prepared to sleep with a gorilla. He telephoned to ask whether he could have time to pay.

O'Reilly is refused a room

O'Reilly is refused a room at a famous hotel. 'I'm sorry, sir, we are full up', said the head receptionist.

'If Prince Philip were to come here', said O'Reilly, 'you'd find a room for him, wouldn't you?'.

'I suppose we would', said the receptionist.

'Well, I've got news for you', O'Reilly retorted. 'He isn't coming. So I'll have his room.'

Drink fast

Like a Scottish wedding reception – plenty for everyone, but you have to be quick. . . .

Procrastination

A visitor to Ireland once asked a Professor: 'What is the Gaelic for "mañana"?'. The Professor replied: 'I regret that we do not have in the Irish language any word which conveys that same sense of urgency!'

Power

Power is wonderful, absolute power is absolutely wonderful.

A capital story

'Where is the capital of Saudi Arabia?'
Answer: 'A third in Switzerland; a third in London;_ and the rest in Germany and the USA'. [*We should be so lucky!* *GJ*]

Airlines

The Lufthansa pilot is reputed to have said: 'You will enjoy yourselves aboard this Lufthansa flight. . . . Zat is an order!'

The following message was allegedly put out by a certain Eastern airline: 'Ladies and gentlemen, we are now flying at an altitude of 27,000 feet. If you look over to your right – that is the starboard side – you will see that we are above the Indian Ocean. If you look carefully, you will note a tiny, yellow speck. That is a life raft. In it there are four people. They are your crew. This message is recorded. . . .'

Training

Two strangers occupied the upper and lower bunks in a sleeper compartment of a long-distance train. They wished each other good night and the man on the lower bunk was just about to drift away when he heard a voice from above him: 'Oy! Am I thirsty! Am I thirsty! Am I thirsty!' Then, after a long pause, it started again: 'Oy! Am I thirsty! Am I thirsty! Am I thirsty! Am I thirsty!'

Exasperated, the man below clambered out of his bunk; fetched a glass of water from the side and handed it up to his travelling companion who thanked him, most profusely. 'God bless you! And good night!', he said.

Five minutes later, just as he was about to sleep, the man in the bunk below heard a voice from above him, moaning out: 'Oy! Was I thirsty! Was I thirsty! Was I thirsty!'

Wrongdoing

When visiting Egypt, one of our guides explained his *modus operandi*. 'If you have to do wrong', he said, 'you must know the right way to do it'.

Discretion

If I know something you do not know, then you know that I cannot tell you; and if I do not know anything that you do not know, you will not want to hear me anyway!

Offensive person

A well known politician is reputed to have met a renowned and unpleasant lady on a dark night in a back street. The following morning he was charged with having an offensive person on his weapon.

Hell

Stalin died and went below. Shortly thereafter, St Peter answered a knock on the door. He found the devil outside, seeking political asylum.

Eggs and baskets

British aircraft manufacturers once suggested to Winston Churchill that he, the Cabinet and 40 other MPs should go up in the newly invented Comet, so as to give confidence to the public. But one of his ministers complained that if anything happened to the aircraft, it would be disastrous. The country would be plunged into over 60 by-elections at the same time.

Reluctantly, the old man agreed. 'It all goes to show', he said, 'that it is potentially disastrous to put all your baskets into one egg. . .'.

Brainwashing

Chief Rabbi Rosen of Rumania tells of his first visit to America. On landing, he was surrounded by press men who asked him some very abrupt and even rude questions. For instance: 'Rabbi, are you not brainwashed in your country?'. He replied: 'Yes, I suppose we are. But then so are you, in a different way. The difference between us and you, though, is that *we* do not believe what *we* read in the newspapers and you do.'

One of the problems of their suspended disbelief is that even when Rumanian newspapers or radio are telling the truth while other people's are lying, Rumanians are so suspicious that they still prefer to believe other people's lies.

Civilisation

Ghandi was asked: 'What do you think of Western civilisation?'. He replied: 'I think it would be a very good idea'.

Never satisfied

The host asked his house-guest: 'Will you have coffee after dinner?'.
'No thank you. Just brandy.'
'Will you have cocoa before you retire?'
'No thank you. Just tea.'
'Will you have tea for breakfast?'
'No thank you – coffee.'
'Would you like boiled eggs or scrambled eggs?'
'One of each, please.'
After breakfast, the host asked his guest: 'How were your eggs?'.
'Not good.'
'Why?'
'You boiled the wrong one!'

Quangos

A quango is like a septic tank – the thick chunks rise to the top. But as the Health and Safety Commission is approved of by both the Labour and Conservative Governments, it will doubtless remain – thus proving the truth of the old saying: 'It takes two to quango'. (*Bill Simpson*)

On distinction

To appear really distinguished, you need grey hair, a wide girth and piles. The grey hair gives you an appearance of wisdom; the girth an appearance of prosperity; and the piles a look of anxiety that can quite easily be mistaken for true concern.

Nobility – and precedence

When the late Aga Khan was due to be guest at a luncheon in the House of Lords, the host wrote to the Garter King of Arms on the question of precedence. After a long wait, he received the following reply: 'The Aga Khan is believed to be a direct descendent of God. English Dukes take precedence. . . .'

When President Nixon told the truth

An opponent said: 'How do you know when ex-President Nixon is lying? When he spreads his hands out, he's telling the truth. . . . When he wags his finger, he's telling the truth. . . . When he shakes his fist, he's telling the truth. . . . But when he opens his mouth. . . .'

Mind your language

A Canadian MP once replied to a suggestion that their proceedings ought to be held from time to time in French by saying: 'If the English language was good enough for Matthew, Mark, Luke and John, it is good enough for us!'

Oil wealth

It's not clever just to have oil, you know. Sardines have oil and they are really stupid. They even get inside the tin and leave the key on the outside. (*Bob Monkhouse*)

Top insult

Bernard Shaw sent Winston Churchill two tickets for the first night of 'St. Joan' – 'one for yourself – the other for a friend – if you have one'.

Churchill wrote back, returning the tickets and regretting that he could not come to the first night. 'But I would like tickets for the second night', he said. 'If there is one. . . .'

Person unknown

A Tory Whip telephoned one of his Members in the middle of the night, to tell him to come in to vote. A woman's voice answered the phone – but he heard a male voice in the background saying: 'Tell him I'm not here. . .'.

'I'm afraid Mr . . . is not here,' said the voice.

Quick as a flash, the Whip replied: 'In that case, please tell the man who is in bed with you, whomever he may be, that he is required at the House of Commons to vote. . .'.

Withdraw

The late Will Paling, MP, once called Churchill 'a dirty dog'. The

Tory benches erupted with cries of: 'Withdraw, withdraw. . . .'
The old man rose to his feet. 'Not at all', he said. 'I do not invite the
Honourable Member to withdraw. On the contrary, I invite him to
repeat what he has said outside this Chamber. And I will then show
him what a dirty dog does to a paling!'

Opposition

To be in Opposition is no disgrace. In fact, it is an honour. But it is
the only honour which politicians do not actively seek! (*Abba Eban*)

Russia

Brezhnev once asked Kosygin: 'How many Jews are there in the
Soviet Union?'. 'About 3 million', Kosygin replies. 'Then tell me: if
we opened the doors and allowed as many Jews to leave as wanted to
go, how many would emigrate?'.
After a moment's thought, Kosygin replied: 'I'd say about 15
million!'.

Heavenly clocks

At the time of the general election in Australia, the following
unkind story was unhappily current (*and may, of course, be amended
for any politicians, local or national, of your choice!*) It was told of
Malcolm Fraser (retiring Prime Minister); Bill Haydon (Leader of the
Opposition); and Donald Chipp (Leader of their equivalent of the
Liberal Party): An Australian died and was transported to the gates
of Heaven, where he found St Peter in a room full of clocks. 'What are
these for?' he asked.
'Oh, these are kept for all politicians', St Peter replied, and took out
his key and wound up a large grandfather clock on the wall. 'This one
is for Malcolm Fraser. Watch', he commanded. Suddenly, the hands
of the clock moved forward twelve hours. 'That happens', said St
Peter, whenever the owner of the clock makes a false promise or tells
an untruth'.
The new arrival pointed at a small carriage clock on the mantel-
piece nearby. 'Whose is that?', he asked.
'Donald Chipp's', replied St Peter, as its hands started leaping
forward.
'Have you got one for Bill Haydon?'
'Of course', said St Peter. 'I keep it on my desk. I use it instead of a
fan!' [*Note: I heard this story told by supporters of each party, with the*

'fan' or sometimes the *'ventilator'* clock given in each case to the most disliked leader. GJ]

Recession, depression – and recovery

A recession is when your neighbour is out of work; a depression is when you are out of work; recovery is when the government is out of work. . . .

Apartheid

During the Second World War, the United States Fleet paid a courtesy call in Johannesburg. A society lady who was running a big dance one night asked the American authorities to send half a dozen of his boys along. Six big black men duly arrived.

'I'm terrible sorry', said the hostess, 'but I'm afraid that there must be some mistake'. 'No ma'am', replied the leader of the party. 'Major Rabinowitz never makes mistakes!'

Family tradition

Franklin D. Roosevelt was asked why he was a Democrat. He replied: 'Because my great grandfather and my grandfather and my father were Democrats before me'.

'What would happen if your great grandfather, your grandfather and your father had been horse thieves?', retorted the questioner.

'In that case', President Roosevelt replied, 'I would have been a Republican'.

One nation

Some Americans say that Yankees from the North are like haemorrhoids. If they come down and then go up again quickly, that's not too bad. But if they come down and stay down, that is a pain in the rear. . . .

Deténte

A Soviet dignitary boasted to an American acquaintance that they had found a new way to make a lion share a cage with a lamb. 'If you don't believe me', he said, 'then when you come to the USSR we will show you. . .'.

True enough, on his next visit the American was taken to Moscow

Zoo and there in a cage was a lion lying in one corner and a lamb in another.

'That's wonderful', said the American. 'You must have a very remarkable lion and a very wonderful lamb. . . .'

'The lion is a good one', replied the Russian. 'But we have a new lamb every morning.'

Misunderstanding

When Dai was first elected to the Council, he voted against the installation of urinals in the High Street.

'Why did you vote against that?' asked his friend, Morgan.

'Well, to be honest', said Dai, 'I don't know the meaning of the word. And I never vote in favour of anything I don't understand.'

Morgan explained the meaning. And Dai leapt to his feet.

'Mr Mayor', he said, 'I know that you cannot reopen the voting just for me. But I would not like it to be recorded that I am against having urinals in the High Street. As a matter of fact, I am also in favour of installing arsenals.'

New Councillor

Dai Jones is elected a Councillor for the first time. Delighted, he goes to the pub to celebrate.

'Your usual Dai?' asks the barman.

'*Councillor* Dai, if you please', Dai retorted.

When he went to collect his coat in the cloakroom, the attendant said: 'Good evening, Dai'.

He replied: '*Councillor* Dai, if you please.'

On the bus, the conductor said: 'Nice to see you, Dai'.

'*Councillor* Dai, if you please', he replied.

And so it went on with everyone he met. And when he got home, he heard his wife's voice from upstairs: 'Is that you, Dai?'

'*Councillor* Dai, if you please', he replied.

'Then you'd better hurry up', his wife called out. 'Dai will be home at any moment!'

Never resign

Frederick the Great intended to dismiss one of his generals. The General wrote to him: 'After the battle, my head is yours. Meanwhile, I intend to use it to best effect on your behalf.'

Why we lost

If you are travelling in a rocky ship and feel seasick, it is quite understandable that you would wish to throw the navigator overboard. (*Dennis Healey*)

Idealism

Yes, India is a country with great ideals – but it is peopled entirely by human beings. (*Mrs Indira Ghandi*) [*Or the UK – or anywhere else! GJ*]

Advice to successor

When Harold Wilson handed over the premiership to James Callaghan, he is said to have left three envelopes in a drawer. They were to be opened in turn, in times of disaster.

Opening the first envelope, after the first disaster, Callaghan read: 'Blame your predecessor'.

After the second, he read: 'Sack your assistant'.

After the third: 'Prepare three envelopes. . .'.

Majority power

If the Arab nations saw fit to declare that the earth is flat, they would get 72 votes at the United Nations – a majority would gladly state that fact to be true. What matters, though, is that they should not believe that the result is accurate. (*Abba Eban*)

Peerless

Jack was made a Peer. His wife said to him: 'What does that make me?'.

Her husband replied: 'The same damn fool that you've always been'.

'Perhaps learned counsel would like to re-phrase that question. . . ?'

86 Law

Transitional period

The Irish government was considering switching its vehicles to driving on the right hand side of the road. Anxious about a transitional changeover period, they decided to effect the alteration 'by stages . . . starting with heavy goods vehicles'.

The rule of law

This country is planted thick with laws from coast to coast. If you cut them down – and you're just the man to do it – do you really think you could stand upright in the wind that would blow then? (*Robert Bolt* – from 'A Man for All Seasons')

Modesty

So I asked myself the question . . . we lawyers frequently ask ourselves questions because in that way we know that we will get prompt and intelligent answers . . . (*Lord Denning*)

Cunning

A teacher in a local school required his class to write an essay on the police. Martin wrote: 'The police is bastards'.

The teacher told the police of the comment. They invited Martin to the station and give him the day of his life. The next day the teacher set the boys another essay on the police. Martin wrote: 'The police is cunning bastards!'.

Speed

An American criminal complained that in New York you are liable to get mugged between the time that you rob the bank and the time that you reach the get-away car.

Case law

'If there was ever a clearer case than this of persons acting in concert, this case is that case. . . .'

Change

A lawyer was interviewed on his hundredth birthday. Journalist: 'I suppose that you have seen many changes in your time?'.
Lawyer: 'Yes – and I have been against them all'.

Forgiving

An old Cockney usher ,used to take visitors to the Lord Chief Justice's Court when Lord Goddard presided: 'Lord Goddard', he would say, 'is famous as a forgiving judge. Very forgiving. For giving five years . . . ten years . . . life. . . .'

Chancery

The court of a well known Chancery judge, now retired (and nameless) became known at the Bar as the 'din of inequity'.

Misunderstanding

As Justice James Cassells was swearing in a jury, one of the jurymen asked to be excused.
'What is your reason?', asked the Judge.
'My wife is about to conceive', he replied.
'I don't think that is what you mean', replied the Judge. 'I think that what you mean is that your wife is about to be confined. But whether you are right or I am right, I agree that you ought to be there. . . .' (*Lord Elwyn Jones*)

Policeman giving evidence of arrest: 'So I cautioned the man and asked him if he could explain his presence, in the early hours of the morning, carrying what appeared to be a house-breaking implement. He made a lengthy reply in a language which I subsequently discovered to be Greek. I told him that I was not satisfied with his explanation and I duly arrested him.'

Good company

Lawyer to judge, well known for his puritanical views and as a pillar of the Church: 'I appear for the plaintiffs – a God-fearing, limited liability company'.

Evolution

In law each of us must look after his 'neighbour' – or, as it is sometimes put, each of us is his brother's keeper. Which reminds me of the monkey in the zoo, discussing the principles of evolution and asking: 'Am I my keeper's brother?'.

[*There is also the ancient shaggy fish story in which a herring was seen without his good friend the whale, whom he always accompanied. When asked by a crab: 'Where is your friend?', he replied: 'I don't know. Am I my blubber's kipper?' GJ*]

Tact

A company official was in the witness box, giving his opinion. 'Do you consider yourself an expert?' asked the cross-examining lawyer.

'Well, no', said the man modestly. 'But I am something of a judge.'

'What is the difference between an expert and a judge?' asked the lawyer.

'An expert sometimes makes mistakes', replied the official. 'A judge – never!'

Written evidence

A man appeared in a lawyer's office: 'I have come to you because God has told me you are the best lawyer in the country.'

The lawyer replied: 'If that happens again, please get it in writing'.

Respected professionals

A foreigner was being shown around Westminster Abbey. His guide pointed to a splendid monument: 'There lies a great and honest man and a most distinguished lawyer', he said.

'That's interesting', the foreigner replied. 'I never knew that in England you buried two men in the same grave!'

Professional courtesies

A lawyer, a priest and a tailor were stranded on a desert island in a shark-infested sea. Eventually, they drew lots to see who should try to swim to the mainland to get help. The lawyer lost; stripped; and plunged into the sea. Within minutes, sharks' fins gathered around him – and moved into formation, on both sides and to the rear.

'There', said the priest, palms pressed against each other, 'my prayers have been answered!'.

'Not at all', said the tailor. 'Mere professional courtesy. . . .'

Split personality

In addressing Sir Gerald Dodson, Common Sergeant of London, at the Old Bailey, counsel apologised for his client's behaviour, saying that he was really two personalities. At home he was sweet, kind and gentle. At work he was a rogue.

'I sentence *both of you* to two years' imprisonment', said the Judge to the prisoner.

Psalms

Counsel quoted the beginning of a psalm, when addressing Sir Gerald Dodson. The Judge then said: 'I recognise the quotation which has been used by your learned counsel, and I regret that he did not quote to you the rest of this psalm, which reads, I think, "As the winds that blow shall ye be swept away". I hereby sweep you away for two years!'

Taking instructions

Judge: 'Does your client think that I am an absolute fool?'.

Counsel: 'Will your Lordship kindly give me just a moment to take instructions?'.

On bias

A well known and particularly unpleasant judge once said after a trial: 'During the whole case, the accused only spoke the truth twice – once when he called the prosecuting counsel a proper bastard – and second, when he said that the judge was biased. . . .'

Frame up

'I know I've not got much of a case', said the client. 'But I've decided how to win it. I'm going to send the judge a crate of champagne.'

'You do that', said the solicitor, 'and you are absolutely certain to lose.'

The case went forward – and to everyone's astonishment, the client won.

'It's just as well that you didn't send the judge that drink', said the lawyer.

'Of course I did,' retorted the client. 'But I put the other man's name on it!'

Guilty?

Magistrate: 'Are you guilty or not guilty?'
Accused: 'If you don't know, why should I tell you?'.

Theft

By unkind tradition, Rumanians are skilled thieves. The following stories are reputed examples:

Railway tracks in Rumania zig-zag, so that the driver can keep an eye on the last coach. . . .

A Rumanian cookery book began: 'First: steal a chicken. . . .'

Two Rumanians met in a spa. One said to the other: 'What are you doing? Taking the waters?'

The other replied: 'No, only the towels'.

Where is it?

A police officer testified that he had observed the accused urinating against a wall. He then left the witness box.

After consultation with her colleagues, the Chairman of the Bench recalled the policeman to the box and asked: 'Officer, just one more question, please. Where is the nearest toilet?'

'Straight out the door behind you, Madam', he said, 'and along the corridor. It's the second door on the left.'

Costs

Two partners fell out and sued each other. Their lawyers tried to settle the disputes, but failed. Eventually, the case reached court.

Outside the courtroom, Morgan said to his Counsel: 'Look, Dai and I used to be very good friends. We were in happy partnership for years. Perhaps we can have a chat and see if we can settle our differences on our own?'

The lawyer replied: 'Why not? But I must warn you. The amount in dispute between you is now less than the legal costs. So even if you settle your dispute, you've got to decide whose going to pay the costs.'

Morgan went to Dai and the two of them disappeared. Half an hour later they returned, beaming.

'Have you settled the case?'

'We have', replied the partners, in unison.

'Well, who's going to pay the costs, then?'

'Oh, that was easy', said Dai. 'We solved the problem. He'll not pay his and I'll not pay mine!' (*Judge Bernard Gillis*)

Trials

At the 1981 Sheep Dog Trials, how many were found guilty?

The law's saddest stories

A Mr Devillez once sued Boots, the chemists, for damages, after he had suffered personal injury caused by their corn solvent. It appears that one night he was in his bathroom, dressed in his birthday suit, with wet hands. The bottle of solvent slipped; the liquid fell against a projection – and it dissolved, thereby greatly reducing his pleasures and recreation. He claimed damages.

Boots protested. 'But we've sold millions of bottles, and it's never happened before!'

'How do you know?' chided the judge, gently.

'Anyway, my lord', counsel for Boots continued, 'what would you have had my client do – put a sign on the bottle saying: "Do not use on your John Thomas"?'

The judge nodded. 'The bottle ought to have had an appropriate warning', he ruled.

Telling this story in Wales, it was capped by the tale of Gwyneth, the village gossip. Bridget approached her one day and said:

'Gwyneth, you have been going around saying that my husband has a corn on his John Thomas!'.
Gwyneth replied: 'Certainly not. I didn't say that. I just said that it *felt* as if he had a corn on his John Thomas!'

Judge's functions

Lord Asquith was discussing the functions of the various branches of the judiciary. He said: 'It is the function of the judge in the Queen's Bench Division to be quick, courteous and wrong. But it must not be supposed that it is the function of the Court of Appeal to be slow, crapulous and wrong – for that would be to usurp the function of the House of Lords.'

Conviction

A famous hanging Judge, Mr Justice Avory, was discussing with Mr Justice Travers Humphreys the unhappy way in which the courts were being conducted by their junior colleagues.
Avory: 'Any of these young members of the Queen's Bench Division can secure the conviction of a guilty man. But it takes an old hand like you or me to make sure that the innocent do not escape!'

Lawyers

It is untrue that lawyers do nothing. They just get together and decide that nothing can be done.

St Peter and Satan had an argument. Satan suggested that they should each consult a lawyer.
'I'm not surprised that you made that suggestion', said St. Peter. 'Lawyers, after all, are so much more accessible to you. . . .'

Alleged motto of the Law Society: The man who is his own lawyer has a fool for a client.

Tradition

It is a long established tradition . . . as Lord Denning would say when he has a new idea. . . .

Brevity

Judge to accused: 'Have you anything to say before I pass

sentence?'.

Accused: 'Yes, guv – for gawd sake keep it short!'.

Punishment for the crime

A man was convicted of a peculiarly unpleasant offence with a dog. The magistrate ranted at him: 'I cannot think of any punishment worthy of this horrible crime. . .'.

A voice from the rear of the court cried out: 'Give him the cat!'.

Unwise counsel

Counsel: 'I hope that you are following me. . .'.
Judge: 'Yes – but where are you going?'.

Counsel pleading with judge to award heavy damages to client with broken jaw: 'Never again will my client be able to bite her bottom with her top teeth. . .'.

Counsel apologises for the length of his speech.
Judge: 'Don't worry – you shortened the winter for us. . .'.

Evidence

Lawyer defending client on charge of causing grievous bodily harm: 'It is our case, my Lord, that there is no evidence that any such affray took place. If it did, we shall prove that my client was not there. If he was there, there is no evidence that he took part in the affray. And in any case, the other man hit him first.'

Justice

A businessman had to leave court before the end of the long, hard-fought trial. He left word for a telegram to be sent to him, to inform him of the result.

At the end of the case, the lawyer sent a telegram as arranged: 'Justice has been done', it read.

The client immediately sent a reply: 'Appeal at once'.

Ducking the question

Lawyer to witness: 'Did you get the letter?'.
Witness (*contemplating whether he should answer Yes or No – and*

after a long pause) 'Not necessarily'.

Contracts

It was a curious contract. The first clause forbids you to read any of the others.

Juries

Welsh juries are against crime – but they are not too dogmatic about it. (*Lord Elwyn Jones*)

A Scottish jury was informed by the judge: 'This is a simple case and no doubt it will not take you long to reach your verdict'.
After jury had been out for three hours, the judge called them in. 'What's happened?', he enquired.
'We had no difficulty in reaching our verdict', he was told. 'But the trouble is trying to elect a foreman. . . .'

The truth

There are three stories in any law suit: the plaintiff's; the defendant's; and the truth.

Oh, hell!

A businessman arrived at the pearly gates and was cross-examined by St Peter. He demanded his basic civil right – to be represented by a lawyer.
'Sorry', said St Peter. 'We haven't any up here.'

Leading counsel

Litigant arrives at court to find that whilst he is represented by junior counsel only, his opponent has both a junior and a leader. He tugs the gown of his advocate: 'How are you going to manage?', he said. 'The other side have a QC and a junior. . . .'
'I'm as good as any two of them', replied the junior.
A few minutes later, the client again tugged at the barrister's gown. 'I'm worried', he said. 'I've noticed that when the QC is talking, the barrister behind him is thinking. But when you are talking, no one is thinking!'

Companies

Lord Thurloe once said: 'A corporation has no body to be burned and no soul to be damned. . .'.

Chinese praise

A Chinese man in the witness box in a stamp theft case was praised by the judge. He replied: 'Philately will get you everywhere. . .'.

Wills

Lecturer: 'When you are constructing a will, try to put yourself in the position of the man who made the will. Try to look at the documents through the testicles of the spectator. . . .'

Justice?

When I was a puisne judge – sitting on my own, in my own court – I could be sure that justice would be done in that court. But now I sit in the Court of Appeal with two brother judges, the odds *against* justice being done in my court are 2 to 1! (*Lord Denning*)

Interviewed on his 81st birthday, Lord Denning was asked whether it was not correct that he bent the law, in order to do justice. He replied: 'Certainly not. I just develop it. . .'.

Perjury

Counsel, cross-examining a man who alleges his arm and shoulder were hurt in an accident: 'Show me how high you can raise your arm, please. . . .' The witness raises his arm a few inches, clearly with great effort and difficulty.
'Now show me how high you could raise it, *before* the accident. . . .'
The arm goes high into the air.
[*This tale is, of course, best told with the appropriate demonstration. GJ*]

Guilt

A man appeared in a Magistrates Court. Magistrate: 'Did you steal these goods?'.
'Yes.'

'Did you take them home?'
'Yes.'
'Did you then sell the goods?'
'Yes.'
'Do you want to say anything to me?'
'Yes. I want a lawyer.'
'What is the point in getting a lawyer when you are so obviously guilty on your own admission?'
'Well, I'm just dying to find out what he'd find to say for me!'

Leave law to the lawyers

There were too many cart drivers in a Russian village, so the municipality decided to issue licences. But each prospective applicant had to pass an examination.

Ivan came for his examination and was asked: 'Suppose that your cart stuck in deep mud, what would you do?'

'I'd lash my whip over my horse's head and I'd cry out: "giddy-up".'

'And if that didn't work?'

'Then I'd get out of the cart and down into the mud and I'd put my shoulder to the back of the cart and I'd push with all my might and I'd at the same time lash my whip above the horse's head and shout "giddy-up".'

'And if that was no good?'

'Then I'd get the passengers out of my cart and they'd have to come down in the mud and push along with me and I'd lash my whip above the horse's head and shout "giddy-up".'

'I'm sorry', said the examiner, 'but you've failed'.

'Why?'

'Because a good cart driver never enters the mud.'

And that explains why you should let your lawyers get on with their job . . . and why you should not enter into matters that come within the expertise of others.

Cross-examination

Fred, the policeman, gives evidence of having observed disgusting behaviour by a courting couple in car. They deny it, maintaining that had he been in a position to observe, they would have heard him coming.

Counsel: 'Was it not a gravel path? What size shoes do you take? Was it not in the silence of the night? I put it to you that had you been

near to that car, they would have heard the tramp of your feet. . . .'
Constable: 'No sir'.
Counsel: 'You say that they would not have heard the tramp of your feet? Why do you say that?'
Constable: 'I was riding my bicycle'.
[*This sort of horror explains why young lawyers are enjoined 'Never ask a question in cross-examination unless you know the answer'. Theoretically, splendid advice. . . . GJ*]

Fellow feeling

A burglar was caught in the garden of a millionaire's mansion, a transistor radio in his pocket.
'What do you want us to do with him?', asked the police.
'Let him go', answered the millionaire. 'We all started small.'

Socialist lawyers

The expression 'socialist lawyer' is a contradiction in terms – like 'military intelligence'. (*Michael Foot*)

Single-handed

Did you hear about the man who asked for a one-armed lawyer? When asked why, he replied: 'I'm sick of being told: "On the one hand this – and on the other hand that".'

International law

Famous Professor, Hersch Lauterpacht, used to say: 'International law is not much good. It creates laws which the wicked do not obey and the righteous do not need.'

Whisky and water

Former Lord Chief Justice, Lord Goddard, was asked what was the difference between whisky and water. He replied: 'If you make the former in private, that is a felony; if you make the latter in public, that is a misdemeanour'. [*Happily, the distinction between felonies and misdemeanours has now been abolished: GJ*]

No charge

PC: 'You are under arrest, sir. I am taking you to the police station where you will have to stay the night.'

'And what's the charge, officer?'

'No charge, sir. All part of the service.'

'When I give my speech tonight, I want everyone *to pay attention. . . .*'

87 Love, sex, marriage and family

Fatherly boast

I have never raised a hand to my son – except in self-defence. (*Lord Janner*)

On stupidity

O'Reilly came home and found his wife in bed with another man. 'What the hell do you two think you are doing?', he asked. The wife turned to the other man. 'There you are', she said. 'I told you he was stupid!'

Problems

Churchill once remarked that there is nothing more difficult than holding up a wall leaning towards you except kissing a girl leaning away from you.

Company

A man is known by the company which he thinks no one knows he is keeping.

Three speech

A woman sued for divorce, claiming that her husband had only spoken to her three times in the course of their marriage. She applied for custody of the three children.

Army legitimates

Four men were talking in a train. The first said: 'I am a brigadier; I am married; I have three sons; and they are all barristers'.

The next said: 'I am a brigadier; I am married; I have three sons and they are all solicitors'.

The third said: 'I am a brigadier; I am married; I have three sons; they are all chartered accountants'.

The fourth was silent. 'Well, aren't you going to tell us about yourself?', asked the first brigadier.

'Very well', he replied. 'I am a sergeant major. I am not married. I have three sons. They are all brigadiers.'

In love

A well known peer married at a comparatively advanced age. His wife is an attractive Mediterranean lady. When the noble lord fell ill, his wife replied to a telephone enquiry as follows: 'He is much better, but he is still under heavy seduction'.

Romance

Fall in love with yourself and you are in for a lifetime of romance. (*Oscar Wilde*)

Love

My first wife liked to talk to me while she was making love. She used to phone me from a motel room. . . . Got me so used to it that she would use me to time a boiled egg. It was always soft boiled. . . . (*Bob Monkhouse*)

Excuses

Dai and Gwyneth were about to celebrate their Silver Wedding. 'What shall we do?', Dai asked. 'Shall we go on a little cruise? Or take a package tour to the Canary Islands? Whatever you like. . . .'

She replied: 'No, Dai. Let's just relive some of our youth. Let's go to places we visited when we were courting – like Petticoat Lane and the zoo, and taking a boat on Regent's Park lake.'

So they did. They started with the market; went on to the boating lake; and then visited the zoo.

In the monkey house, the happy couple explained the importance of their visit and the keeper invited them to enter the gorilla's cage, one at a time. Gwyneth went first, while Dai stood outside the bars.

Suddenly, the gorilla attacked Gwyneth and threw her to the ground, tearing up her dress. 'Help, help', she shouted. 'Dai, what shall I do?'

Dai replied: 'Why don't you just tell him you've got one of your headaches, dear?'.

Love and money

'If I lost all my money, darling, would you still love me?'
'Of course I would, darling. But I'd miss you. . . .'

Curses

Dealer shows woman a magnificent diamond. 'This, madam, is the Plotnik diamond. Is it not beautiful? It is one of the largest in the world and is very valuable. But there is a curse which goes with the Plotnik diamond. . . .'
Customer: 'What curse is that?'
Dealer: 'Mr Plotnik!'

Life's purpose

Confucius says: 'I am asked why I buy rice and flowers? I reply: I buy rice to live and flowers so that I have something to live for.'

Uncertain future?

A sex questionnaire to college students included: 'Are you a virgin?'.
One girl replied: 'Not yet'.

Marriages

A parson had two ties – a black one for funerals and a white one for weddings. One day, he arrived at a wedding wearing a black tie.
'Why are you wearing a black tie, Parson?', he was asked. 'That's the wrong one. . . .'
'Have you seen the bride?', he replied.

Invitations

Wife, going through list of possible invitees: 'Eadie Brown? No, we'll not ask her. Eleanor and Martin Green? No. Arthur Harris – he won't be able to come. Splendid – let's invite him.'

Secretaries

Sign on noticeboard of large insurance company: 'Managers are asked to take advantage of their secretaries as early in the day as possible!'

Wives

Behind every successful man stands an amazed woman.

Window cleaner

Raquel Welch once went on a brass-rubbing tour of the Gorbals. She was in bed one morning when she saw a window cleaner outside her room. She lifted back the covers and showed him one shoulder. He kept on working. She removed her nightdress and showed him her better points. He still kept on working. So she jumped on to the bed as God made her. The window cleaner opened the window; looked in; and said: 'Madam – have you never seen a window cleaner before?'.

Adultery?

Witness: 'I have never committed adultery with anyone other than my husband'.

Naked truth

Man comes home and finds wife, lying naked on the bed. 'Why aren't you wearing anything?', he asks.

'I keep telling you', she replies. 'I haven't anything to wear. . . .'

He marches over to the cupboard, throws open the door and then says: 'Hello, Persian Lamb . . . , Hello, Ocelot . . . , Hello, Mink . . . , Oh, hello Sam . . . ! Hello, Persian Lamb . . . , Hello, Coney. . .'.

Suicidal

Daughter phones from America. 'I'm happy to tell you that I have fallen in love.' 'Congratulations', says father. 'Who is he?'

'Well, he's got frizzy hair – but he's very nice.'

'A black?'

'Yes. He's a Catholic. Rather badly disabled, I'm afraid. Only one eye. But you scarcely notice his speech impediment or his hunchback.'

'Well, never mind. Bring him home and we shall be delighted to meet him. You *must* get married over here.'

'But where will we stay? He has no money.'

'Never mind. You can have our room. Mother will sleep on the settee in the living room.'

'But what about you, Daddy?'

'Don't worry about me. As soon as I put the receiver down, I shall drop dead.'

To whom it may concern

David suffered a severe heart attack. When he recovered, he asked his wife to return to marital intercourse. She said: 'Not without a doctor's certificate. . . .'

So David went to his doctor who examined him and wrote out a certificate.

'Doctor', said David, 'please mark it: To whom it may concern. . .'.

Necessity?

Chaim came home and found his wife in bed with his best friend. He looked down at him sadly and said: 'Moishe – *I* have to – but *you*!'.

Tired

Two men were visiting a brothel on the top floor of a twenty-story block. The lift broke down and they started to climb. One said to the other: 'Wouldn't it be awful if we got to the top and found that the girls weren't there'.

After ten floors, the other replied: 'Wouldn't it be awful if we got to the top and the girls were there!'.

What for?

Two old men were sitting on a bench in a boulevard. One said: 'Do you remember how we used to run up and down here when we were young, chasing girls?'.

The other replied: 'I remember running up and down – but I've forgotten what it was for'.

Thanks

At his wife's request, a husband gave her as a birthday present a plot of land in the local cemetery. The following year he refused to give her a birthday present at all.

'Why no present, darling?', she asked.

'Because you haven't used the one I gave you last year', he replied.

Raffles

A girl came home one night with a fur coat. Her husband said: 'Where did you get that from?'. 'I won it on a raffle', she replied.

The next night, she arrived home wearing a diamond ring. 'And where did that come from?', her husband enquired. 'I won it on a raffle', she said.

The next night, the girl arrived in a Rolls Royce Silver Cloud. 'All right, darling', said her husband. 'I know. . . . You won it on a raffle . . . .' She nodded.

The girl said: 'Darling, be a pet and run my bath for me'.

Shortly after, she came upstairs and found that the bath had only an inch of water in it. 'What's the matter, darling?', she said. 'Why don't you run me a decent bath?'

'Oh, sorry, darling . . . but I didn't want your raffle ticket to get wet. . . .'

A prisoner went round the cells, selling tickets for the Warder's Ball. One of his mates complained: 'I don't want to buy a ticket for any screw's dance!'. The seller replied: 'It's not a dance. It's a raffle!'

Contribution

Mary goes to the doctor with pain in her stomach. She returns home and asks her husband: 'Don't you want to know what the doctor said?'.

'All right then, tell me.'

'I must have sexual intercourse at least twenty times a month.'

'Ah, I see. Then put me down for four.'

Contraceptives

You can always recognise a Welsh contraceptive because it has a leek in it; a Scottish one because of the patch over the leak; and an Irish one because there's a patch which is *not* over the leak.

Wrinkles

Two old ladies in an old people's home* decide to go streaking. A retired sailor is sitting with his wife watching them. She says: 'Look at those two. What are they wearing?'

'I don't know – but whatever it is, it needs pressing!' [*This may be adapted for a named hotel, club or other institution. GJ]

Jewish wedding

The Jewish bridegroom traditionally treads on glass, breaking it into thousands of pieces. Why? 'To celebrate the last occasion when he will be able to put his foot down. . . .'

Tribute by host to wife

I would like to thank my wife for working so hard and so expensively for the success of this function. She deserves all the credit for this lovely affair – I hope that she will get it from the hotel. . . .

Training

The difference between education and training? If your daughter comes home and says that she has been having sex education at school, you would doubtless rejoice. But if she says that she has been having sex training, you would have due cause for alarm.

Wrongdoing

Mabel, aged 18, arrived home at four in the morning – wearing a mink coat.
'Did I do wrong?', she asked her mother.
Mother replied: 'I don't know whether you did right or wrong, dear – but you certainly did well!'.

Pensioner's marriage

Two pensioners married. On their honeymoon night, the husband reached for his wife's hand – and held it tenderly. On the next night, he did the same. On the third night, he reached out for her hand but it was not there.
'What's the matter, Mary?', he asked.
'I am sorry, dear', she replied. 'I am too tired tonight. . . .'

Wrapping it up

David was away on business. He telephoned his wife. 'Any news?', he asked.
'Yes. The cat has died.'
'How terrible. But fancy you telling me like that. Why didn't you wrap it up. . . . Like saying: "The cat's not well . . ." or "The cat is up a tree . . ."?'

The next time he was away, David phoned his wife: 'Any news?'.

Wife: 'Yes. I'm afraid mother-in-law's not well. In fact, she's up a tree. . . .'

Wedding present

A father-in-law gave his son-in-law five thousand shares in his business. 'There you are, lad', he said. 'Anything else I can do for you?'

The son-in-law replied: 'Yes, Dad. Please would you buy me out?'

Helping hand

In the middle of a snowy winter, a farmer complained to his neighbour: 'I'm tired of your lad. He keeps widdling his name in the snow outside my window. . . .'

Neighbour: 'Oh, it's only boyish pranks. . .'.

Farmer: 'It would be normally – but the trouble is that they are in my daughter's handwriting!'.

Sex

I asked your chairman for details of the people I would be speaking to today – numbers, broken down by age and sex – and he replied: 'Yes, they are. . .'. (*Clement Freud*)

Always right

Wife: 'I have my faults. But being wrong isn't one of them.'

Premarital

Two businessmen talking:

'I never slept with my wife before I married. Did you?'

'I don't know John. What was her maiden name?'

Tolerance

Irish New Yorker returns home one evening to tell his mother that he had got engaged. To whom? 'To a prostitute', he replied. She fainted.

The son said: 'I didn't know you were so prejudiced as to object to me marrying a prostitute'.

'Oh', said the mother, 'did you say a *prostitute*? *That's* all right. I thought you said Protestant!'

Prostitutes

A prostitute is covered by the Factories Act because she is employed for the demolition of temporary erections.

Welsh virgins

The day after his wedding, Dai returns home. 'What's happened?', asked his mother.

'I found out that Bridget is a virgin', he said. 'So I left her.'

'Quite right', said his mother. 'If she's not good enough for the rest of the boys in the village, why should she be good enough for you'.

Not again

Three Viking boats approach beach in Sussex. Head man leaps ashore and yells out: 'Boat 1 – tonight – looting'.

'Hurray!', cry the men.

'Boat 2 – tonight – burning', shouts the leader.

'Hurrah!', cry the men.

'Boat 3. . . .'

A small voice cries out: 'Oh, God, not rape again!'.

Aspirations

Dai informs his wife that he is buying a new suit. 'It's very modern', he said. 'It includes a fourteen-inch zip.'

'Dai', she answers, 'you remind me of that company director across the road. He has a double garage and rides out every morning on his bicycle.'

Insurance

The favourite uncle at a wedding dinner announced that he was going to give the bridegroom a life insurance policy. The bride burst into tears. When she was finally calmed, she blurted out: 'I don't like it . . . I don't like it . . . I don't want father to set light to Harry like he did to the warehouse. . . .'.

Wills

A man climbed to the top floor of a block of apartments, to the home of a well known call-girl. As she opened the door, he had a heart attack and dropped down dead. His executors asked their lawyers this question: 'Are we bound to carry out the testator's last wish?'.

The angel of death

A girl died in the arms of her elderly lover. He was charged with manslaughter. He explained his sad situation to the judge thus: 'My arms were around her; her arms were around me. Her legs were around me and mine around her. My lips were on her lips and her lips on my lips. Her breasts were on my chest and my chest on her breasts. My lord, I do not know how the angel of death managed to get in!'

'And this one, Miss Forbish, is the direct line. . . .'

88 Religious and ethnic

Faith

An Italian priest was walking along a cliff top when he slipped and fell – but was caught by a slender sapling, growing out of the cliff. He looked down 300 feet at the sea and up at heaven and cried out: 'Is there anyone up there – help, help!'. And a mighty voice cried out: 'I am here. Fear not. Let go of the tree and I will keep you safe.' The priest looked down 300 feet at the raging sea and the rocks. Then he cried out: 'Is there anyone else up there – help, help!'.

Also: A nun was driving her little Fiat along the road when it ran out of petrol. She left the car and walked 10 miles to the nearest filling station. Regretfully, they said that they had no jerry can and no other container of any sort. 'Surely you have something which I could put the petrol into', she pleaded. Thoughtfully the attendant said: 'Well, I can only offer you an old chamber pot. . .'.

Gratefully, the nun accepted. The pot was filled with petrol; she walked back to the car. And as she was pouring it into the petrol tank, a passing motorist leaned out of the window, saying: 'Well, sister, I wish I had your faith!'

Who likes fish?

In 1958 the Rumanian Minister of the Interior announced that permission would be given for people to go to Israel. Instead of sending off those who had long since applied to join relatives, they invited applications. Thousands of Jews queued up to apply.

Chief Rabbi Rosen went to see the Minister, who said: 'What do you want, then? Is this not what you have always been asking for?'

The Rabbi told him the story of another Rabbi who issued an invitation to people in the village to join him for a fish dinner. When they arrived, he gave them nothing to eat.

'What's this, Rabbi?', they protested. 'We thought you were going to give us dinner?'

'Oh, no', replied the Rabbi, 'I just wanted to know which of you liked fish'.

'Well, Minister – I think that you are just trying to find out which of us like fish. . .', said Chief Rabbi Rosen.

He was right. It was not until much later that the flow of emmigration began. They simply wanted to know how many Jews would leave if given permission.

Whose religion?

Father Brown (Roman Catholic) and the Reverend Green (Anglican) were arguing furiously over a theological matter.

The priest held up his hand: 'Come, let us not quarrel!', he said. 'You and I are both doing God's work – you in your way and I in His!'

Contorted logic

It appears that only some 30 per cent of serious road accidents are actually caused by drunken driving. In the remainder of cases the drivers were sober. It follows that sober drivers are more of a danger than drunken ones.

Prescriptions

A down-and-out tries to beg a pound from a passer-by.

'What it is then? Drugs?'

'Don't indulge.'

'So I suppose you smoke yourself silly?'

'As a matter of fact, I never smoke at all.'

'Then there is only one answer. Gambling. . . .'

'Certainly not. That's a mug's game. . . .'

'Then never mind the quid. You come into the car with me and let me take you home to meet my wife. I would like her to see what happens to a man who doesn't drink, take drugs, smoke or gamble . . . .'

Sign over chemist's shop: 'We dispense with accuracy'.

Jewish jokes

A Jewish joke is a joke which Jewish people have heard and non-Jewish people would not understand.

Terrorism

The Mafia Godfather arrived at the Pearly Gates.

St. Peter: 'I'm not sure that we will have you in here. I'll have to ask The Boss.'

'I haven't come to be invited in', said the Godfather. 'I have come to give you three minutes to get out.'

Love of Russia

An old man was studying Hebrew on a park bench in Moscow. A KGB man came up to him and said: 'What are you reading?'.

'I'm studying Hebrew.'

'What's the use of that to you?'

'It's the language of Israel.'

'Old man – you will never get there. . . .'

'Never mind, then. It's the language of Paradise.'

'But what happens if you go to the other place, then?'

'That will present no problem. I already speak Russian.'

A load of old hay

There was only one person at the service at the local church. The Vicar said to him: 'Shall I carry on?'.

Congregant: 'I am only an old cowhand. If there is only one cow in the field I still feed him.'

So the Vicar carried out the whole service. On his way out he said to the congregant: 'How did you like it?'.

Congregant: 'I am only an old cowhand. Even if there is only one cow in the field I still feed him. But I do not feed him the whole load of hay!'

Solutions

As a Jew you should understand that it is better to have a problem with no final solution than a final solution with no problem! (*Professor Chouraqui*)

Optimism

An optimist thinks that all is for the best in the best of all possible worlds. But they say in the Vatican that a pessimist is one who thinks that he is right.

Ten Commandments

If Moses had had to descend from Mount Sinai and submit his Ten

Commandments to the scrutiny of Israeli's Parliamentary Committee, I doubt whether they would ever have become law. (*Abba Eban*)

Phrophesies

It is very difficult to make a prophesy as to the future . . . and in Israel, it is very difficult to be a prophet at all, because of the competition. . . .

Epistle

An epistle is the wife of an apostle. . . .

Brilliance

A Rabbi visited a kibbutz on the edge of the desert. He said: 'You kibbutzniks are so clever. . . . You know how to settle where the trees are!'

Barmitzvah baskets

A well known Rabbi was addressing a Jewish boy on his Barmitzvah (*his confirmation, at the age of 13*) He said: 'You have a special responsibility, Brian. You are an only child. Your parents have, as it were, put all their eggs into one basket – and you are that basket!'

Many of my best friends . . .

When King Khaled of Saudi Arabia first greeted US Secretary of State, Henry Kissinger, he launched into his renowned attack on the Jews and Israel . . . and how they had taken over the world banks and financial institutions, its communications and its newspapers, its television and its radio. 'They have even infiltrated into positions of high power in the Foreign Ministries of the world', declaimed His Majesty.

Then, realising what he had said, the King added: 'But you, sir, we welcome warmly – not as a Jew, but as a great human being. . .'.

Secretary Kissinger replied quietly: 'Your Majesty, many of my best friends are human beings. . .'.

A woman of worth

After the marriage service, the bridegroom thanked the Rabbi and said to him: 'What do I owe you?'.

'Give me as much as you think that the bride is worth', the Rabbi replied.

The groom handed him a crumpled fiver.

The Rabbi looked at the bride – and gave the groom £4 change.

Anti-anti-semitic

A Jewish man was sitting in the corner of a compartment, while two other travellers sat chatting. One said to the other: 'Where are you going?'.

'To Brighton.'

'Oh, that used to be a nice place. But it isn't any more. It's full of Jews.'

'Where are you going, then?', asked his friend.

'To Bournemouth.'

'Bournemouth! You talk of Brighton but you should see what's happening to Bournemouth, with all those Jewish hotels. . . .'

The Jew lowered his newspaper and looked at them over the top. 'You know where you two boys should go', he said. 'You should go to hell. There are no Jews there!'

Food

A man at a well known restaurant (*let us call it Grubbs – but you can insert any name you wish. GJ*) asked for everything to be piled on his plate in huge quantities. And he ate it with his fingers. The proprietor said: 'Sir, you are behaving like a pig!'.

'Yes', replied the man. 'I was doing the same at Claridges and they said to me: "If you want to eat like a pig, go to Grubbs. . ." '.

A man came into Grubbs with an alligator on a leash. He said: 'Do you serve Jews here?'.

Mr. Grubb replied: 'Of course we do'.

'In that case', said the man, 'I'll have two salt-beef sandwiches for me and a Jew for my alligator. . .'.

Persistence

A woman was lying on a beach in Miami. She turned to a man lying alongside her and asked: 'Excuse me, are you Jewish?'. He replied: 'No, I'm not'.

A few minutes later, the woman turned again to the man and said: 'Are you sure you're not Jewish?'. He replied: 'I'm certain'

Five minutes later, the woman again addressed the man: 'Excuse me, are you absolutely certain that you're not Jewish?'.

He replied, angrily: 'All right. So I'm Jewish.'

The woman paused: 'Now, isn't that funny', she said. 'You don't look Jewish!'

Fowl language

A man was standing on the steps of the Cathedral, shooing away the pigeons. 'Bugger off . . . , bugger of . . . , bugger off . . .', he said.

A priest emerged and listened to this performance. 'My man', he said, 'you really shouldn't talk to pigeons like that. Not on the steps of of this House of God. You should say: "Shoo . . . , shoo . . . , shoo . .

'Look', he said. 'I'll demonstrate, shoo . . . , shoo . . . , shoo . . .', he said to the pigeons. They all flew away.

'There', said the priest to the visitor. 'I told you all you had to say was: "Shoo . . . , shoo . . . , shoo . . .", and they'd all bugger off, just the same!'

Who?

Salome was the young lady who took off her clothes and danced in front of Harrods.

God?

Suffragette: 'Put your trust in God. *She* will provide.'

Repeat business

A tailor made a suit for an Anglican parson. He refused to accept any charge. The parson sent him a lovely bible.

Two weeks later, the same tailor made a suit for a Roman Catholic priest. Again, he refused to charge. The priest sent him a magnificent prayer book.

The tailor was later visited by a Rabbi and made a suit for him. He made no charge. The Rabbi sent him another Rabbi.

The choice before us

Vicar, blessing all parties before British Election: 'We shall have three hymns today. In honour of the Conservatives: Now Thank We All Our God. . . . In honour of the Labour Party: Oh God Our Help In Ages Past. . . . And in honour of the Liberals: God Does Move in Mysterious Ways. . . .'

An ancestor's mistake

Why is it that the children of Israel beat their breasts on mention of the Promised Land?

Because of the terrible mistake of their ancestors. If Moses had turned right instead of left, they would have had the oilfields and the Egyptians and Saudis would have had the Promised Land. . . .

Enemies

A priest was called in to administer the last rites to a dying parishioner. 'Fergus O'Reilly', he said. 'Do you renounce the Devil, now and forevermore?'

'Oh, Father', replied the dying man. 'This is no time to be making enemies – anywhere.'

'*Last thing I remember, everyone was drinking my health. . . .*'

89 Your health

Mother-in-law

'I hear that your mother-in-law is in hospital!'
'That's right.'
'How long has she been there?'
'In three weeks, please God, it will be a month!'

Illness uncured

A man suffering from constipation went to his doctor who provided him with a suppository, telling him to leave it in his back passage overnight and that if it did not do the trick, to come back in a couple of days.

Two days later, the patient returned. 'It was useless', he said.

'Did you do as I recommended', asked the doctor.

'Well', said the patient, 'we haven't got a back passage in our house. So I put it on top of the refrigerator. For all the good it did me, I might just as well have shoved it up my rear end!'

Glass houses

Two guests at a cocktail party. One says to the other: 'Look, old man I shouldn't drive if I were you. Your face is getting all blurry.'

Inferiority

A man told his psychiatrist that he was suffering from a severe inferiority complex. The psychiatrist said: 'I am sorry sir, but I cannot help you.'

'Why not?'

'I am afraid that you *are* inferior!'

Dentist

Dentist to patient: 'Now, we're not going to hurt each other, are we?'.

Animal behaviour

Letter from professor, concerned to prevent new limits on vivisection: 'I teach animal behaviour to my students. . .'.

Hospitals

A man cut off his hand with a circular saw. Clutching the hand, he rushed off to the London Clinic. They demanded £3,500 to sew it on again. So he ran down Harley Street. There he found Mick O'Brien – surgeon – who sewed it on for £350. He returned to the clinic to complain at their extortionate prices . . . shook his fist at them . . . and it came off! [*This one needs action. GJ*]

Medical prophecy

An American doctor gave his patient six months to live – and sent him a bill for $500. By the end of the six months, the bill was still not paid. The doctor then gave his patient another six months. . . .

Real ale

A barren woman attended her doctor's surgery for artificial insemination. 'What will happen?', she asked.

'I just get a bottle from the fridge and spray you with a syringe', he replied.

He went out to the refrigerator but found the bottle was empty and the syringe missing. He walked back into the room, wearing no trousers.

'What's happening now?', asked the woman.

'I'm afraid we've run out of bottled', he said. 'You'll have to make do with draught!'

Mad?

A psychotic builds castles in the air; psychopaths live in them; psychiatrists collect the rent.

Listen!

Man visits a psychiatrist's office and says: 'My trouble is no one listens to me'. The psychiatrist says: 'Next. . .'.

Doctor's etiquette

The luscious blonde lay on her doctor's couch. 'Kiss me, doctor', she demanded.

'Madam', he replied, 'you ask me to kiss you? I struggled for years to get through my medical examinations . . . my parents sacrificed for me . . . I am now qualified and at work . . . and you ask me to kiss you. . . ? Why', he said, withdrawing his hand from beneath her skirt. 'I shouldn't even be doing this!'

Lost voice

A singer who has lost his voice knocked on the door of his doctor's surgery. A nurse appeared. The man whispered: 'Is Dr Jones in?'. The nurse whispered in reply: 'No – come in quickly'.

The doctor arrived after about fifteen minutes, wrote out a prescription and recommended 'plenty of ice cream'.

The singer duly lodged the prescription with the chemist and went off to the ice cream parlour. He whispered: 'What flavours of ice cream do you have?'.

The ice cream man replied, whispering: 'Strawberry and vanilla'.

Singer: 'Do you have laryngitis too?'.

The ice cream man whispered: 'No – just strawberry and vanilla'.

Safety in theatres

A woman who had been sitting towards the back of the stalls left her seat during the interval. When she returned, she found a man lying across the seat. She asked him to move. He just groaned. Eventually, she called the manager. 'Come on, come on, my man . . . please move along', he said. The man opened his eyes and said nothing. 'If you don't move, I'll have to call the police', said the manager.

Eventually, the policeman arrived, with his notebook. 'Very well, where do you come from?', asked the officer.

'From the balcony', the man groaned.

Rat catching

A farmer told his friend how upset he was at the way that rats were overrunning his farm. The friend said: 'You ought to try setting traps and putting down poison'.

Farmer: 'I've tried both, but it's hopeless'.

'Then the only thing left is to bung up their holes.'
Farmer: 'I know – but you've got to catch the little blighters first!'.

Anatomy

The Scottish riding school was economising by using only one spur – on the principle that if you get half a horse to go, there is a good chance that the other half will follow.

Drink and drive?

A Scottish hotel applied for a drinking licence. This was refused because 'the roads in the vicinity of the hotel are unsuitable for drunken driving'.

Only average

There was once a Russian doctor who bustled into the ward and said: 'I'm in a terrible hurry. Please give me the average temperature of all the patients. . .'. (*Shimon Peres*)

Nurses

Occupational nurses are a race apart. I once asked one what you do when you have a patient brought in with a bleeding leg? She replied: 'You bind up the bleeding wound; you elevate the bleeding leg; and you call in the bleeding doctor'.

Problems

Psychiatrist says to woman patient: 'Now just relax'. Five minutes later: 'Well, that's solved my problem. What's yours?'

Evidence

I once sat in the surgery of Dr Henry Shifman, then the Israeli Parliament's own doctor. I noticed items on his shelf, which gave a clear indication of the needs of his patients. Bottles included: adrenalin; nitroglycerin; aspirin; anusol; morphine; laxatives; and a huge drum of Valium – empty.

Ambition

The Minister of Health visited a hospital and was introduced to three international rugby players, lying in adjoining beds. He asked the first man: 'What's the matter with you?'.

'I have piles, sir', replied the man.

'And what are they doing for you?'

'They give me a brush and some ointment and I apply it to myself.'

'And what's your ambition now?'

'To get back to the rugger field to play for England, sir, as soon as possible.'

'Well done, my boy. I wish you luck.' And he turned to the second man.

'What's the matter with you, then?'

'I'm afraid that I've got venereal disease.'

'Oh dear. And what treatment are they giving you?'

'They give me a brush and some ointment and I apply it to myself.'

'And what's your ambition?'

'To get back to the rugger field to play for England again, as soon as possible', he said.

'Well done, my boy', nodded the Minister and turned to the third bed.

'And what's your trouble?'

'I have laryngitis', the man whispered.

'What are they doing for you?'

'They give me a brush and some ointment and I apply it to myself.'

'And what is your ambition?'

'To get the brush before the other two fellows. . . .'

Oedipus

A Jewish couple sent their son to a psychiatrist. He returned and his mother enquired what had happened. 'Nu?', she said.

'He says I've got an oedipus complex.'

'Oedipus shmoedipus', his mother retorted. 'You just go on loving your mummy!'

Rare?

Patients in a psychiatric hospital were undergoing group therapy. One asked: 'Why are we all here?'. Another immediately replied: 'Because we're not all there. . .'.

'*It'll be a much better speech if you don't read from your notes. . . .*'

90 *Miscellany of wit – and the end*

Us

We are proud of the inhabitants of our island. There are the Scots who take themselves seriously – as well as anything else they can lay their hands on; the Welsh, who pray on their knees and on each other; the Irish, who will die for what they believe in, even if they do not know what that is; and the English, who proclaim that they are self-made men, thereby absolving the Lord from a heavy burden.

Optimism

An optimist says that the bottle is half full – a pessimist that it is half empty.

Age

The young look forward; the old look back; and the middle-aged look around.

You are young if it is as easy to go upstairs as it is to go down; you are middle-aged if it is easier to go down than up; and you are old if it is just as difficult to go in either direction.

Irish fall from grace

An Irishman fell 80 feet from a scaffold. By good fortune, he managed to clutch hold of a rope about 20 feet from the ground. After a few moments, he let go and fell on his head.

His friend picked him up and said: 'Mike – why did you let go of that rope?'.

He replied: 'I was afraid it was going to break'.

Only blood

A Scottish friend of mine always carried a hip flask of whisky. One day he fell and felt damp around his hip. 'My God', he said. 'I hope it's only blood!'

Ugh!

A Scotsman was found wandering on the rooftops. The drinks were on the house.

Spoilsport

The advantage of having a Scottish granny is that though she doesn't prevent you from falling into sin, she does prevent you from enjoying it. . . .

Take your time

An El Al plane was landing in New York. The pilot announced: 'Ladies and gentlemen, we hope that you have enjoyed this flight on El Al and that we shall have the pleasure of your company on future flights'. Then, forgetting that his loudspeaker was still switched on, he added: 'Now all I need is a nice cup of coffee and a woman!'

A pert air hostess rushed up the gangway towards the cockpit. An old Mama put her hand gently on her passing arm: 'Don't hurry, darling', she said. 'Give him time to have his coffee!'

Recognition

For many years, Charlie in London and Bill in New York were pen pals. They had never met.

One day, Charlie received a letter from Bill, saying that he intended to come to London. 'Please cable back if it's convenient', Bill wrote.

The following exchange of cables then ensued:

Charlie: 'Delighted to welcome you. Will meet you at station.'

Bill: 'Thanks – am black. Charlie.'

Charlie: 'Don't care if black. Come. Will meet you at station.'

Bill: 'Am Catholic.'

Charlie: 'Don't care if black Catholic. Come. Will meet you at station.'

Bill: 'Am hunchback.'

Charlie: 'Don't care if black Catholic hunchback. Come. Will meet you at station.'

Bill: 'Have only one eye in centre of forehead.'

Charlie: 'Don't care if you are black Catholic, hunchback with only one eye in middle of forehead. Will meet you at station. But how do I recognise you?'

Mistaken identity

Years ago, we visited India. At that time, our daughter Laura was a small child. Her hair was cut short and she wore jeans and a T-shirt. We were served lunch in our hotel by a turbanned waiter, wearing a traditional Indian coat, known as a 'dhoti'.

The waiter asked me: 'Would the little boy like some more?'.

Laura piped up: 'Isn't that funny. *She* thinks I'm a boy!'

Rebel

I wouldn't wish to belong to a club that would have me for a member. (*Groucho Marx*)

Class distinction

When I was serving in the British Army of the Rhine, I found a notice on our HQ board at Christmas. It read: 'Christmas parties will be held as follows: Officers and their ladies, 24 December; non-commissioned Officers and their wives, 25 December; and other ranks and their womenfolk, 26 December'.

Irish

Pat put on a clean pair of socks every day. The problem was that by the end of the week he couldn't get his shoes on.

Three men go into car wash. How do you spot the Irishman? He's the one on a motorbike.

Philosophy

If you do not know where you are going, you will probably end up somewhere else. . . .

Non sequitur

Lord Birkett liked to tell the tale of the woman in the train who watched the man opposite her tearing up a newspaper and every now and again throwing tiny pieces out of the window.

'Why are you doing that, sir?', she enquired.

'To keep the elephants away', he replied.

'But there are no elephants', she protested.

'Yes', he answered. 'It is indeed wonderfully effective.'

Temptation

Do not blame the mouse – blame the hole in the wall. (*Talmud*)

The twist

Don't turn around, but look behind you!

Tact

Dai the bread, Morgan the tailor and Evan the bookie went to the races. Unfortunately, a horse leapt over the rails and smashed into poor Dai, knocking him down and killing him. Morgan and Evan considered the problem: 'Who should tell Mrs. Jones?'.

Morgan said: 'I'm only a tailor. I have no tact. Evan, you tell her. You're a bookie, so you know how to explain losses. . . .'

So Evan went to the village and knocked on the door of the Jones's terraced home. A lady came to the door.

'Excuse me, madam', said Evan. 'I'm sorry to disturb you. But are you Widow Jones?'

'There's no Widow Jones here', she replied.

'Do you want to make a bet?', asked Evan.

Isolationist

A man once sat in a boat, boring a hole under his seat. 'Don't worry, shipmates', he said to his fellow travellers. 'It's only under *my* seat, not yours. . .'. (*Talmud*)

A floral tribute

Everyone is condemned to the sadness of attending funerals – I treasure one anecdote which has added a moment of consolation to many a cremation service.

An elegant lady cousin had to attend both a funeral and a wedding on the same summer's afternoon. So she donned a smart, navy blue suit but put her magnificent, new, floral hat into a paper bag. As it was covered with gay and realistic, artificial flowers, it was hardly suitable headgear for a cremation.

In the entrance of the crematorium, a solemn black-clad man – obviously a cloakroom attendant – held out his hand for her parcel and she gave it to him. Then she sat quietly at the back.

Moments later, the coffin was wheeled noiselessly into the funeral hall. It was crowned with a magnificent floral tribute – her hat!

My cousin sat transfixed during the service, which reached its silent climax as the doors at the far end of the hall slid apart and the coffin rolled gently away, still bedecked with her hat.

The service over, she joined the mourners around the back where all the wreaths had been laid against the chapel wall, accompanied by a simple sign: 'In Memory of the Departed'. She stood silently – wondering whether she dared remove her floral tribute from the rest. Watching the sad faces of the family of the deceased, she decided that her hat must be sacrificed. She went to the wedding hatless. When she returned that evening, her hat had gone.

Well clad

In a class in a Leicester comprehensive school, I asked the pupils what newspapers they had in their homes.

'Who gets the Mirror?' A forest of hands went up.

'The Sun?' More hands.

'The Express?' A few.

'The Mail?' Another few.

'The Leicester Mercury?' Everybody.

'The Times?' One hand.

I asked the girl who put her hand up so surprisingly: 'What does your father do?'.

'The crossword', she replied.

Will

An old man was dying. His children and his grandchildren were gathered around his bed, waiting patiently. Every few minutes, the old gentleman pointed down to the floor with two fingers of his right hand. Eventually, the eldest son said: 'He is trying to tell us that's where he's put the money. . .'.

So they started pulling up the floorboards all over the house – but found nothing.

That evening, the father rallied and started to chat. Eventually, the son said to him: 'Tell me, father, what were you pointing two fingers at the floor for?'.

'Oh that', replied the father. 'I was just too weak to point them upwards.'

Index